Productivity Improvement Manual

Dedicated to

Harold Martin, who inspired
many people in many countries
to think more deeply about
productivity

Productivity Improvement Manual

Alan Lawlor

Q

Quorum Books
Westport, Connecticut

Published in the United States and Canada by
Quorum Books, Greenwood Press, a division of
Congressional Information Service, Inc., Westport, Connecticut

English language edition, except the United States and Canada,
published by Gower Publishing Company Limited, England

First published 1985

Library of Congress Cataloging-in-Publication Data

Lawlor, Alan.
  Productivity improvement manual.

  Includes bibliographies and index.
  1. Industrial productivity–Measurement.
2. Efficiency, Industrial.   I. Title.
HD56.25.L39   1985   658.3′14   85–12194
ISBN 0–89930–148–7 (lib. bdg.)

Library of Congress Catalog Card Number: 85–12194

ISBN: 0–89930–148–7

Printed in Great Britain

Contents

Part III Improving Productivity

Illustrations

Preface

This book brings together some twenty-five years' study into productivity by my colleague the late Professor Harold Martin, and my own work over the past fifteen years. It has taken nearly two years to prepare and write and consequently has been influenced by the changing picture of productivity over this period of time.

Though the book does provide practical guidance on how to measure and improve productivity it must be emphasised that in such a complex field there can be no easy short-term answers. Equally the need for a more effective means of managing resources in a fast-changing world does demand concerted and continuing attention by governments and individual organisations alike. This is particularly necessary in the prevailing conditions of fierce competition and cuts in government expenditure. But it is not just these changes that have to be contended with. We are living in times of rapid rates of change where nothing stands still. Therefore, the task of improving productivity in its totality must include learning how to adjust to change and the accompanying new standards of performance, some of which will be higher than those currently existing.

We have to abandon the narrow view of productivity associated with production and labour efficiency. It is now much more than this and needs to take account of increased energy and raw material costs along with a growing concern with unemployment and the quality of working life. This book attempts to widen the horizons to include the productivity needs of the year 2000 and to suggest ways of beginning to address them now. This is done by showing how to deal with three questions, which together form the central theme of the book:

'Where are you now?'
'How much better could you be?'
'Where should you be?'

The text is divided into four main parts. The first one sets the productivity scene, and provides readers with an opportunity at the end to carry out an assessment of their own organisation. Part II presents a framework for measuring productivity in any kind of organisation. The often-overlooked task of getting the information to do the measuring is also dealt with, and a chapter is devoted to simple low-cost methods for obtaining information that may not exist. The techniques described are called participative: the idea is that involving people in the collection of productivity information increases the likelihood of their becoming committed to using it to improve performance. Throughout this section well-tried methods for assessing productivity are included which can be modified to suit particular needs.

Part III provides practical guidance on setting up and running productivity improvement programmes. It deals also with the human problems of improving productivity. Chapter 8 describes the action learning approach: what it is, how it works and some applications. More a philosophy than a technique, action learning is an effective means of bringing about organisational change. It is now used in many parts of the world, in firms employing two people and in organisations employing many thousands. Over the last few years it has been developed for the specific task of improving productivity. Three applications are described in Chapter 9. The first one involved twelve different manufacturing companies and comprised a productivity audit, external action learning meetings and in-plant improvement groups. A second case study describes an in-plant action learning programme in a large electronics firm. The last one is a dynamic form of interfirm comparison involving twenty-four garden centres. In the first and last cases a multiplier effect was created through assisting a number of companies at the same time. The second case study illustrates the power of in-plant action learning for changing attitudes and bringing about organisational change.

By this stage the elements of productivity will have been explained together with practical ways of improving it. The last part of the text examines the new perspectives necessary to deal with the question 'What should you be doing?' The following nine factors are examined. These are considered to be the keys to success as we move towards productivity 2000.

1   The changing role of energy and materials
2   What is wealth and how will it be created?
3   New concepts of viability
4   The emerging challenges for industry
5   New-style measurements as we approach 2000
6   The increasing significance of white collar productivity in an information age
7   Computer conferencing as a means of bringing together large numbers of people to study the productivity issue and how it might be improved
8   Reward systems appropriate to new-style organisations
9   The prevailing attitudes to productivity.

Two appendices are included, a glossary of terms and a list of organisations throughout the world which have an interest in productivity.

Productivity is a dynamic subject, and my views have been influenced by the changing scene even as I committed my thoughts to paper. My apologies if my reaction to these changes may, at times, appear confusing. I am continuing my study of the subject and to enrich the work I welcome comments, of any kind, from readers.

Alan Lawlor

Acknowledgements

The writing of a wide-ranging book on productivity has involved the co-operation and encouragement of many people. Some have provided direct help while from others the help has been of an indirect kind.

The initial inspiration came from my longstanding colleague, the late Harold Martin, and latterly his dear wife Jackie. Simcha Bahiri of Tel Aviv University has contributed much to the sections on technical aspects of measurements and my partner, George Boulden, contributed to the chapter on action learning.

For all of the practical experience which I hope shines through the material on the technical aspects my thanks go to more people than space will permit. The Manpower Services Commission through their faith and support enabled the productivity improvement programme to get started, and it was through the wisdom of Alan Strickland of the Horticultural Trades Association that the dynamic interfirm comparison concept was introduced. In addition there are a large number of managers, supervisors and operators who have unwittingly provided considerable guidance and have helped me to keep my feet on the ground.

The wider horizons evident throughout the book, and especially the last chapter, owe much to the radical thinking of Stafford Beer, Hazel Henderson, John Naisbitt, Howard Odum, Reg Revans, Nicholas Georgescu-Roegen and Ernst Schumacher. Fay Hughes of Birmingham Public Reference Library gave untiring assistance in obtaining this reference material. The inspiration for the idea of electronic action learning is solely due to Jack Grayson of the American Productivity Center with his pioneering work on computer conferencing; and for keeping me abreast of international attitudes to productivity my thanks go to Tony Hubert of the European Association of Productivity Centres in Brussels. The development of the computer software for the dynamic action learning programme described in Chapter 9 owes a good deal to the perseverance and interest of my son Derek.

My appreciation to Annette Treeby, who somehow managed to translate what at times seemed indecipherable scrawl into an understandable draft. To Malcolm Stern, my editor at Gower, who gave his initial and continuing support to the project, goes my special gratitude.

Lastly I thank my dear wife Nancy, who through her patience, gentle encouragement and critical comments enabled me to press on with what at times seemed a difficult task.

                                                                    AL

Part I
Setting the Scene

1 Productivity: the key to prosperity

Views about productivity from around the world present a mixed picture. In the United States there was talk in 1983 of a productivity fire. On the other hand in the same year a senior industrialist who took part in a computer conference (described in the last chapter) said '... There is no question in my mind that the forces loose in the world today will inexorably force us to face the problem of producing competitively or sinking from the scene as did Greece and Rome.'

During the same period other countries provided similar contrasts. Norway had a national productivity year in 1982. In the UK there was talk about a productivity miracle about to start, (1) but at the same time the Confederation of British Industry was expressing deep concern about the adverse position of unit labour costs compared with other countries. As Tony Hubert (the Secretary General of the European Association of National Productivity Centres) said in the May 1984 issue of *Euro Productive Ideas*: 'Are we looking at a new world, a brave new world or simply an evolving world of productivity? No doubt something of everything.'

Surprisingly there still seems to be just as much misunderstanding about what productivity is as about how to measure it. Even the word 'productivity' is part of the problem. For many people it is still associated with production and labour productivity. Yet in a world where energy and materials costs have soared, competition has become fiercer and budgets are drained by welfare-oriented societies, the need for a more effective management of resources has never been higher. Productivity should therefore be a number one priority in every country and the organisations within them. But there is also a need to move perceptions away from the narrower view of efficiency on the factory floor to the task of improving total productivity. This total approach will necessitate getting more for less and at the same time reducing the environmental effects of mass production. A consequence of this change in attitude will be a greater concern for the quality of working life (QWL) than for growth in material consumption, which became predominant in the 1960s. So as to achieve this shift in attitudes we need to be made aware of the total nature of the problem, with the caution that there are certainly no quick remedies in the task of improving productivity.

The American Productivity Center (APC) in Houston, for example, has devoted considerable energy to arousing top American leaders to three activities.

1   Promoting understanding on the simple question: What is productivity?
2   Developing better methods of measuring productivity at both national and individual organisational levels.
3   Creating awareness of what needs to be done to arrest the serious decline in the productivity of American industry.

A consensus view from an international state of the art conference on productivity in Fontainebleau, France, in 1982 (2) came to similar conclusions: it's a total problem and there are no choices; survival and prosperity depend upon a continuous attack on the productivity issue. Therefore, the state of the art must be full commitment, especially from top managers, to the task of a productive and human use of all resources at the disposal of government and individual organisations.

WHY STUDY PRODUCTIVITY?

While productivity is receiving increased attention in many countries, the underlying problem of improving it is still meeting mixed reactions. The reasons for this are understandable. They include crippling national debts and, for individual companies, the daunting task of trying to survive in a fiercely competitive world. In these conditions pleas for concerted programmes of productivity improvement are met with such reactions as lack of time, confusion as to where to start, apathy and indifference. But amidst these varying attitudes there are at least five compelling reasons why productivity must receive serious and continuing attention.

1 The world's markets have become very competitive, with survival consequently dependent upon maintaining the right balance between price, quality and delivery.
2 Manufacturing industry has now been redistributed to include the Third World. This means that the older industrialised countries must compete with their new low-cost competitors or else design and make entirely new products.
3 The economic and social wellbeing of people, and in turn the peace of the world, depend upon organisations of all kinds making effective use of the limited resources at their disposal. This includes generating sufficient income to meet daily needs and a surplus, which may be called wealth, for investment in the future.
4 An appropriate social infrastructure (eg education, health provision and public transport) necessitates the generation by industry of sufficient income and wealth to support it. Moreover, because this section of economies, especially in the Western World, now consumes a significant proportion of national incomes, these public organisations also have a responsibility to manage their productivity more effectively.
5 The undesirable effects of inflation can be reduced by the efficient production of an adequate supply of goods and services by the industrial and public sectors for everyone, including the employed and unemployed, retired people and the young.

MANAGING CHANGE

An important factor in the productivity problem is the need to adjust to change. The task of improving performance requires attention to all aspects of the organisation – the total approach; improving one part may be detrimental to the rest. Equally, it is a continuing activity due to the fast-changing world in which we all live; a highly efficient and committed workforce will not survive if the organisation cannot adapt to its new circumstances. Indeed, Stafford Beer (3) states that a viable organisation is one which can adjust to changes in its environment not foreseen when it was first set up. Reg Revans (4) calls this a learning organisation and one which is on its guard against outdated, possibly harmful, experience or 'P' for programme knowledge. Instead we need to develop the skill of asking the totally new question 'Q'. The organisations that survive will be learning or adapting at least in keeping with the rate of change they are facing. If they do not, they will eventually fade away, as shown by the British motor cycle and shipbuilding industries. A graphic illustration of the rate of change, its relationship to 'P' and 'Q', and the adaptation process is shown in Figure 1.1. This shows that where the rate of change is, slow existing knowledge 'P' is appropriate. But in the conditions of rapid change indicated by the near vertical part of the curve, the generation of fresh thinking stimulated by new question 'Q' is essential.

The understanding and management of change have a vital part to play in improving productivity. Each change is generally accompanied by higher standards of performance: for example computer-controlled manufacturing systems have caused Japanese industry to aim for zero set-up times. So apart from the fact that organisations won't have any productivity to improve if they do not change, standards of performance are constantly being updated. The range of changes to be contended with are examined in depth in the last chapter, but the significant ones are listed briefly below:

1 The staple industries of basic chemicals, steel and textiles are being replaced by new-style information/knowledge-based ones. This was described by Drucker (5) in the 1960s as the Age of Discontinuity, and by Toffler (6) as the transformation from second wave 'smokestack' industries to a third wave information age. Hawken in his penetrating analysis (7) calls it 'The Next Economy'.

2 The growth in output, wages, standard of living and productivity which reached its peak in the 1960s was founded on seemingly abundant supplies of cheap energy and raw materials. While there has been a fall in energy prices since the dramatic increase of 1973, indications are for a trend upward, and in any event we shall never return to the low prices prevailing prior to the OPEC rises. This is already having profound effects on the structure of economies and particularly manufacturing industry.

3 Information-age technology based upon the microcomputer opens up organisational and manufacturing process controls not thought possible a few years ago.

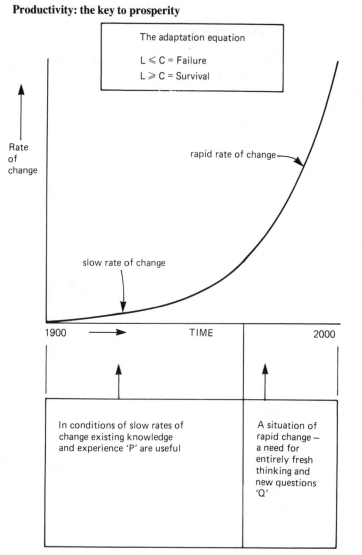

The adaptation equation

$L \leqslant C$ = Failure
$L \geqslant C$ = Survival

Rate
of
change

rapid rate of change

slow rate of change

1900   →   TIME   2000

In conditions of slow rates of change existing knowledge and experience 'P' are useful

A situation of rapid change – a need for entirely fresh thinking and new questions 'Q'

Figure 1.1 The influence of change –
with acknowledgements to Professor Reg Revans

There are other changes, like the redistribution of industry already mentioned and the contrast of a shorter life cycle for some products alongside 1-million-mile-intervals between overhauls developed by an American truck maker. It all adds up to rapid and complex changes which should be of prime concern to anyone interested in productivity.

PRODUCTIVITY: WHAT IS IT?

The answer to this question is dealt with in detail in subsequent chapters but does require some outline examination now. At its simplest, productivity is the relationship between goods produced and sold or services provided – the output, and the resources consumed in doing it – the input. This is usually stated as

$$\frac{\text{Output}}{\text{Input}} = \text{Productivity}$$

The problem, as we shall see, is using appropriate output and input information to obtain reliable measurements. At the outset we also need to distinguish productivity from a number of misbeliefs about it. For example, judging performance simply by output, as is often the case, can be misleading. Output may be rising without productivity also increasing, if, for instance, input costs have risen disproportionately. Satisfactory profits and productivity are also assumed to go together. But if profits have been maintained or increased through price recovery, it is possible productivity could be stagnating and even deteriorating. Furthermore we can delude ourselves into believing that cost cutting exercises also improve efficiency, whereas, done indiscriminately, they can make matters worse. Part of the APC's awareness campaign in America is directed at increasing understanding of the question 'What is productivity?' and, of equal importance, appreciating what it is not.

MEASUREMENT

PREREQUISITES FOR IMPROVEMENT

Part of the foundation of a sound productivity improvement programme is a reliable measurement system. Lord Kelvin's dictum 'To know something properly you must first measure it' is still sound advice for anyone interested in improving productivity. Moreover, it is doubtful if productivity can be improved until we have measured the current position; how can we judge whether performance is better unless we know what conditions were like at the outset? As one manager who took part in the productivity project described in Chapter 9 said, 'The monthly figures gave us a new insight into our business never previously provided ...'.

For this reason the measurement of productivity receives a lot of attention in subsequent chapters.

One of the bases of the success of the Japanese economy is their regard for information as a crucial resource, including productivity measures. In 1976 Dr Frank Jones, in an address to the UK Institution of Mechanical Engineers, (8) suggested to the Central Statistical Office that the kind of detailed industrial information that is produced regularly in Japan should also be made available in the UK. Table 1.1 is an example of the exact measures of industrial efficiency which are on public display in Japan. As Frank Jones said, 'There are no absolute measures of efficiency ... one can be as wasteful in men and money as one likes, as long as the competition is doing even worse, one will survive.' But information of the type shown in Table 1.1 keeps us on our toes and, as you will see in Chapter 9, a dynamic form of interfirm comparison also keeps us aware of the changing standards that have to be achieved to remain successful.

Table 1.1
The creation of wealth in 416 Japanese manufacturing companies in the year ending 31 March 1974.

Men	Employees	2,393,343
Money	Total assets	£67,000m

	£
Net tangible assets (building, plant and machinery) at depreciated value	18,271m
Total assets per employee	27,994
Net tangible assets per employee	7,634
Performance per employee	
Sales	26,743
Raw materials and services bought in	19,357
Added Value per employee	7,386
Wealth created per £ of total assets employed	£0.264
Wealth created per £ net tangible assets employed	£0.968

With acknowledgements to Dr F. E. Jones, 'The Economic Ingredients of Industrial Success', James Clayton Lecture, Institution of Mechanical Engineers.

BASICS OF MEASUREMENT

In general an effective measurement system should show in various ways how efficiently available resources are used to generate useful output. The resources comprise people, services necessary to use physical assets, and wear and tear costs (ie depreciation). Output should be useful in the sense that it is required. In addition to knowing how efficiently resources are utilised we need to have regular information on four other factors: i) the degree to which organisational aims are being attained; ii) what is being achieved compared to what is possible – a measure of potential; iii) how we compare with other organisations and countries; and iv) the growth, stagnation or deterioration aspects over time, that is, productivity trends.

PITFALLS

Practical experience suggests that a sound system of measurement should take account of the following factors:

1. It must be used and lead to action.
2. Information that is produced only when someone asks for it is generally ineffective; productivity measures need to be published on a routine, regular basis.
3. Productivity information must be believed by and understandable to those who have to use it.
4. Too much information and too little are equally bad. The former creates confusion and the latter blind ignorance.
5. Aggregating figures to give averages may obscure significant variations in performance.
6. Many productivity indicators are only partial measures and therefore reveal only part of the story, whereas total factor productivity provides a fuller picture. In the former case only single inputs are used, while total factor measures embrace all of the inputs consumed in the output generating process.
7. The measurement system needs to be under constant review; dispense with the parts not used and introduce new measurements to suit the changed circumstances.

MACRO MEASUREMENTS

The indicators of performance (the macro measurements) at national level, although not easy to understand or even believe,

are still useful for at least two reasons. Firstly, they give an indication of a country's standard of living. Secondly, for industrial
enterprises they provide comparisons of performance, that is
degrees of competitiveness.

The most common macro measurement is Gross National
Product (GNP) per capita. GNP is the indicator of a country's
economic performance and more particularly its standard of living.
GNP can be defined either as the total of wages/salaries, rents,
profits, dividends, interests and royalties or as total expenditure. If
income from abroad is deducted it is called Gross Domestic
Product (GDP). So as to avoid double accounting, the purchase of
materials, energy and services between individual enterprises is
excluded. Therefore, GDP is the national equivalent of added
value at company level – a point that is elaborated upon in later
chapters. An extract from the World Bank report for 1984, shown
in Table 1.2, shows the GNP per capita for all the main regions of

Table 1.2
World GNP per capita at market prices
Year 1980

Major regions	GNP per capita Average * (US $)	% Growth in GNP 1979 to 1980	Population millions
North America	11460	+ 9.1	252
Japan	9020	+ 7.8	118
Oceania	7810	+ 11.6	23
Europe	7540	+ 11.5	449
USSR †	4040	NA	264
Middle East	5790	+ 34.3	38
South America	2070	+ 19.6	236
Central America	1740	+ 7.4	111
Africa	760	+ 8.6	459
Asia	330	+ 6.5	2193

* An indication of the standard of living
† Figures for 1979; 1980 figures not available
With acknowledgement to the *World Bank Atlas*.

the world. It can be seen that the older industrialised countries
achieve the highest standard of living. North America, Japan and
Europe, which form a significant proportion of this part of the

world, give a range of performance (highest to lowest GNP per capita) of 1.5 to 1. While this is a crude indication of productivity, it does suggest that some countries are managing their resources

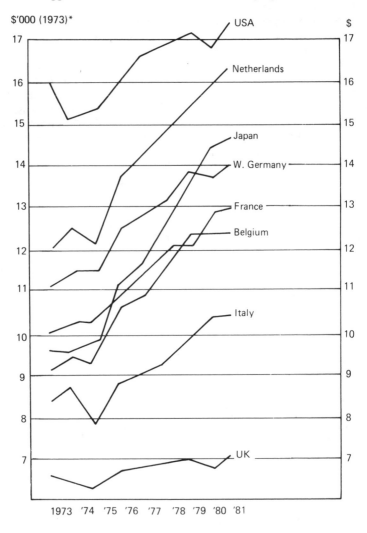

* adjusted to the value of the American dollar in 1973

Acknowledgements to A. D. Roy, National Institute of Economic and Social Research

Figure 1.2 Manufacturing output per worker–year for eight countries

more efficiently than others. The report also reveals the time delay problem with international figures; by 1984 these were the latest statistics available.

A more refined version of GNP per capita is output per worker for the manufacturing sectors of countries. It is virtually GNP for all the people employed in industry. A study made by the National Institute of Economic and Social Research (NIESR) (9) in the UK for eight industrialised countries revealed that West Germany was achieving nearly twice as much output per worker as the UK, with Japan showing the greatest growth of all countries over the period 1973 to 1981. The results of the study are shown in Figure 1.2. While output per worker is in widespread use we should bear in mind the following reservations:

1 It is difficult to take account of the effects of differing degrees of inflation and exchange rates in the countries compared; NIESR did acknowledge these difficulties and tried to minimise their effects.
2 Output per worker is only a partial measure and therefore excludes labour costs, the costs of purchased services and capital changes.

Evidence from countries which are measuring these other aspects reveals that though labour productivity (ie output per worker) was improving, capital productivity showed a decrease with a consequent adverse effect on total productivity. The APC in their awareness-promoting campaign in the United States have proposed to the Bureau of Labor Statistics that they take account of these other inputs and adopt a total factor form of measurement. Norway and Israel are examples of countries which are taking a similar approach.

A number of other methods are used to compare the productivity of countries – often tons of steel or cars per worker; they are certainly easy to understand and do claim the attention of the average person. On the other hand such comparisons, even with their popular appeal, only tell part of the story; labour costs and capital are not included. The European Management Forum based in Geneva produce a comprehensive annual report on productivity for the 22 member countries of the Organisation for Economic and Cultural Development (OECD). An extract from the industrial efficiency part of the report for 1983 (10) is shown in Table 1.3. It can be seen that Japan remains in the top position for 1982 and 1983, with a number of countries moving down the list and five improving on their 1982 performance. This particular study is interesting for its attention to the numerical assessment of efficiency, but an evaluation of the more qualitative factors like

role of the state, the use of resources, whether the country was
outward looking, and innovative characteristics and stability were
also included. Though some countries, notably Japan and Switzer-
land, tended to rank high on overall scores, for the ten separate
factors individual countries varied in their position, some being
high on certain factors and low on others.

While international productivity measurements are difficult to

Table 1.3
Industrial efficacy: a summary of 22 OECD member
countries arranged in 1983 rank order

Rank Orders 1982	Rank Orders 1983	Country	Change 1982 to 1983
1	1	Japan	NC
2	2	Switzerland	NC
14	3	Austria	+
11	4	Netherlands	+
5	5	Ireland	NC
3	6	United States	—
9	7	Greece	+
NR	8	Turkey	NP
4	9	Germany	—
8	10	Denmark	—
21	11	Spain	+
16	12	Sweden	+
6	13	Canada	—
10	14	Norway	—
17	15	Finland	+
18	16	Australia	+
13	17	United Kingdom	—
12	18	Belgium/Luxembourg	—
7	19	France	—
19	20	Portugal	—
20	21	Italy	—
15	22	New Zealand	—

Notes:

NC = no change
+ = improvement
— = deterioration
NP = not possible to make a
         comparison
NR = not ranked in 1982

understand and may be inaccessible to the people who are affected by them, they do provide valuable guides to levels of competitiveness. What is required is credible information which has an impact on management and the general public. The kind of approach adopted by the Japanese and illustrated in Table 1.1 should be adapted to suit local needs. Survival in a highly competitive world will require ongoing information on the standards to be reached. Handy (11) suggests that the iron law of international comparison will necessitate an annual improvement in efficiency of 3 per cent just to stand still. This raises the daunting challenge of even greater growth if more jobs are to be created, or using the growth above 3 per cent to pay more wages to the existing workforce.

MICRO MEASUREMENTS

Macro indicators form an important part of the total productivity picture, but performance information at the individual organisation level is of greater interest to most managers. This information falls under the general heading of micro measurements. Within each enterprise some form of overall measurement will be found. For the commercial organisation the finance function tends to have a strong influence on the measurements used, such as return on capital employed (ie profit divided by total assets employed in the business) or profit to sales. A whole range of other indicators will be found, including sales or profit per employee and the more physical ones like output per hour. The former is influenced by accountants while the latter is the kind of measurement used by engineers. As pointed out already measures of profitability may indicate that money is being made but this will not necessarily mean that productivity is satisfactory. The reverse also follows from this argument: you can be productive in spite of poor profitability, eg not selling what is being produced under the most efficient conditions. Liquidity is a third crucial factor. An enterprise could be both profitable and productive and yet find itself in severe difficulties due to lack of working capital. Therefore a good measurement system should provide controls on profitability, productivity and liquidity.

In Part II macro and micro measurements are dealt with in considerable detail. The general principles of measurement are examined. The measurement of productivity should be an interlocking system right from such macro indicators as GNP per capita to sales per employee in the typical enterprise. As we shall see the individual organisation also needs a family of supporting measurements. This cascade effect, with each one giving information on its main areas of operation right from the macro to micro indicators, is shown in Figure 1.3.

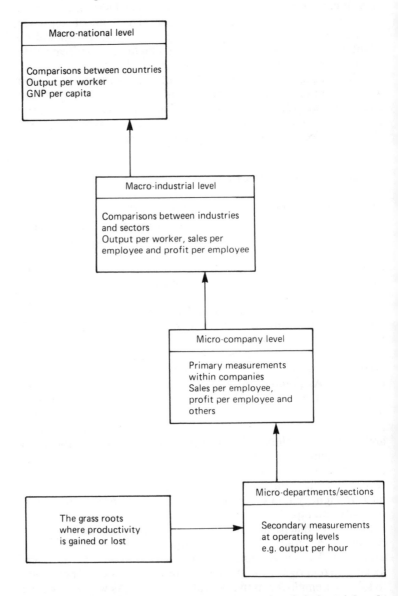

Figure 1.3 Productivity measurement at national, industrial and company levels

For the single enterprise or a particular industry regular information is required on three heads: i) its own performance, ii) its trend over time and iii) how it compares with others. Table 1.4,

Table 1.4   Productivity performance for UK industries for the years 1982 and 1983, arranged in rank order of profit per employee for 1983

With acknowledgements to Inter Company Comparisons Ltd London *Industrial Performance Analysis* 9th Edition 1984

No	Industry	Sales per employee				Profit per employee			
		1981/2 £	RO a	1982/3 £	% b	1981/2 £	RO c	1982/3 £	% b
1	Distillers	69700	1	79800	+14.5	10020	1	13404	+33.1
2	Drop forgers	25800	6	32300	+25.2	4281	2	6505	+51.9
3	Housebuilders	50900	2	64400	+26.5	4848	3	5590	+15.3
4	Supermarkets	38300	3	51200	+33.7	1272	4	1752	+37.7
5	High St traders	29300	5	36100	+23.2	1192	5	1362	+14.3
6	Bakeries	15200	9	17000	+11.8	316	6	315	NC
7	Steel producers	33900	4	33800	NC	276	7	−1400	−607
8	Machine tools	14400	10	16200	+12.5	913	8	−1419	−255
9	Agricultural equipment	24800	7	27600	+11.3	601	9	−1675	−378
10	Commercial vehicles	24200	8	29900	+23.6	−4595	10	−4401	+4.2
d	Variation of profit per employee					16.7 to 1		42.6 to 1	

Notes:

a   rank order of sales per employee for 1981

b   percentage change from 1982 to 1983

c   rank order of profit per employee for 1982/3

d   ratio of highest to lowest ignoring losses

NC   virtually no change

extracted from the UK Inter Company Comparisons survey for 1984 shows the comparisons of sales and profit per employee for ten UK industries, and their percentage change (trend) from 1982 to 1983. It is also interesting to note that the variation in profit per employee (the range of performance expressed as the ratio of the highest to lowest) varies considerably, ie 42.6 to 1. This situation is due to a combination of three factors:

1   The reliability of profit per employee as an indicator;
2   The variation in the conditions in which different industries operate;
3   A more effective management of resources by some enterprises.

All three factors have an influence on productivity improvement. Clearly measurements that mean what they portray and are believed and used are necessary. If external conditions are becoming unsatisfactory it is within our power to control if we have the will to do so. Lastly, learning how to make better use of resources embraces the first two – that is, a good measurement system, and an awareness of the need to adapt to a changed environment plus the more difficult task of actually improving existing performance.

KEYS TO SUCCESS

NEW AGE SOLUTIONS

During the last few years many well-known companies have failed or are operating on a reduced scale. Even countries have found themselves in serious economic circumstances. So the answer to the question, 'What are the keys to success?' is likely to be uppermost in the minds of many people at macro and micro levels. Pledges to sustain economic growth, the rescheduling of debts and attacks on inflation are some of the various ways of seeking a more prosperous future. At the same time enterprises of all kinds, large and small, public and private, have responded by cutting costs and resolving to be more efficient. Since we are in the midst of a third or even fourth wave transformation, these are all anachronistic palliatives, although they seem to give some short-term relief. Solutions more in keeping with the new age are needed. We should not delude ourselves that there are any quickfire answers to the kind of productivity problem now briefly outlined. As Toffler (12) has said, 'the subterranean structure on which our economies are based is now, itself, shifting, cracking ... we are dealing with surface phenomena rather than focusing on the deep structure, where the really big changes are occurring.' There would seem to be two keys to success:

1 Learning how to adapt to change on a continuing basis.
2 Information at all levels that is believed and made use of.

Learning from success

While we should be wary of trying to repeat the success of others, they can help to make us aware of our own areas of weakness.

The Japanese experience provides some insight into the ingredients of success. Henri-Claude de Bettigines, Director of the Euro-Asia Centre at INSEAD, France, speaking at the State of the Art Conference, (2) summed up Japan's industrial success under eight headings:

1 Information is regarded as a strategic resource;
2 Highly flexible organisations;
3 A willingness to 'unlearn' and hence to challenge existing beliefs;
4 A world vision of the future;
5 Personalised relations and individual acceptance at all levels of problem ownership;
6 Commitment to technological advance as a major objective;
7 Technical co-operation with suppliers;
8 Life-time employment as a national goal.

There are parts of the Japanese economy which do not exhibit these qualities and are operating at much lower levels of productivity. Even so, just their awareness of a need to unlearn is an important pointer for us all.

Nearer to the grass roots, the characteristics of the above-average American companies are reported in the popular Peters and Waterman book *In Search of Excellence*. (13) The companies in the study, which included MacDonalds and Texas Instruments, were chosen for their above-average growth and innovation performance record over a twenty-five-year period. Although the companies were using modern technology, it was the simple things that made them excellent. In all the firms studied, people who had good ideas were encouraged – some companies called them 'product champions', customer needs were given high priority and there was a strong orientation to action.

The eight attributes common to these excellent companies are listed below:

1   Action-orientation or just getting things done
2   Keeping in tune with the customer
3   Creating and fostering a climate of innovation
4   Involving people in productivity
5   Hands-on commitment of top management
6   Sticking to what you are good at
7   A simple and lean organisation structure
8   Getting the right balance between freedom of action and control.

The innovation and involvement aspects have similarities with the Japanese experience. But whereas the Peters and Waterman study is more to do with grass roots, micro, levels of performance, the Japanese points are of concern to the strategic macro factors.

FOCUSING PRODUCTIVITY

The productivity issue as now described is a complex one involving many factors. So that we can focus our attention the following eight factors have been selected as having the greatest bearing on productivity:

1   Economic climate: this includes the buoyancy of world trade, fluctuations in interest and exchange rates and the price of energy and raw materials;
2   Markets: these exhibit characteristics of growth alongside stagnation, where the right balance of price, quality and delivery is essential for survival;
3   Change: this is the rate of technical, social and economic change that has to be understood and managed;
4   Organisations: a climate and structure have to be created which enable people to adjust to the external rate of change and meet the new standards of productivity;
5   People: the attitudes, values and beliefs of people working in organisations have to be respected if their commitment to change is to be gained together with the achievements of new standards of performance;
6   Rewards: the necessary improvements in performance must be rewarded in both financial and psychological terms;
7   Information: productivity improvement depends upon a good information system which must be relevant, simple and

credible, have an impact on people and be available at the
right time;
8   Technology: the most up-to-date technology will be in-
    effective if the other seven factors are overlooked. Equally,
    technology should embrace design, methods, systems and
    appropriate techniques.

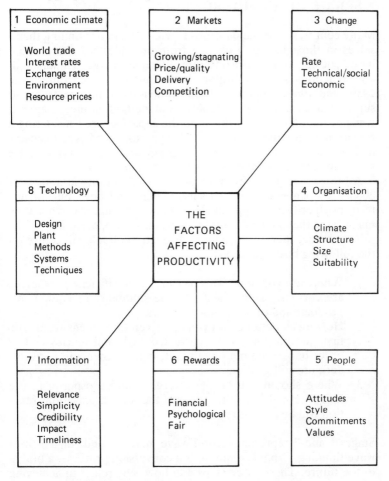

Notes:

1   Factors 1, 2 and 3 are external and tend to be regarded as uncontrollable variables

2   Factors 4 to 8 are internal variables and should therefore be within the control of
    the organisation

Figure 1.4   Focusing productivity

Difficult as it will be, these eight factors should be viewed as a whole and not in isolation. They are all interdependent. In the chapters that follow the interdependency aspect is expanded and so are the eight factors summarised in Figure 1.4.

A BRIDGE TO THE FUTURE

Many countries and the enterprises within them are finding themselves in the midst of a change from an Industrial Revolution-based society to a totally different information age. Understandably reactions are based upon the attitudes built up during the 1950s and 1960s. At one extreme individual firms are trying to survive using traditional technology and methods of measurement, while at the other end of the scale the Japanese are considering a replacement for the outdated GNP per capita and American car makers, in response to the rise in energy and materials costs, are saving millions of tons of materials used in motor cars.

A bridge is required from the present to the future and the year 2000. Companies do have to survive here and now, but longer-term prosperity will depend upon radical changes in what they make, how they make it, and the markets they operate in.

The theme, therefore, running through the book will centre on the following three questions:

1 Where are you now? This concerns how efficiently resources are currently being used and the suitability of equipment, products and organisation structure.
2 How much better could you be? Even though answering the first question may have corrected such deficiencies as low order books and outdated plant, improvements in performance are still possible.
3 Where should you be? For survival and prosperity in the longer term drastic alterations in the way organisations function will be necessary.

Stages 1 and 2 represent second wave methods and stage 3 third wave thinking. What is required is a conversion process – a bridge to the future. These three steps and how they relate to achieving full potential are illustrated in Figure 1.5.

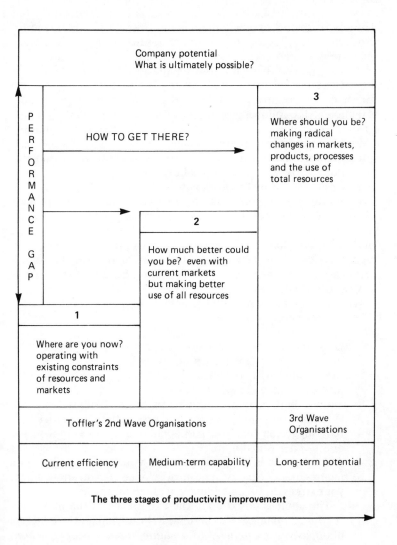

Figure 1.5 The basics of productivity improvement

SUMMARY

The object of this opening chapter has been to set the scene for productivity improvement. It is a complex task which is affected by many interrelated factors and consequently there are no quick, easy answers. But this is not to say solutions are not possible; they are. However, achieving more lasting improvements to the performance of countries and their organisations will necessitate attention to the following points:

1 Learning how to adapt to change;
2 Making people aware at all levels, through credible information, of the real state of productivity;
3 Commitment by top leaders to the productivity problem;
4 Improving performance in the short term and making longer-term radical changes in everything we do.

In the chapters that follow the techniques of productivity improvement blended with practical case studies are described. The aim is to facilitate the conversion process from where you are now to where you should be.

Before you make a start on the next part you could consider the following questions:

1 Do you think the varying growths in productivity are due to:
   (a)   inherent problems within countries
   (b)   a worldwide problem
   (c)   unreliable measurements.
2 Should there be improved national productivity statistics?
3 What do you believe are the real productivity priorities?
4 It is suggested that you and some colleagues complete the questionnaire in Figure 1.6 and then use it as a basis for discussion. It is an audit to assist you to reveal the main factors influencing current performance. It will show where your strengths lie and equally areas requiring attention.

    The audit is based upon the experience of the more successful companies, who all tend to be strong on the 8 factors of *objectives, customers, information, money, people, action, ideas* and *doing what you do best.*

There are two statements for each of the eight factors, making a total of 16 statements. Your response to each statement can range over a score of 1–10. Statements tending to 1 are on the left-hand side and 10 on the right. For each of the 16 statements place an N (for Now) above the number 1–10 that best indicates your assess-

OBJECTIVES

1 We are not clear on our goals, consequently there is no concerted action to achieve them.

1 2 3 4 5 6 7 8 9 10

Everyone knows exactly where we are going and we are committed to getting there.

2 We rarely review where we are going and make adjustments to our objectives.

1 2 3 4 5 6 7 8 9 10

Objectives are regularly reviewed in the light of changing market conditions.

CUSTOMERS/MARKETS

3 We take the market for granted.

1 2 3 4 5 6 7 8 9 10

We do everything we can to meet the needs of customers and the market.

4 We do not have information about our market. We hope we can sell what we make and buy.

1 2 3 4 5 6 7 8 9 10

We have a clear understanding of our market and concentrate on satisfying it.

INFORMATION/CONTROLS

5 Information is so mixed that it causes confusion.

1 2 3 4 5 6 7 8 9 10

Our information is so clear that there is rarely any confusion as to where our priorities lie.

6 Our controls are tight on trivialities and loose on important matters.

1 2 3 4 5 6 7 8 9 10

We have freedom to act within understood policy guidelines.

MONEY MANAGEMENT

7 We only make sporadic use of financial information.

1 2 3 4 5 6 7 8 9 10

We all make regular use of financial information to manage the business.

8 We do not regularly involve staff in our sales/cost position.

1 2 3 4 5 6 7 8 9 10

Getting the right balance between sales revenue and costs is understood by everyone.

Figure 1.6 Organisational assessment questionnaire

PEOPLE INVOLVEMENT

9 We do not involve   1 2 3 4 5 6 7 8 9 10   We have a highly moti-
   people in product-   vated team and encourage
   ivity improvement   them in every way we can.
   projects.

10 Our procedures   1 2 3 4 5 6 7 8 9 10   We keep our company
   and communications   organisation, procedures
   are complicated and   and communication very
   confusing.   simple.

ACTION

11 We dilly dally   1 2 3 4 5 6 7 8 9 10   We've got it almost right.
   too much in too   We don't rush into
   many instances.   decisions but don't have
                                                unnecessary delays.

12 We act without   1 2 3 4 5 6 7 8 9 10   Our actions are based
   reliable informa-   upon sound market and
   tion.   financial information.

IDEAS

13 We don't encourage   1 2 3 4 5 6 7 8 9 10   We encourage ideas, even
   ideas; we kill them   the risky ones.
   by default.

14 We are not aware   1 2 3 4 5 6 7 8 9 10   Business opportunities
   of the fresh oppor-   are identified by careful
   tunities for our business.   product/market studies.

DOING WHAT YOU
DO BEST

15 We are confused   1 2 3 4 5 6 7 8 9 10   We are well aware what
   about what business   business we are in.
   we are in.

16 We don't know what   1 2 3 4 5 6 7 8 9 10   We know what we're good
   we do best.   at and concentrate on it.

Fig 1.6 (concluded)

ment of your company as it is now. Then place a D (for Desired) above each number 1–10 for all 16 statements to show what you desire for the company. In other words, N represents how things are now and D how you would like them to be. Draw two lines to connect all the Ns and Ds, shade in between the lines and you will get some idea of gaps in the company. Get colleagues to do the same thing and compare your results.

Be as honest as you can.

REFERENCES

1 Hogg, Sarah, 'How to add up the productivity sums', *The Times* 2 April 1984
2 'Productivity – The New Direction – A State of the Art Conference', INSEAD, European Institute of Business Administration, Fontaine bleau, France, 11–13 July 1982
3 Beer, Stafford, *Heart of Enterprise*, John Wiley, 1979
4 Revans, Reg, *The Origins and Growth of Action Learning*, Chartwell Bratt, 1982
5 Drucker, Peter, *The Age of Discontinuity*, Heinemann, 1969
6 Toffler, Alvin, *The Third Wave, The revolution that will change our lives*, William Collins, 1980
7 Hawken, Paul, *The Next Economy*, Holt, Rinehart and Winston, 1983
8 Jones, Dr F. E., 'The Economic Ingredients of Industrial Success', *Journal of The Institution of Mechanical Engineers*, Vol 190, 16/76, 1976
9 Roy, A. D. 'Labour Productivity in 1980: An international comparison', *National Institute Economic Review*, Number 101, August 1982
10 *Report on International Industrial Competitiveness 1982–1983*, European Management Forum, Geneva 1983
11 Handy, Charles, *The Future of Work*, Basil Blackwell, 1984
12 Toffler, Alvin, *Previews & Promises*, William Morrow and Co., New York, 1983
13 Peters, Thomas J. and Waterman, Robert H. Jnr, *In Search of Excellence*, Harper and Row, New York, 1982

Part II
Measuring Productivity

Introduction to Part II:

The Elements of Productivity Measurement

In Part I we saw that the survival of any organisation will depend a good deal upon the skilful management of its resources. Even so in the present conditions of uncertainty, when enterprises in many countries have dramatically reduced their costs and there still does not appear to be much improvement, appeals for better productivity measurements may seem out of place. All the same the aim in Part II is to show that good productivity information is the important first step to convincing ourselves that productivity improvement, in its widest sense, is a necessity.

It is recognised that productivity measurement is only one part of the whole task of improving productivity. Even so information on all aspects of organisations will need to be regarded as a crucial resource. Equally, it will require intelligent use; that is, the information collected has to be converted into meaningful measurements which tell us how well we are managing the resources at our disposal. Moreover, they are used to bring about improvements. An effective management information system, the prerequisite of skilled productivity analysis, should take account of the following factors:

- *Awareness*: it needs to make us aware of the existing productivity position, both internally and externally.
- *Action*: it should lead to change in the current position; in other words, it is used.
- *Confusion*: the system should filter out the irrelevant information which confuses and diverts our attention.
- *Comprehensibility*: everyone who receives productivity information must understand it.
- *Defensiveness*: the defensive reactions to figures, especially the adverse ones, have to be overcome.
- *Timeliness*: information has to be available in sufficient time for action to be taken.
- *Validity*: actual changes in productivity are accurately reflected in the measurement system.
- *Dynamism*: it must be sensitive to the changing internal and external conditions; tomorrow's problems cannot be solved with yesterday's measurement system.

These eight points could be summed up in four words: simple, credible, flexible and used. Chapter 3 includes a more detailed method of information auditing, but in the meantime try assessing your current information system against these eight factors.

The principal aim of Part II is to set the scene for measuring productivity. It is a long section which reflects the key role of measurement and information in increasing organisational performance. The three chapters that follow cover the following areas:

1 The common misunderstandings about productivity, the five aims of an effective measurement system and an examination of the basic types of output and input classification necessary for measuring productivity.
2 Techniques for obtaining the information necessary for measuring productivity. Low-cost methods for improving productivity are also included.
3 How to measure productivity at the primary and secondary levels of organisations.

Our objective is to present a blend of the technical aspects of productivity measurement combined with practical guidance on how to use it. As Robert Heller (1) has said, 'There are managers who cannot calculate percentages but still have a natural flair to make profits.' Harold Martin (2) gave this advice on productivity improvement: 'It is not only necessary to measure it, but to use the information for remedial management decision making and control.'

REFERENCES

1   Heller, Robert, *The Naked Manager,* Barrie & Jackson, London 1974
2   Martin, Professor Harold, 'Productivity Costing and Management', *Management International Review*, No. 7, 1970.

2 What is productivity?

Productivity, as previously stated, is the relationship between goods produced, or a service provided, and the resources consumed in doing it. Productivity, therefore, in its very many forms is stated as some variation of the ratio:

$$\frac{\text{OUTPUT}}{\text{INPUT}}$$

The problem with productivity measurement is deciding which are the best outputs and inputs to use. To answer this question we first have to have a clear idea of what productivity is and what it is not. So at the outset we should clear up the common misunderstandings about productivity.

1. 'Increased output increases productivity.' This is only true if costs have not gone up at a greater rate. We should guard against being activity-oriented with insufficient attention to results; the output/input relationship is the important guide. Moreover, increases in output compared to previous years should take account of price increases and inflation.

2   'Profit and productivity are synonymous.' If profits have been obtained through price recovery this is not necessarily true: productivity may have gone down. Conversely, good productivity does not always go with high profits, eg the goods produced efficiently may not be required.

3   'Cutting costs improves productivity.' In depressed economic conditions reducing costs is regarded as necessary for survival. However, a short-term cutting of expenditure, especially if done indiscriminately, could make matters worse in the long term.

4   'Profits today and tomorrow are possible.' We may have to forgo short-term profits, even incur losses, so that we can invest in projects for longer-term survival. Such projects could include productivity improvement programmes.

5   'Partial productivity improvement is worthwhile.' Organisations are interdependent units; the performance of one part affects the rest. Therefore, a piecemeal approach is generally not successful: eg productivity measurement on its own is not enough. Figure 2.1 illustrates the experience of the American Productivity Center in Houston, that companies who take a total approach are more successful in productivity improvement.

6   'Productivity only applies to production.' Productivity is relevant to any organisation, public, private, non-profit-making, manufacturers, retailers and service businesses alike.

All these factors can influence our attitudes to productivity. As Alvin Toffler (1) has said, 'It depends on what is measured and who does the measuring'.

DEFINING PRODUCTIVITY

All organisations should be concerned with how they convert their resources (inputs) into some form of output. This implies that all organisations are output systems. Output can take the form of products manufactured, goods sold and services provided. So productivity can be defined as how efficiently inputs are converted into outputs. Around this simple definition there are many opinions about the best ways of measuring conversion efficiency. Many companies may judge their performance purely in output terms, eg sales and products made, but this is not productivity. While accountants use financial indicators like return on capital employed, engineers tend more to physical measurements, for example output per labour-hour. All of these methods have a part to play in productivity measurement, but we shall be working from the definition overleaf.

Approach	Unsuccessful programmes					Successful programmes				
	Companies					Companies				
	A	B	C	D	E	F	G	H	I	J
Management support		●				●	●	●	●	●
Measurement system				●		●	●	●	●	●
Objectives				●		●	●	●	●	●
Strategic plan						●		●		●
Appraisals			●			●	●	●	●	●
Organisation						●	●	●	●	●
Quality								●		●
Teams			●				●		●	●
Quality circles	●					●	●			●
Sharing gains					●					●
Multiple skills						●	●		●	●
Communications		●				●	●	●	●	●
	Piecemeal approach					Total approach				

Figure 2.1   Productivity improvement: total and piecemeal approaches

With acknowledgement to the American Productivity Center

Productivity is a comprehensive measure of how efficiently and effectively organisations satisfy the following five aims.

1 Objectives: the degree to which principal objectives are achieved;
2 Efficiency: how efficiently resources (inputs of labour materials, purchased services and capital) are used to generate useful outputs, useful in the sense that goods made or services provided are actually needed;
3 Effectiveness: what is achieved in output and input terms compared to what is potentially possible;
4 Comparability: how productivity compares with other organisations, industries and countries;
5 Trends: the productivity performance record over time, ie the decline, static or growth aspects.

These five factors are fundamental to any productivity measurement system and therefore require detailed examination.

OBJECTIVES

We need to know whether our main organisational objectives have been achieved. Many accountants, businessmen and economists regard maximisation of profit as the chief objective. While there will be different interpretations of the meaning of maximisation and profit, certainly in commercial organisations profit is important. But there are other competing aims. Paying satisfactory wages for employees, meeting the bills of outside suppliers, and setting aside a fund for wear and tear (ie depreciation) and future investment are also important. Adam Smith, (2) the father of private enterprise economic theory, stated some 200 years ago that the sole end purpose of any organisation is to make a viable living for everyone involved in it and to sustain its fixed and circulating capital.

The advice of Adam Smith and present-day experience point to something more than just profit as the basic aim. Indeed, Nobel Prize-winning economist Samuelson and John Galbraith have both argued that profit is only a form of interest. Enterprises do not fail, at least in the short run, when they cease to make a profit but when losses have so reduced their working capital that they cannot pay their wages and creditors. In the light of this analysis the following primary objective developed by Harold Martin (see reference 2, page 92) is more appropriate: 'To assure an adequate total fund to meet all of the demands on the organisation'.

This fund is called total earnings and forms the basis of the productivity measurement system described in this book. For manufacturers and retailers total earnings is simply sales less all materials actually contained in the sales. For organisations which do not consume materials in this sense (eg agriculture, mining and service organisations), sales and total earnings are the same thing.

Total earnings is thus the fund which includes all wages and salaries, purchased services (eg electricity, gas, oil, water, rent and telephone), depreciation, profit and taxes. Furthermore, giving equal priority to all stakeholders is more socially acceptable than just concentrating on profit. The rate at which this total fund is generated is also consistent with the efficient use of all resources and can therefore be applied as a total factor productivity measurement. The main divisions of total earnings are shown in Figure 2.2.

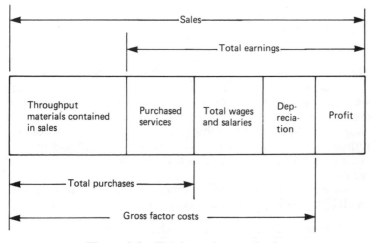

Figure 2.2   Total earnings and sales

EFFICIENCY

Measurements of efficiency provide answers to the question in Chapter 1, 'Where are you now?' They tell us how well output is being generated from available inputs and are an indication of the utilisation of available capacity. Efficiency is therefore a measurement of the way an organisation is currently using the resources at its disposal. Stafford Beer in his penetrating productivity analysis (3) calls this 'actuality' or what we are managing to do now, with existing resources, under existing constraints. Efficiency measurements should reveal two broad aspects of existing organisational performance:

1 The output to input relationship, that is, the output generated by available inputs, bearing in mind whether the output is useful in the sense of being required now or at some future time. For this reason planning for useful outputs should play an important part in productivity, especially in manufacturing and retailing concerns.
2 The utilisation of resources or the quantity of inputs utilised compared to the total capacity available.

Where-we-are-now efficiency is bound to include varying degrees of wasteful, as well as the more efficient, use of resources; our efficiency indicators should tell us where the inefficiencies lie.

We also need to be aware of how engineers and accountants treat efficiency. It is implicit in engineering systems that you cannot get more out than you put in, in other words, efficiency will always be less than 100 per cent; the conversion of inputs into outputs results in losses (eg heat, noise and vibration). This point is important when measurements of potential efficiency are taken. Theoretically efficiency ratios greater than 1 are not possible.

Accountants on the other hand aim for output/input ratios which are above 100 per cent. All commercial undertakings will seek a rate of sales income which will provide a margin over and above operating costs. It is this surplus or profit which gives performances ratios above 100 per cent. Remember also that profit is not a good productivity indicator because of the influence of price recovery.

Industrial and commercial enterprises then will aim to achieve an efficiency ratio greater than unity. This can be stated as:

$$\frac{\text{Output}}{\text{Input}} = \frac{\text{Input} + \text{Profit}}{\text{Input}} \qquad \frac{O}{I} = \frac{I + P}{I}$$

In contrast the engineer's concept of efficiency is

$$\frac{\text{Input} - \text{Losses}}{\text{Input}}$$

The positive and negative (ie profit and loss) link between these two viewpoints can be shown as

$$\frac{\text{Output} - \text{Input}}{\text{Input}} = \frac{O - I}{I} = \frac{O}{I} - 1$$

This shows that I deducted from the productivity ratio of O/I gives the profit productivity ratio. The measurement of performance in all commercial organisations will be influenced in varying degrees by the profit-oriented financial indicators of the accountant and the more physical ones of the engineers. The American Productivity Center have done considerable work on how to relate these financial and physical aspects. Their method for relating profitability, productivity and price recovery is illustrated in Figure 2.3. A further development of this price recovery method is described in the *Harvard Business Review*, May/June 1984.

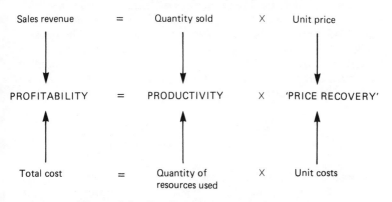

Figure 2.3   Profitability and productivity

With acknowledgement to Carl G. Thor, Vice-President, American Productivity Center, Houston, Texas, USA.

EFFECTIVENESS

Though efficiency and effectiveness are related they are different aspects of productivity measurement. Efficiency measures the existing state of affairs, but effectiveness compares present achievements with what could be done if resources were managed more effectively. This concept of effectiveness includes an output target to be reached, achieving a new standard of performance, or a more idealistic potential which would be possible if all constraints were removed. There are therefore two levels of organisational effectiveness.

1   Reaching improved standards of performance through better organisation and the use of management techniques (eg work study). The target is to make use of the full capability

of resources such as plant, a design department, a piece of land or a hospital. Even with the current constraints of unsatisfactory resources and a low level of demand, could we be better if we really worked at it?

2   Aiming for an ideal potential if constraints, both internal and external, were removed. As Russell Ackoff (4) points out, all organisations should pursue goals which may at the time seem unattainable.

Level 1 is concerned with the question 'How much better could you be?' or what Beer (3) describes as increasing our capability, but being aware that if we do not take advantage of our increased capability productivity goes down. Level 2 focuses on the question 'What else should we be doing?'

Effectiveness is thus a measure of what output could be achieved compared with how efficiently resources are utilised. The relationship to output/input is shown below:

$$\frac{\text{Output}}{\text{Input}} = \frac{\text{Effectiveness (what could be achieved)}}{\text{Resources consumed}}$$

In practice there will be many levels of effectiveness combined with just as many degrees of resource consumption. Therefore productivity improvement will involve some combination of increasing effectiveness and a better use of available resources. We have avoided using efficiency in the denomination of the above ratio as this would imply that if efficiency goes down productivity goes up. Eilon (5) suggests that output can vary between a present actual and a maximum with input varying between an actual and a minimum. A modified version of Eilon's framework for analysing the range of outputs and inputs is shown in Figure 2.4. This shows four basic ratios:

1   Actual output divided by actual input, a status quo;
2   Higher output divided by current actual inputs, that is, higher results are there to be had but capability has not changed;
3   Actual current output divided by lower inputs; capability has increased but is not being used;
4   The highest level of effectiveness, maximum output divided by minimum input.

The following example shows the options open to a company which wants to improve its use of stock.

A manufacturing company is currently achieving an annual rate of stock turn of four times based upon sales for the year of £6 million and total average stocks of £1.5 million. It would like to match the Japanese average of 8, a new level of effectiveness.

		Output range	
I n p u t		Actual	2 levels of effectiveness
r a n g e	Actual	1 Where you are now	2 High output possibility Low capability
	Range of resource consumption	3 High capability Low output effectiveness	4 Where you should be

Figure 2.4   Range of outputs and inputs

There are three possible ways of doing this:

1   Increase sales to £12 million, ie a 100 per cent increase, and maintain existing stock levels;
2   Decrease stocks to £¾ million, ie a 50 per cent decrease, and continue with sales as they are;
3   Adopt a combination of increased sales and reduced stocks.

Whichever option is adopted the lessons are twofold:

1   Current levels of efficiency must be assessed and targets of effectiveness determined.
2   Productivity improvement involves trade-offs; each part of an organisation affects the rest; it is a total problem.

COMPARABILITY

A good guide to an organisation's performance is comparison with other organisations. Indeed no matter how good the productivity ratio, on its own it does not tell us much; without some form of comparison it is useless. If, for example, a retail shop has increased its sales from £20,000 in a month to £30,000 with the same staff of ten, it will be pleased. But suppose a similar business is earning £50,000 with nine people. Comparisons of this kind open our eyes to higher standards, but, more important, they act as a spur to improve.

It is not only comparisons between organisations that require attention. In a fiercely competitive world which is also becoming smaller due to the communications revolution, managers will have to be more aware of international comparisons. Ignoring them will jeopardise survival for any company that depends upon world markets.

Interfirm comparisons are also measurements of effectiveness because they expose the performance of one organisation to the standards of others. They therefore provide targets to aim for. Furthermore, if we regularly compare ourselves with others we shall be kept informed of what needs to be achieved in order to remain competitive. In Chapter 5 an interfirm comparison programme is described, called 'productivity audits', which has been used successfully in a wide range of companies.

TRENDS

Comparisons inform us how our level of productivity sizes up to others. Trends in productivity performance over time are also an essential part of any measurement system. The comparison of current performance with that of last month or the previous year will reveal whether any growth has taken place. It is worth emphasising that while comparisons and trends are two important aspects of productivity measurement they are often confused. For example, the American Productivity Center reminds United States industry that in 1983 it was both first and last in productivity: first in comparison with other industrial countries and last in growth trend.

There are two cautions we need to bear in mind when comparing productivity levels and tracking them over time periods. One is to allow for price increases and the effects of inflation and the other to consider differing mixes of output and inputs.

Adjusting for inflation

If total sales in two consecutive years were £2,000,000 and £2,140,000, this suggests a trend of plus 7 per cent. However, if inflation was 6 per cent the apparent growth becomes less impressive. It can be argued that when output and input costs have gone up similarly, inflation will not affect productivity ratios. This belief that inflation will equally affect prices charged and such costs as wages may be satisfactory in some circumstances. The important point is to be aware of the effects of price increases and inflation and to make conscious decisions. Like most managerial decision making the amount of risk depends a great deal on how much information we have.

There are two methods for allowing for increases in prices and costs. One is to maintain an annual index of output and inputs and compare the change with nationally published inflation and retail indices or, where they are available, specific indices for your industry. The indexing method consists of giving the basic period an index of 100 and then comparing subsequent actual figures with this index. The other method, used by the American Productivity Center, is to deflate actual output and input by the average price/cost increases in the company.

Table 2.1 The indexing method for comparing inflation rates: sales output analysis

Base year 1982		Results 1983				
Total sales £'000	Index	Total sales £'000	Index	Actual growth	Inflation rate	Real growth
1	2	3	4	5	6	7
5000	100	5400	108	+ 8%	105.6	+2.4%

Table 2.2 The indexing method for comparing inflation rates: input costs (wages and salaries) analysis

Base year 1982			Results 1983					
Total wages and salaries £'000	Index	% Sales	Total wages and salaries £'000	Index	Actual growth	% sales	Retail cost of living index	Real growth
1	2	3	4	5	6	7	8	9
1000	100	20	1220	122	+22%	22.6%	107	+15%

Tables 2.1 and 2.2 provide illustrations of method 1. Table 2.1 shows an output index of 108 or an apparent 8 per cent growth, but when allowance is made for an inflation index of 105.6 the real growth is only 2.4 per cent, ie 8 per cent − 5.6 per cent. The actual wages and salaries incurred for the above outputs are shown in Table 2.2. This indicates an adverse trend for the company, with wages to sales now 2.6 per cent up in 1983, at 22.6 per cent. For employees the picture is better, with their remuneration 15 per cent up after allowing for a retail cost of living index rate of 7 per cent. We can also derive two productivity indices from these figures as shown below:

1 $\dfrac{\text{Output index 1983}}{\text{Input index 1983}} = \dfrac{108}{122} = 0.88$

2 $\dfrac{\text{\% wages to sales 1982}}{\text{\% wages to sales 1983}} = \dfrac{20}{22.6} = 0.88$

In both cases there is a deterioration in productivity.

The analysis of productivity trends should come as close as possible to the actual physical changes that have taken place. For this reason individual organisations should try and keep track of their own record of price and cost increases. In the case of the figures shown in Table 2.1 an analysis of price increases for all product groups revealed an average increase of 6 per cent (ie 0.4 per cent more than the inflation rate of 5.6 per cent). It was also found that the total hours worked for the two years were 178,039 and 194,648 respectively. This information and that shown in Table 2.1 and 2.2 makes it possible to deflate outputs and inputs and to calculate deflated productivity measurements, shown in Table 2.3. This is the method developed by the American Productivity Center. The analysis continues to reveal adverse trends in productivity; in 1982 every £1 of wages was generating £5 of sales, while in 1983 this had fallen to £4.5. Similarly one hour produced £28.1 of sales in 1982 and £26.2 in 1983. Through this method of deflating for price and cost increases a physical indicator of productivity is obtained. It also gives a link with the financial position. For example, if wages in 1983 had generated sales at the 1982 level (ie £5 of sales for every £1 of wages), £700,000 additional sales would have resulted (ie 5 × 1,220,000 = 6,100,000 − 5,400,000). There is, of course, the difficult task of getting the necessary improvements in efficiency, but first we need to keep track of price and cost changes and their effects on productivity.

Table 2.3 Deflated sales, wages and productivity

Item	Base year 1982 1	Results for 1983 Details 2	% change 3
Actual sales	£5,000,000	£5,400,000	+8
Price deflator		1.06	
Deflated sales (actual sales ÷ 1.06)		£5,094,339 c	
Price generated sales (Item 1−Item 3)		£305,661	+6
Actual wages	£1,000,000	£1,220,000	+22
Wage deflator (retail cost of living index)		1.07	
Deflated wages (actual wages ÷ 1.07)		£1,140,186 d	
Wages generated by retail cost of living index (Item 5−Item 7)		£79,814	
Total hours worked	178,039	194,648	+9.3
1982 sales ÷ hours worked	£28.1		
1982 sales ÷ wages	£5		
Deflated sales ÷hours worked		£26.1	
Deflated sales ÷ wages		£4.5	
Hourly productivity 1982/1983		$\frac{26.1}{28.1} = .93$	
Sales/wages productivity 1982/1983		$\frac{4.5}{5} = .9$	

Remaining wage increases are due to additional hours worked and wage drift.

Account should also be taken of other cost increases, e.g. energy, materials and so on. The internal system should maintain movements in price increases and the various cost increases.

The net sales value if prices had remained constant.

Wage costs if there had been no retail cost of living increases.

Allowing for different output/input mixes

When making comparisons or trends analysis, account should be taken of different mixes of outputs and inputs on productivity measurement. In organisations where there are only one or two outputs and inputs are fairly stable this aspect is not important. But in the majority of enterprises such a situation is unlikely, so a system of weighting is generally used. This is a method for reducing seemingly unlike outputs and inputs to some common basis of comparison. The weighting factors may be materials, labour, energy, prices or capital depending upon which one is common to all outputs. For example, the company shown in Tables 2.1 to 2.3 produces three groups of castings. A labour weighting analysis would give the results shown in Table 2.4. This shows that if the output of castings in groups B and C had been produced with the labour intensity relative to group A 38,000 more tons would have been produced. A similar analysis could be made for 1983 and enable output in equivalent tons to be compared.

Table 2.4 Labour weighting analysis
Sales 1982 £5,000,000

Casting product group	1 Labour content hours/ton	2 Labour content relative to A	3 Output actual tons	4 Product A* equivalent tons
A	25	1.00	50,000	50,000
B	40	1.6	30,000	48,000
C	50	2.00	20,000	40,000
Totals			100,000	138,000

Note:
* Column 3 × column 2

For ease of reference the elements of a productivity measurement system are shown in Figure 2.5.

OUTPUTS

The next step to increase our understanding of productivity is to clarify the types of output used at the organisation and national levels. We believe you should be able to relate the outputs used at national level to those used within individual organisations. Though they appear difficult to many people, country-level statistics are not much different from what is found within a company.

The principal outputs used are described below. So as to simplify future use the outputs described have each been given a letter prefix. For quick reference a glossary of terms is also included as an appendix. Much of the analysis that follows is based upon the extensive studies of productivity made by Harold Martin and Simcha Bahiri of Tel Aviv University.

1 OBJECTIVES	2 EFFICIENCY	3 EFFECTIVENESS	4 COMPARISONS	5 TRENDS
Generating a satisfactory total fund to meet all demands on the organisation consistent with an efficient use of resources	1 Current output compared to inputs used 2 Quantity of inputs used compared to total capacity available	What is currently being achieved compared to what is possible	Productivity comparisons between organisations, industries and countries	Comparisons of productivity over time within organisations and for growth comparisons between industries and countries
Am I meeting the basic needs of the organisation?	Where am I now?	How much better could I be? Where should I be?	How do I compare with others?	Am I growing, standing still or in decline?
			1 Adjust for inflation, price and cost increases	
			2 Allow for varying mixes of output and inputs	

Figure 2.5 Productivity: the five aims

1 *Gross sales revenue, 'S':* the total income received from goods produced or goods sold in the case of retailers. At the national level the grand total of all sales of all companies is called gross output.

2 *Profit, 'P':* the amount remaining after all costs including depreciation have been deducted from sales. We should note that profit is only one form of output and does not on its own reveal the degree of profitability or productivity.

3 *Gross total earnings, 'T':* gross sales revenue less the throughput materials or bought-out products consumed in the sales. As stated earlier, total earnings is the basic fund from which all the demands on the organisation have to be met. In the case of service organisations, agriculture and extractive industries, where there are no throughput materials, total earnings equals sales.

4 *Gross value added (GVA):* not to be confused with total earnings, is gross sales revenue less all outside purchases used in the conversion process (ie throughput materials plus all purchased services such as electricity, gas, water, telephone and rents). At the national level 'GVA' is called Gross Domestic Product, 'GDP' or net national output; Gross National Product, 'GNP', as noted in Part I, is merely 'GDP' plus net income from

abroad. Thus 'GVA' is the company equivalent of 'GDP'.

5   *Net value added, 'NVA':* 'GVA' less depreciation. 'NVA' is
    finding increasing use in net value added productivity and is
    also being developed by UNIDO (United Nations Industrial
    Development Organisation) for what they call social surplus
    productivity, described next. At the national level NVA = net
    domestic product; Net National Value Added is a more refined
    version of 'NVA' which is GVA less depreciation charges and
    all repatriated payments (ie interest, profit, royalties and
    salaries).

6   *Social surplus, 'SS':* the UNIDO project aims to study the
    difference between commercial and national profitability. This
    is mainly directed to increasing the efficiency of generating
    social surplus, an important figure especially for developing
    countries. It can be simply defined as the total of all retained
    interests, rents, royalties and profits. Social surplus – NVA less
    labour costs.

7   *Gross contribution margin, 'CM':* used in management
    accounting, is gross sales revenue less all variable costs. Con-
    tribution margin is what is left from sales after meeting variable
    costs and is thus the contribution to fixed costs and profit.
    While 'CM' is more often associated with cost we are classify-
    ing it as a form of output. It also means output that can be sold
    or used in the period being measured.

These are the seven divisions of output used for the primary
measurement of organisational productivity. Their national
equivalents have also been stated where appropriate. Secondary
measurements at the 'shop floor' levels require more detailed
outputs, such as:

   Cars produced
   Tons of castings made
   Number of sales calls
   Number of customers served
   Clients consulted
   Design drawings completed
   Letters typed
   Operations performed
   Patients seen
   Passengers carried
   Plants grown

These are a mixture of outputs for industry, retailing, professional services, health care, transport and horticulture.

INPUTS

Now for an examination of the inputs which in various ways are consumed in the generation of the outputs described. Letter prefixes are similarly used.

1 *Gross factor costs, 'F':* the total of all costs incurred in making products, selling them or providing a service. This includes throughput materials where appropriate, purchase services, wages, depreciation and as also illustrated in Figure 2.1.

2 *Throughput materials, 'M':* 'M' in the case of manufacturers are materials and bought-out parts actually contained in the product made. For retailers or wholesalers it is the products purchased from a manufacturer or distributor for sale to a customer. For the purpose of measuring conversion efficiency, throughput materials are regarded as a temporary investment in the company. This input cost is irrelevant for service organisations (eg solicitors, banks, government departments etc), some parts of agriculture, and extractive industries (eg mining and oilfields).

3 *Total purchased services, 'PS':* these are the total of all services purchased from various sources and used in the process of converting materials into outputs. Purchased services are divided into two groups: (i) running costs consisting of energy (electricity, gas and oil), water, telephone, postage, consultants' fees, indirect production materials, processing materials, travelling and hotel expenses, and catering; and (ii) capital costs, consisting generally of rents, local taxes, insurance, leasing and royalties.

   Throughput materials and purchased services together comprise all outside purchases and will be prefixed 'X'.

4 *All wages and salaries, 'W':* total employee costs include everyone working in the organisation from chief executive to cleaners and embrace not only wages and salaries but all other benefits.

5 *Depreciation, 'k':* depreciation charges, on the one hand, are nominal in the sense that a tangible cost is not actually incurred on a regular basis. On the other hand, they are real wear-and-tear costs and should therefore be included in the period total conversion costs.

6 *Total conversion costs, 'C':* for better or for worse, with all the

existing inefficiencies, these are the costs of converting materials and parts into, preferably, useful output. These costs are the total of all wages and salaries, purchased services and depreciation or W + PS + k = C. Moreover, though conversion implies making some kind of product conversion, these costs are relevant to any form of organisation.

7 *Total capital charges, 'K':* in general these are the total of all costs associated with fixed assets, ie buildings, plant equipment and land. The charges included are total purchased service, 'PS', or capital costs, ie rents, local taxes, insurance, leasing, royalties, plus running costs and depreciation 'k'.

All of the costs described can be divided into fixed and variable elements. That is, some costs will tend not to vary even though the level of output has changed. On the other hand, some costs are very sensitive to output changes. The best example of variable cost is throughput materials, which is also the best example of a truly avoidable cost.

A simple division of conversion costs will be used as shown in the three basic categories in Figure 2.6.

Total remuneration	Purchased services	Depreciation
All wage and salary costs	Everything purchased from outside and used in the conversion process including capital costs 'k'	Wear and tear costs incurred in the conversion costs

Notes:

1 Throughput materials are regarded as a temporary investment in the enterprise rather than a cost. The above three costs are consumed in converting throughput materials into useful outputs.

2 Some capital charges are included in purchased services, as are energy costs. For more refined productivity measurements these may need to be isolated.

Figure 2.6 Conversion costs

There are other inputs we shall need to use, the more common of which are listed below:

1 Total people working in the organisation with part-timers adjusted to a full-time basis;

2   Physical space used. In the United States and Great Britain square footage is used, with square metres in Europe. Where volume occupied is important, as in retail establishments and warehouses, cubic measurements are more meaningful.

3   Stock, or to give it the more comprehensive term, inventory, is an important input especially for retailers and manufacturers.

The other input we should consider is time. Whether it be a manufacturing plant, a design department, the typing pool, the local supermarket or a hospital, the productivity potential is dependent on how the time available is used. The maximum or upper theoretical limit that any organisation can be operated is 24 hours per day for 365 days per year. But this assumes that everyone starts and finishes on time and there are no other interruptions. A more realistic capacity must take into account interruptions leading to lost time, and will be called feasible capacity.

This practical view of capacity is based on the ability of the organisation to generate its particular form of output. This does not take into account idle time, which is caused by lack of work to be done. After allowing for lost and idle time the remaining time can be used in two ways which will be called productive work and ancillary work. These two terms will be dealt with in more detail later on. For the time being productive work is what makes the greatest impact on the organisation's objectives. Ancillary work supports productive work activity. For example, in a plant making motor cars, productive work is when labour or plant is actually transforming materials in some way, with one kind of ancillary work being moving materials from one operation to another. These main divisions of time are summarised in Figure 2.7.

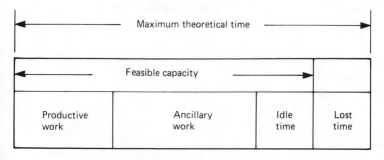

Note: Productive work time tends to be less than ancillary work time

Figure 2.7 Divisions of time

For both productive measurement and planning work an agreement on feasible capacity is an important starting point. There are a number of ways of finding out the capacity that is available. These methods include obtaining a consensus between the main functions (eg senior management, production, sales and accounts), recording devices on equipment and activity sampling.

SUMMARY

The common language of outputs and inputs we have described forms the basis of analysing productivity whether at the organisational, industrial, sector or national levels. Figure 2.8 shows the relationship between the outputs and inputs used. A reliable productivity measurement system should also take account of the effects of price increases and inflation. We will need to have the answers to such questions as, 'Is our present profitability due to increased prices or improved productivity?' 'How do we really compare with last year when our sales, profits and costs are deflated to allow for price changes and the effects of inflation on costs?' 'What level of profitability could we have had from improved productivity?' The method for relating profitability, productivity and price recovery pioneered by the American Productivity Center provides answers to these questions. Busy managers need to relate productivity measurements to bottom-line considerations like profitability. Equally, they should appreciate that profits from improved productivity give better long-term security than those from price recovery.

In the next chapter more practical definitions of information for measuring productivity are described. Before you make a start on measurement we suggest you deal with the following questions:

1   In the light of the eight points in the introduction to Part II, how effective is your productivity information system?
2   Do you have misunderstandings about productivity?
3   Have you been taking a partial approach to productivity improvement?
4   Do you distinguish between efficiency and effectiveness?
5   Is something other than profit needed to measure organisational objectives?
6   Does your measurement system separate profitability from productivity?
7   Is allowance made for price increases and the effects of inflation on costs? What method do you use?

8 Have you any measurements that reveal your utilisation of resources on productive work?

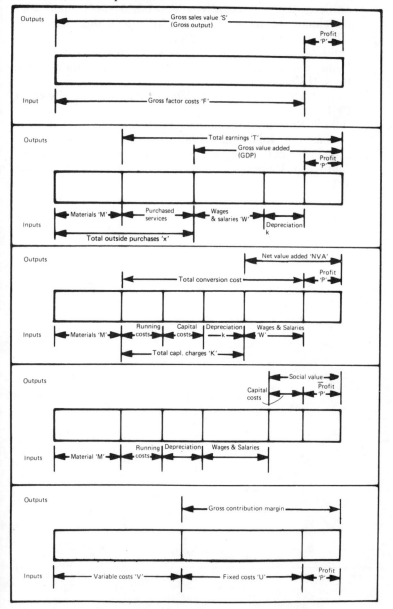

Figure 2.8 Divisions of outputs and inputs

REFERENCES

1   Toffler, Alvin, 'Productivity depends entirely upon what we choose to measure – and who does the measuring', *Observer*, London, 31 May 1981.
2   Smith, Adam, *The Wealth of Nations*, The Modern Library, Random House, New York, 1937, Book I Chapter 8 and Book II Chapter 1.
3   Beer, Stafford, *Brain of the Firm*, John Wiley, 2nd edition, 1981.
4   Ackoff, Russell L., *Creating the Corporate Future – Plan or Be Planned For*, John Wiley, 1981.
5   Eilon, Samuel, 'Use and Misuse of Productivity Ratios', *Journal of Management Science*, Vol. 10, No. 6, pp 575–80, 1982.

3 Information – the crucial resource

For the purposes of productivity measurement there are two kinds of information. Firstly, there is the basic information necessary to calculate the measurements. Secondly there are the resulting measurements. In this chapter the aim is to examine the problems of obtaining the necessary information of the first kind. Information gathering may not be an easy task. The facts and figures that we take for granted, particularly in the smaller company, are quite often just not there, at least on a regular basis.

There is now little doubt that information will be regarded as a resource equally as important as equipment and people. Indeed Peter Drucker(1) predicted in the 1960s that information and knowledge would be the new growth industries. *The Next Economy*, (2) written in 1983, proposes that the manufacturers who survive will have to design information and intelligence into their products and manufacturing processes and, of significance to this book, will have an adequate flow of operating information.

This chapter will attempt to define information, describe the difficulties of obtaining it, and establish such aspects as how often it should be used, who should provide and who receive it, and how it should be controlled and monitored.

WHAT IS INFORMATION?

Most organisations, especially those with a computer, will not be short of information. Indeed, the people concerned may have too much, may not be able to understand what reaches them or may misuse it. In productivity measurement and the preceding basic information, we define information, whether verbal or written, as something that causes change to take place. We shall also be treating productivity measurement as information which is published on a routine and regular basis. Haphazard, irregular figures generally reflect a panic reaction and are therefore not classed as part of a productivity measurement system. Any information collected should be seen as a means to improving productivity. The simple but demanding test is 'Is it put to practical use?' If not then it is questionable whether the effort should continue. At the same time, with so much change taking place, information systems will need to be under regular review.

Experience suggests that some organisations may be starved of information that is needed, and even may be unaware that they need the information. This situation may arise for two reasons:

1   The organisation filters out, as Ackoff (3) describes it, the important information. In everyday terms people unconsciously distort communications and completely omit some aspects. Still more insidiously, filtering is done for political and manipulative purposes. The second phenomenon is difficult to overcome, but we can prevent the first.

2   We need to improve our skill at asking what Revans (4) calls the totally new question, 'Q', and to be on our guard against the dangers of relying on our existing programmed knowledge and experience, 'P'. As we have said elsewhere, nothing can be more harmful to effective productivity measurement than relying on yesterday's information to measure tomorrow's productivity, and not being aware of it. As Ackoff (3) reminds us: 'If managers do not know how to use the information they need ... giving it them will only increase their information overload.' A good information system must therefore help managers to learn what they need. Creating conditions where 'P' and 'Q' are understood will help to do this. Chapter 8 shows how the critical climate in action learning groups confronts our possibly outdated information and incorrect assumptions.

At this stage, if you have not already done so, you could be evaluating your current information system against the following eight factors mentioned in the introduction to this part of the book.

1 Awareness
2 Action
3 Confusion
4 Comprehensibility
5 Defensiveness
6 Timeliness
7 Validity
8 Dynamism

WORKING DEFINITIONS

In Chapter 2 the more technical language of outputs and inputs was presented. But for everyday use we require practical working definitions of the information needed. It is this basic information that is often not interpreted the same way between organisations and in many cases even within them. For example the much-published sales per employee figure, if used for interfirm comparisons, depend upon what is meant by sales and employees. We shall be defining sales as gross sales in monetary terms less any credits to customers less sales tax, eg Value Added Tax. Employees are everyone working in the organisation, with any part-timers adjusted to a full-time basis. Similar precise definitions are necessary for all the other information used in productivity measurement. The views of everyone concerned should be sought and then the definitions can be published, remembering the previous caution for a regular review.

Lists of definitions already used for productivity audits for a wide range of manufacturers and retailers are shown in Figures 3.1 and 3.2. We shall be coming back to these definitions in Chapter 5 when the productivity audit system is described. We believe that agreeing and obtaining a routine supply of the kind of information indicated in these illustrations is a first step to reliable productivity measurement. All organisations, particularly the commercial ones, require a constant flow of information on the forces affecting business internally and externally. The information in the illustrations is used to calculate the productivity of resources in the interaction of these internal and external environments. The principal forces at work are shown in Figure 3.3 together with the main points where decisions, both long- and short-term, have to be made, based on the information available.

Item No	Item	Definition
1	Sales value	Total sales value (rounded off to nearest £) less VAT and credits.
2	Materials and Bought out parts	All raw materials, bought out parts and packaging materials actually consumed in the sales for the month. By definition it cannot exceed sales value. This item is regarded as a temporary investment in your company to be converted into sales as quickly as possible. If you have difficulty estimate it by adjusting your sales value by your average percentage of materials/bought out parts. For example, if this is 40%,multiply your monthly sales figure by .4.
3	Total earnings	Sales, item 1, less materials, item 2. This is the total fund to meet all the demands on your business.
4	Total employees	Everyone working in the company. Adjust your part-timers to a full-time basis by totalling their hours worked and dividing by the hours for your full-time week.
5	Total wages and salaries	Total wages and salaries and all other employment costs (ie holiday pay, national insurance and pensions) for everyone working in the company.
6	Total purchased services	All purchases from outside other than materials and bought out items. This includes energy costs (coal, electricity, gas and oil), rent, rates, telephone, postage, leasing, hire purchase, processing materials, insurance, bank charges, professional services, sundry purchases, car expenses, travel, hotels and meals.
7	Depreciation	The wear and tear costs of running the company. Unlike the other costs above (eg items 5 and 6) these do not appear as costs every month, but they are there. For ease of calculation take your annual balance sheet figure and divide by 12.

Figure 3.1 Definitions of information for manufacturers

Item No	Item	Definition
8	Total cost	The sum of items 5,6, and 7. This is the total cost of running your company, what it really costs to convert your materials/bought out goods into sales and, more importantly, total earnings. Remember, get a feel for the percentage of costs to sales and watch for changes.
9	Average inventory	Take the average of your opening and closing inventory (raw materials, work in progress and finished goods) and express the figure at sales value so as to obtain comparable rate of stock turn figures. Sales and inventory need to be in the same terms, ie in sales value. As with materials consumed in sales for the month (item 2) you may have difficulty in establishing your inventory on a monthly basis. If so, provide estimates. You can do this by adjusting your last physical stocktake by sales and purchases since then. It may not be accurate but is still good enough to give a fair indication of your rate of stock turn.
10	Net profit	Item 3 (total earnings) less item 8 (total cost). Note this is your conversion profit and does not include changes in inventory.

Figure 3.1 (Concluded)

Item No	Item	Definition
1	Sales value	Total sales value (rounded off to the nearest £) less VAT and credits.
2	Purchased goods in sales	All purchased goods at bought in prices less VAT. These are the goods, including any packaging materials, actually contained in the sales for the month. Note that by definition this figure cannot exceed sales value. If it gives difficulty try your average percentage of purchase goods to sales. For

Figure 3.2 Definitions of information for retailers

Item No	Item	Definition
		example if your average is 64% multiply your sales value figure by .64.
3	Total earnings	Sales, item 1, less purchased goods, item 2. This is the total fund to meet all the demands on the business.
4	Total employees	Everyone working in the company, paid and unpaid. Adjust your part-timers to a full-time basis by totalling their hours worked and dividing by your hours for a normal full-time week. To be realistic include anyone working 80 hours or more as two people.
5	Total customers	Total customers for the month. You should be able to obtain this figure from your daily till roll.
6	Sales area in square feet	Include all space involved in selling, ie display and walkways or everywhere customers have access to. Do not include store rooms, offices, and warehouses.
7	Total wages and salaries	This is the total employment cost for everyone. Include all wages, salaries, National Insurance, holidays and pension payments.
8	Overheads	These are all your purchased services: include rent, rates, electricity, gas, oil, coal, water, telephone, bank charges, professional charges, postage, car expenses, catering and sundry purchases. For utilities like electricity, gas etc, and rates take the previous year totals, adjust for likely increases and divide by 12.
9	Depreciation	The wear and tear costs of running your business. Unlike with other costs, you do not have monthly evidence of these costs but they are there. For ease of calculation take your annual balance sheet figures and divide by 12.

Figure 3.2 (Continued)

Item No	Item	Definition
10	Total cost	The sum of items 7, 8 and 9. This is the total cost of running your company, what it really costs to convert your purchased goods into sales and, more important, total earnings.
11	Average stock	This is the average total stock at sales value less VAT carried during the month. Include all stock in displays and store rooms. It is recognised that many retailing companies may not maintain monthly stock figures, but it is a key factor in retailing efficiency. If it presents difficulties, provide estimates for the time being. You can do this by adjusting your last physical stocktake by sales and purchases since then. It will be inaccurate, but still good enough to give a fair indication of your rate of stock turn.
12	Net profit	Item 3, total earnings, less item 10, total cost. Note this is your conversion profit and does not include changes in stock.

Figure 3.2 (Concluded)

DIFFICULTIES

The elements of productivity measurement are relatively easy to understand. The big difficulty, particularly for the smaller enterprise, is in obtaining a regular supply of information to do the measuring. For example, many small manufacturing and retailing enterprises do not maintain monthly stock figures. Yet keeping a close watch on the relationship of stock to the sales it generates, ie the rate of stock turn, is information they cannot do without.

The following points will provide practical guidance on overcoming the usual difficulties.

- *Will*: there has to be a will and perseverance to get the information and keep getting it.
- *Accuracy*: to obtain essential information on time you may have to sacrifice accuracy; estimates of monthly stock figures that are 5 per cent inaccurate are better than none at all.

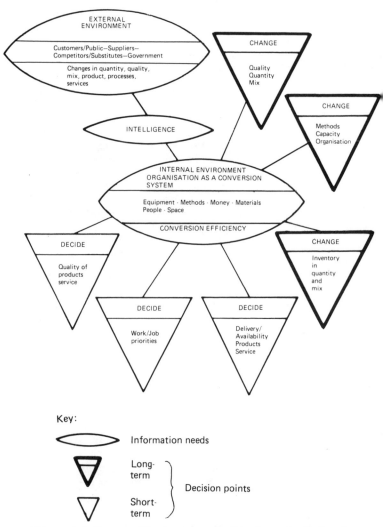

**Figure 3.3 Forces affecting organisational productivity: the
information needs**

● *Records*: existing information should be put to better use.
   For example:
   – Simplify stock control by dividing stock into three
     groups, 'A' the most expensive, 'B' moderately costly,
     and 'C' the cheapest items. In Chapter 7 the technique
     of Pareto analysis shows how to do this in more detail.

When you have divided stock in this way have your supplier and sales paperwork identified in the same categories. In this way you can maintain a 'paper' stock figure.

- Have preprinted stock lists to ease the periodic physical stock take. Categorise the list as above into A, B, and C.
- Examine all existing forms, both those you create and those produced by external people like suppliers, and see how they could be modified to give you the information listed in Figures 3.1 and 3.2. For instance, as well as providing data for productivity measurement you can also use the information to monitor cost trends.
- Discuss with your accountants how productivity-type information could be integrated with the existing financial system.

● *Activity Sampling:* this technique is also described further in Chapter 7. It is a simple low-cost method for collecting information on a wide variety of activities. Bahiri (5) and Norman (6) trained factory foremen in a very short time to use the method to obtain data on the utilisation of plant and direct labour in 45 different companies. It has also been used by shop assistants to obtain valuable information on customer flow and staff activity in very small retail establishments. The involvement of people in activity sampling also gains their commitment to improve what they observe.

FREQUENCY

A European working group (7) who studied 'Corporate Early Warning Systems' found that the frequency with which information is made available is an important factor in monitoring company performance. What matters is not only when the figures should be produced but how soon after the expected time they are actually available. We have found that this gap can be up to six weeks. Just getting an improvement in timeliness can be a significant step forward.

The other factor revealed by the above study group is the differing frequencies for various items of information. Some information is necessary on a daily basis, even hourly for sensitive processes. There will also be figures that are only required on a monthly or less frequent basis. Getting these decisions right can have a significant influence on the effectiveness of the measurement system. As a general guide the frequency should be based on how much notice is required to take any remedial action. In a retail shop, details of customers, sales and the consequent average sale per customer need to be available on a daily basis. On the other hand monthly figures are adequate for calculating overall company productivity.

With the decreasing cost and increasing capacity of the micro-computer more continuous analysis of information is now a possibility, even for smaller enterprises. Computer programming methods for filtering information are now becoming available. Cyberfilter, described by Espejo,(8) is a method which can analyse information flowing in a company and provide managers with signals of significant changes, enabling them to take action before there is any damage to the enterprise. It is a kind of electronic management by exception.

The overriding requirement is to be aware of the frequency decision, involve people in it, set targets and insist they are kept.

PROVIDERS AND RECIPIENTS

Once the information required has been agreed, the routine is not complete until the providers of it have also agreed to supply it by the specified times. In some cases, especially the smaller enterprise, information of the kind described in Figures 3.1 and 3.2 will be supplied and converted into productivity measurements by the same person. For larger organisations this process will probably involve a number of people. Whatever the case, a senior member of management should be known to be responsible for the productivity measurement figures. At the receiving end are the various people who make practical use of the measurements created.

The names of suppliers and users of information should be made known together with the target dates when information should be available. You will find that the action group meetings described in Chapter 8 are the best means of maintaining good information. As we noted earlier, the real test is whether the information leads to change. This simple aim keeps the system alive and relevant and ensures there is a continuing link between measurement and action.

CONTROL

An effective information system should have good control characteristics. It should lead to the necessary changes in the system it is measuring; this is the action requirement previously mentioned.

Equally, it should control itself. It must change to suit the changing circumstances of whatever is being measured. We shall be dealing with the first point in Chapter 4, but the second is relevant to the analysis of information.

To ensure information meets the criterion of being used, every two to three months productivity information should be reviewed in the light of the following questions:

1   When was the information last used?
2   When was the information last produced?
3   Does it need changing in any way?
4   What new information is now necessary? Who will produce it?

INFORMATION AUDIT

As we have stated, obtaining productivity information raises a number of problems. These are principally:

● getting more information than we need, the irrelevancy problem:
● not knowing which information is required to measure productivity, the 'Q' problem;
● using outdated information, the 'P' problem;
● lacking the skill to make use of productivity information.

The principal purpose of this chapter is to help you deal with these problems. What to do with the information is examined in the following chapters. In this chapter we are concerned with what is needed now – methods for evaluating existing information systems. What do we need to know in order to assess productivity? Just as productivity audits are necessary, audits of information are also required. Information audits for manufacturers and retailers are shown in Figures 3.4 and 3.5. These have been found to be useful in productivity improvement programmes sponsored by the Manpower Services Commission, described in later chapters.

Information audit: Manufacturers

Regard information as a crucial resource like materials, money, people and plant. Therefore a regular supply of it that you understand and use is important. The operative word is *use*. Overleaf is an audit of the essential information you need.

INSTRUCTIONS

Below are ten statements about information in *your* company as it is *now*. Information is defined as a *routinely published item* and is made *available* for *managing your business*. Any information you get when there is pressure to do so is not included. The statements relate to the main areas of *materials, people, plant, products, and sales*.

You are asked to assess each statement in degrees of *truth* ranging from completely *untrue* at 1 to *absolutely true* at 7. Just circle the score that best fits your response. In your answers keep constantly in mind the above definition.

MATERIALS

1 We have complete information on costs and usage of materials.

Completely   ├──┼──┼──┼──┼──┼──┤   Absolutely
untrue   1   2   3   4   5   6   7   true

2 We maintain a monthly check on rate of stock turn.

Completely   ├──┼──┼──┼──┼──┼──┤   Absolutely
untrue   1   2   3   4   5   6   7   true

PEOPLE

3 People are used for productive work.

Completely   ├──┼──┼──┼──┼──┼──┤   Absolutely
untrue   1   2   3   4   5   6   7   true

4 Measurements of indirect staff productivity are maintained.

Completely   ├──┼──┼──┼──┼──┼──┤   Absolutely
untrue   1   2   3   4   5   6   7   true

PLANT

5 Key items of plant are utilised on productive work.

Completely   ├──┼──┼──┼──┼──┼──┤   Absolutely
untrue   1   2   3   4   5   6   7   true

Figure 3.4   Information audit for manufacturers

6   We know the workload for key items of plant.

Completely ├───┼───┼───┼───┼───┼───┤ Absolutely
untrue   1   2   3   4   5   6   7   true

PRODUCTS

7   We have information on significant changes in product mix.

Completely ├───┼───┼───┼───┼───┼───┤ Absolutely
untrue   1   2   3   4   5   6   7   true

8   We know how long it takes to get products through the factory.

Completely ├───┼───┼───┼───┼───┼───┤ Absolutely
untrue   1   2   3   4   5   6   7   true

SALES

9   We regularly monitor the real movement in sales after allowing
    for price changes.

Completely ├───┼───┼───┼───┼───┼───┤ Absolutely
untrue   1   2   3   4   5   6   7   true

10 We keep a regular check on the relationship of sales to costs.

Completely ├───┼───┼───┼───┼───┼───┤ Absolutely
untrue   1   2   3   4   5   6   7   true

Now do a total assessment of your information system against the
five areas below. Just enter your score, the one circled, against the
appropriate statement number.

MATERIALS   PLANT
1   _____   5   _____
2   _____   6   _____
Total _____   Total _____
Average _____   Average _____

PEOPLE   PRODUCTS
3   _____   7   _____
4   _____   8   _____
Total _____   Total _____
Average _____   Average _____

Figure 3.4   (Continued)

SALES
9   _____
10   _____
Total   ════════
Average _____

Any average score below 4.0 needs study and below 3.0 urgent attention.

Figure 3.4 (Concluded)
With acknowledgements to *Improve Your Own Productivity*,
Manpower Services Commission, 1984, by the author.

Information audit: Retailers

Good down-to-earth retailing information about such things as your local markets and which stocks turn over the best is essential: you cannot afford not to have it. You need a regular supply of productivity information that you *understand* and *use*. Here is a check on some of the essential information needed in retailing.

INSTRUCTIONS

Below are ten statements about information in *your* company as it is *now*. Information is defined here as a *routinely published item* and is made available for managing your business; any information you only get when there is pressure to obtain it is not included. The statements relate to the main areas of displays/space, markets/ competitors, products, staff and sales. You are asked to assess each statement in degrees of truth of the statement as it applies to *you*: your response can vary from *completely untrue* at 1 to *absolutely true* at 7. Just circle the score that best fits your response.
  In your answers keep constantly in mind the above definition.

DISPLAYS/SPACE
1   We have complete information on the productivity of displays.

Completely |—+—+—+—+—+—+—| Absolutely
untrue   1   2   3   4   5   6   7   true

2   We regularly measure our sales per square foot.

Completely |—+—+—+—+—+—+—| Absolutely
untrue   1   2   3   4   5   6   7   true

Figure 3.5   Information for retailers

MARKETS/COMPETITORS

3   We know the size and type of our market (eg no. of house-holds).

Completely   ├──┼──┼──┼──┼──┼──┤   Absolutely
untrue   1   2   3   4   5   6   7   true

4   We maintain regular information on the competition.

Completely   ├──┼──┼──┼──┼──┼──┤   Absolutely
untrue   1   2   3   4   5   6   7   true

PRODUCTS

5   We know which products make the greatest contribution to sales.

Completely   ├──┼──┼──┼──┼──┼──┤   Absolutely
untrue   1   2   3   4   5   6   7   true

6   We maintain information on the profitability of our product lines.

Completely   ├──┼──┼──┼──┼──┼──┤   Absolutely
untrue   1   2   3   4   5   6   7   true

STAFF

7   We measure staff productivity (eg per cent of wages to sales).

Completely   ├──┼──┼──┼──┼──┼──┤   Absolutely
untrue   1   2   3   4   5   6   7   true

8   We measure staff/customer ratios.

Completely   ├──┼──┼──┼──┼──┼──┤   Absolutely
untrue   1   2   3   4   5   6   7   true

Figure 3.5   (Continued)

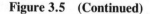

SALES/STOCKS

9   We maintain movements in our sales adjusted for price.

Completely untrue |———+———+———+———+———+———| Absolutely true

           1   2   3   4   5   6   7

10   We keep monthly rate of stock turn figures.

Completely untrue |———+———+———+———+———+———| Absolutely true

           1   2   3   4   5   6   7

Now do a total assessment of your information system against the five areas below. Just enter your score, the one circled, against the appropriate statement numbers.

Displays/Space		Markets/Competitors	
1	_____	3	_____
2	_____	4	_____
Total	_____	Total	_____
Average	_____	Average	_____

PRODUCTS		STAFF	
5	_____	7	_____
6	_____	8	_____
Total	_____	Total	_____
Average	_____	Average	_____

SALES/STOCKS	
9	_____
10	_____
Total	_____
Average	_____

Any average score below 4.0 needs study and below 3.0 urgent attention.

Figure 3.5   (Concluded)

With acknowledgement to *Improve Your Own Productivity*, Manpower Services Commission 1984, by the author.

Summary

Productivity measurement requires a regular supply of what we have described as basic information; the most reliable indicators are little use if there is difficulty in obtaining the necessary facts and figures. At the same time the collection of information does incur some cost, so it must be put to practical use. Our simple definition of information provides the answer to this dilemma; information must lead to change. If information and the eventual productivity measurements are constantly assessed against whether they are used there should be no wasted clerical effort.

We have suggested that there are a number of low-cost ways to overcome the difficulties of information collection. The acknowledged productivity leaders are Marks and Spencer, but Lord Sieff (9) puts their success down to a simple system that tells his managers how the business is doing in all its facets.

So often there is confusion on apparently simple terms like sales and employees. To overcome this problem clear definitions must be agreed by all the providers and users of information which is then published. But information needs to adapt to a changing world so it requires regular appraisal. Indeed as Revans (10) states, organisations which have learnt how to cope with change have recognised that it depends on 'their capacity to grasp the significance that information ... or lack of it ... has in releasing the latent talents of the enterprise to solve its problems.' Moreover, the aim of an effective information system is to get information to the right place at the relevant time to deal with the problems of the moment.

Clear definitions are essential, but so too is the frequency of availability. There are no clear rules on this but some guidance has been provided. The important point is to be aware of the importance of when information is available. It is worth the time and effort involved in getting managerial agreement on what information should be available and by when. An up-to-date and relevant information system is controlled just as much as the productivity it measures.

Finally, before you set up your effective productivity measurement, Figures 3.4 and 3.5 provide you with the opportunity to assess your current information on the key aspects of productivity. As Peters and Waterman found in their *Search for Excellence*, above-average performance depends upon the simple things. One of these is good basic information that you use. It is fitting to end with the simple advice of Ernest Schumacher, (11) who said that 'figures should be made to sing.' He meant that productivity measurements must be more than cold quantitative figures, and have an inner quality and hence meaning to those who use them. How can you make your figures sing?

REFERENCES

1 Drucker, Peter, *The Age of Discontinuity,* Heinemann, 1969
2 Hawken, Paul, *The Next Economy*, Holt, Rinehart & Winston, 1983
3 Ackoff, Russell J., *Creating the Corporate Future: Plan or Be Planned For*, John Wiley, 1981
4 Revans, Reginald W., *The Origins and Growth of Action Learning*, Chartwell-Pratt, 1982, pp. 710–11
5 Bahiri, Simcha, 'How To measure Productivity', *Management Today, July 1970*
6 Norman, R. G., 'Productivity Measurement in Manufacturing Industry', *Works Management*, March 1971
7 *Corporate Early Warning Systems. An Interim Report*, European Association of National Productivity Centres, Brussels, 1982
8 Espejo, R., 'Cybernetic Filtration of Management Information', Working Paper Series No. 126, University of Aston Management Centre, Birmingham, UK, February 1979.
9 'How M & S stays on its guard', *Observer*, 15 July 1979.
10 Revans, R. W., *Studies in Factory Communications*, ALP International, 1973
11 Schumacher, E. F., 'The search for significant measurements in coal mining', in Kirk, Geoffrey (ed.), *Schumacher on Energy, Speeches and writing of E. F. Schumacher*, Abacus, 1983.

4 Basic productivity measurement

The aim of the previous chapters has been to prepare the reader for the task of setting up a sound productivity measurement system. It was considered that the following aspects should be covered before starting this task:

1 Distinguishing between what productivity is, and what it is not;
2 Describing the basic outputs and inputs used in any kind of productivity measurement;
3 Examining the practical problems of obtaining the necessary information to measure productivity;
4 Producing working definitions of the information to be used.

SYSTEMS CONCEPT

It is now generally recognised that all organisations are composed of numbers of interdependent sub-units. The performance of one unit affects all the others. If we improve the efficiency of one function it could lead to a deterioration in others. For example,

73

more sales without the capacity to produce more could worsen efficiency. Hence, as stated earlier, a total approach to productivity measurement is necessary. This interdependency or systems approach is equally relevant to relations between organisations, industries and countries. These wider, more macro, aspects of systems are, of course, influenced by complex political attitudes, but nevertheless they are having an increasing influence on productivity considerations and are now receiving serious attention; the North/South debate (1) is one example of the acceptance by some that a balanced use of the world's finite resources is now necessary. But this chapter is concerned with the functional relationship between various departments and their effects on productivity measurement.

Martin and Bahiri (2) describe the systems concept as a way of thinking about problems, processes and information and their relationships with one another and with their environment. The forces affecting these relationships were illustrated in Figure 3.4 in the previous chapter. Industrial systems may be subdivided into product systems, processing systems, accounting systems, inventory systems and so on. Similar divisions could be made for other organisations such as service industries, hospitals and non-profit-making bodies. What is desirable is a general productivity measurement system which could be used for any organisation, that is, a total system approach with an interlocking family of secondary measurements which affect the whole picture. Each of these secondary indicators should pinpoint where deficiencies exist. Martin's (3) study was aimed at developing this common measure of productivity with a number of supporting indicators. Much earlier Davis, (4) acknowledged by some as having had a powerful influence on productivity measurement, suggested that the views of accountants, economists and engineers should be reconciled and a total approach was necessary. He also stressed the case for adjusting for price changes.

A model of a functioning productive system is shown in Figure 4.1. This shows the importance of adding to the working capital or at least ensuring it is not eroded. It also highlights total earnings as the important fund for meeting all the system's demands. Models along these lines can also be produced for retailing, service and public organisations.

TYPES OF MEASUREMENT

The types of measurement used in assessing productivity are generally classified as follows:

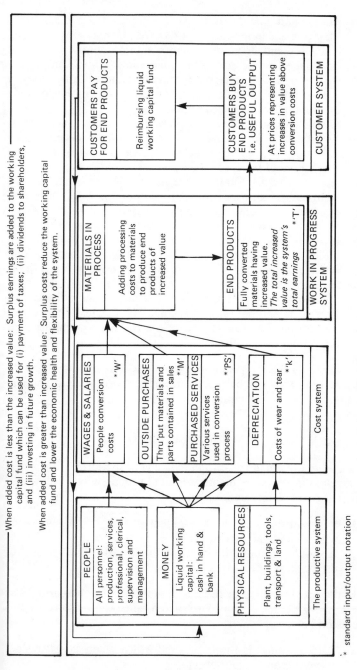

When added cost is less than the increased value: Surplus earnings are added to the working capital fund which can be used for (i) payment of taxes; (ii) dividends to shareholders, and (iii) investing in future growth.

When added cost is greater than increased value: Surplus costs reduce the working capital fund and lower the economic health and flexibility of the system.

CUSTOMER SYSTEM

CUSTOMERS PAY FOR END PRODUCTS

Reimbursing liquid working capital fund

CUSTOMERS BUY END PRODUCTS i.e. USEFUL OUTPUT

At prices representing increases in value above conversion costs

WORK IN PROGRESS SYSTEM

MATERIALS IN PROCESS

Adding processing costs to materials to produce end products of increased value

END PRODUCTS

Fully converted materials having increased value. *The total increased value is the system's total earnings* *'T'

Cost system

WAGES & SALARIES

People conversion costs   *'W'

OUTSIDE PURCHASES

Thru'put materials and parts contained in sales *'M'

PURCHASED SERVICES

Various services used in conversion process   *'PS'

DEPRECIATION

Costs of wear and tear   *'k'

The productive system

PEOPLE

All personnel: production, services, professional, clerical, supervision and management

MONEY

Liquid working capital: cash in hand & bank

PHYSICAL RESOURCES

Plant, buildings, tools, transport & land

.* standard input/output notation

Figure 4.1   A model of a functioning productive system

1   Macro and micro: these were referred to in Chapter 1. Macro measurements are used for comparisons between countries and economic sectors within countries, with individual organisations using micro indicators. Output per worker or added value per worker in manufacturing industry is an example of the former, with sales per employee being one kind of micro measurement.

2   Simple and compound indices: where the outputs and inputs are stated in the same terms these will be called simple indicators, eg wages to sales as a percentage is a simple measurement because wages and sales are both expressed in monetary terms. On the other hand, sales per employee is a compound indicator since the output (ie sales) is stated financially and employees are expressed as units.

3   First and second order indices: a first order measurement involves only one index and a second order two connected indices. For instances, GDP per employed person (GDP divided by number of employees (NE)) is a first order index (it is also a macro and compound measurement). GDP/NE divided by GDP/NE of others is a second order indicator. To express it another way, a second order index is useful for comparing the productivity of one country, organisation or department with others.

An analysis of these types of measurement and how they relate to the five aims of productivity measurement stated in Chapter 2 will be made later in this chapter.

PRIMARY PRODUCTIVITY MEASUREMENT

The studies over many years by the late Harold Martin were aimed at developing a primary measurement of productivity which would satisfy the following requirements:

1   It would measure the attainment of the primary objective which is common to any kind of organisation.

2   It should be stated in an output/input ratio which relates to the primary objective.

In the previous chapter the case was stated for total earnings as the primary objective. For ease of reference the reasons for this are listed below:

1   Total earnings is the basic fund which meets all of the demands on any organisation.

2 Ensuring a flow of total earnings above conversion costs is necessary for a healthy working capital fund. Figure 4.1 illustrates the importance of this aim.

3 Total earnings gives equal priority to all claimants (ie employees, suppliers, shareholders and tax collectors) and is therefore more socially acceptable.

4 It is appropriate to any kind of organisation, private, public, commercial and non-profit-making alike; all of these enterprises should aim for total earnings above their operating costs. Moreover, while it may be difficult to measure outputs in non-commercial undertakings, the inputs inherent in total earnings are common to all kinds of organisation.

Obtaining a high level of total earnings thus ensures a healthy organisation. At the same time, if the rate of generation of total earnings (T) per unit of conversion cost (C) is also high, the enterprise is productive as well. Consequently the primary total earnings productivity (prefix E) is

$$E = \frac{\text{Total earnings}}{\text{Conversion cost}} = \frac{T}{C}$$

Since profit (P), or surplus for non-commercial organisations, is total earnings − conversion cost, or $T - C$, a secondary profit productivity 'Ep' index can be derived thus:

$$Ep = \frac{P}{C} = \frac{T - C}{C} \text{ or } \frac{T}{C} - 1 = E - 1$$

Therefore 1 deducted from total earnings productivity 'E' equals profit productivity 'Ep'. For example, if total earnings are £100,000 in a particular month and conversion costs for the same period are £75,000, total earnings and profit productivity are

$$E = \frac{100,000}{75,000} = 1.33$$

$$Ep = \frac{100,000 - 75,000}{75,000} = 0.33 \text{ or } 1.33 - 1 = 0.33$$

This means that for every £1 of conversion cost, £1.33 of total earnings and £0.33 of profit have been generated. Productivity and profitability are therefore linked; increase productivity and profit is also increased. However, in conventional accounting practice profit includes allowance for changes in stock value. This concept of profit may be described as conversion profit. It is the surplus or profit remaining after allowing for the costs of converting the materials used in the period in question. Inventory productivity is dealt with at a later stage.

Furthermore, total earnings productivity is a total factor measurement. The numerator, total earnings, is a basic output objective and the input of conversion costs includes all of any organisation's operating costs. These costs, described in Chapter 2 and repeated here for ease of reference, include,

- total wages and salaries 'W': the people costs in Figure 4.1
- total purchased services 'PS', which is divided into running costs and capital costs
- depreciation 'K' or wear and tear costs.

In order that the productivity of each of these input costs can be assessed, more detailed indicators are necessary. These will be presented later in this chapter and the next one.

The relationship between total earnings 'T' – which is an engineering concept of added value, that is the value of conversion output – and the economist's version of added value 'AV' is $T = S - M$. It will be remembered that S = sales and M = throughput materials. $AV = S - X$ or $T - PS$ where X equals total outside purchases, including throughput materials 'M' and purchased services 'PS'. As stated in Chapter 1, added value is used extensively for comparisons of productivity between countries. To complete the picture the cost accountant's view of contribution margin 'CM' can be related to total earnings in the following way: $CM = S - V = T - CV$ where $V = M + CV$, where CV, is that portion of conversion costs which varies in direct proportion to the level of output activity. In the short term only throughput materials 'M' and some parts of purchased services 'PS' (eg energy costs) are variable, or they can be avoided. Figure 2.8 (page 53) illustrates the relationships between total earnings, added value and contribution margin.

SECONDARY PRODUCTIVITY MEASUREMENT

Total earnings productivity 'TEP' (E) reveals a primary or overall measurement of efficiency for any kind of organisation. It also shows two other aspects of conversion efficiency:

1   The rate at which input generates output.

2 The quantity of inputs used to generate a given output.

What is less apparent is an important third item of information, namely:

3 The potential output which could be obtained from a given input; the measurements of effectiveness described in the previous chapter.

Secondary productivity measurements provide the answer to this requirement.

TEP answers the question 'Where are you now?' In other words, total earnings are obtained for varying input efficiencies; some plant may have a high utilisation while other items of equipment are little used. Output is produced, or value added, only to the extent that available resources are utilised to convert inputs into outputs. It can, therefore, be argued that the ratio of utilised resources to the total costs of all available resources is a secondary measure of productivity. Consequently, the total conversion cost includes two main divisions:

1 The costs incurred when resources (people and equipment) are productively utilised. These costs can be further subdivided into productive work costs and ancillary work costs. The sum of both costs will be called processing costs, prefix 'Cd', with productive work costs being prefixed 'Ce' and ancillary work 'Ca'.
2 Unutilised or idle resource costs 'Ci', when people and equipment are wholly idle.

These divisions of costs and their relationships to the similar divisions of time shown in Figure 2.7 (page 51) are illustrated in Figure 4.2. It will be seen that total conversion costs have been spread across feasible capacity. This is based on the concept of the availability of resources for productive and ancillary work. For industrial work, products only incur processing cost when they occupy resources. The method for allocating costs, which was developed by Harold Martin, is called Productivity Costing and is described later in this chapter.

We can now state resource or conversion utilisation productivity as follows:

$$\frac{\text{Time or costs incurred on productive and ancillary work}}{\substack{\text{Total time available or total conversion costs, which} \\ \text{includes idle time}}} = \frac{\text{Cd}}{\text{C}}$$

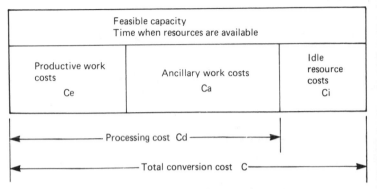

Figure 4.2   Divisions of conversion cost

An even more basic resource productivity indicator is to relate pure productive work 'Ce' to total conversion costs thus,

$$\frac{\text{Time or costs incurred on purely productive work}}{\substack{\text{Total time available or total conversion costs,}\\ \text{which includes ancillary work and idle time.}}} = \frac{Ce}{C}$$

Truly productive work, distinguished from ancillary work, is what directly adds value to materials.The concept of productive work forms an important part of productivity measurement. Harold Martin (5) proposed the following definitions for manufacturing and retailing:

Manufacturing: productive work is work which changes the shape, physical characteristics or appearance of materials, or which joins (assembles) one material to another, or separates one material from another during the process of converting production materials into (saleable or usable) products;

Retail Selling: productive work is work which, in contact with a potential customer, induces them to make a purchase. Such inducements can be performed by staff or in an inert way by displays.

While it is more difficult to define, the concept of productive work is just as relevant to professional and service-type organisations as it is to those who convert throughput materials. Design departments, retail shops, hospitals, typing pools and government should all seek to agree and measure their particular productive work. The very discussion to decide what it is is the first step to improving the use of these precious resources.

There are two other measurements which fall under the general heading of secondary measurements. These are working capital and inventory productivity. Industrial and commercial organisations cannot ignore the key aspect of working capital, therefore its productivity requires measuring. So as to maintain consistency with the use of total earnings as an output measurement, the productivity of working capital is stated as:

$$\frac{\text{Total earnings}}{\text{Thru'put materials + conversion costs}} = \frac{T}{M + C}$$

This gives total earnings per unit of working capital employed or the rate of turnover of working capital. Similar ratios could be employed using sales or profit as the outputs, ie $S/(M + C)$ and $P/(M + C)$.

The productivity of inventory (ie total materials, work in progress and finished stocks) is similar to working capital, but should include a carrying charge to cover the time the inventory has been in the system. These carrying charges can be substantial – up to 25 per cent of inventory costs. The inventory productivity indicator that includes this carrying charge, 'Cinv', is:

$$\frac{\text{Total earnings}}{\text{Thru'put materials + carrying charge}} = \frac{T}{M + Cinv}$$

The more usual way of measuring the productivity of inventory is the rate of stock turn, which is:

$$\frac{\text{Sales}}{\text{Average stock carried}}$$

For industrial and commercial organisations the efficient use of working capital and inventory should be high on the list of managerial priorities. Just as the relationship between profitability and productivity must be understood, so too must the working capital and money aspects; it is little use being profitable and productive if there is no money to manage day-to-day affairs.

PRODUCTIVE POTENTIAL

The potential total earnings of an organisation generated by the total conversion costs is what total earnings would have been obtained if all inputs had been fully utilised – with no idle capacity costs and all resources engaged in productive and ancillary work. In other words, Cd and C are equal. This is unlikely to be achieved in practice, however. To measure potential total earnings, if all conversion costs were utilised on 'Cd' work the potential total earnings 'Tpot' is:

$$\text{Tpot} = \frac{T}{\text{Total Cd}} \times C$$

For example, if total earnings for a period are £100,000, total conversion costs £75,000, processing costs £48,000 and productive work costs £30,000, the following results are obtained:

$$\frac{\text{Utilisation}}{\text{productivity}} = \frac{Cd}{C} = \frac{48,000}{75,000} = .64$$

Just under two-thirds of resources are occupied productively and nearly one third are idle. The existing and potential total earnings are shown below:

Existing total earnings = £100,000

$$\text{Potential total earnings} = \frac{T}{Cd} \times C = \frac{100,000}{48,000} \times 75,000$$

$$= £156,250$$

It can be seen that productive work has a big lever effect on total organisational productivity, with a similar effect on profit. Even more dramatic results are obtained if all resources were utilised only on productive work. Japanese industry is aiming for setting up times of zero (set ups form a large part of ancillary work), and with the application of high technology this may become a possibility. In the above example, potential total earnings with all resources being occupied on purely productive work 'Ce' would be:

$$\frac{100,000}{30,000} \times 75,000 = £250,000$$

This shows that only 40 per cent (30,000 ÷ 75,000) of conversion costs are utilised solely on productive work. If the other 60 per cent were similarly used total earnings would increase $2\frac{1}{2}$ times, ie 250,000 ÷ 100,000.

Comparisons made between overall total earnings productivity, T/C, and total earnings productivity with idle costs removed reveal large differences. Table 4.1 is taken from a study by Martin (3) and illustrates the differences for the two productivity indicators, total earnings T/C, profit P/C and the same two less idle costs, ie T/Cd and P/Cd. It will be seen that the productivity of company 'A' doubles when idle costs are excluded, thus indicating their total earnings potential. The average range for all companies is 1.5, with profit productivity more than doubling at 0.80 compared to 0.35 when idle costs are included. If pure productive work 'Ce' were used the results would be even more startling. The problem is how to achieve it. This is dealt with in later chapters.

Table 4.1   Interfirm productivity comparisons

Company code	1	2	3	4	5
	Overall company productivity		Productivity less idle costs		Range *
					3 ÷ 1
	T/C	P/C	T/Cd	P/Cd	
A	1.70	0.70	3.60	2.60	2 : 1
B	1.66	0.66	2.16	1.16	1.3 : 1
C	1.61	0.61	1.92	0.92	1.2 : 1
D	1.42	0.42	1.93	0.93	1.4 : 1
E	1.39	0.39	1.93	0.93	1.4 : 1
F	1.36	0.36	2.26	1.26	1.7 : 1
G	1.36	0.36	1.82	0.82	1.3 : 1
H	1.32	0.32	1.65	0.65	1.3 : 1
I	1.06	0.06	1.15	0.15	1.1 : 1
J	0.94	−0.06	2.14	1.14	2.3 : 1
K	0.86	−0.14	1.73	0.73	2 : 1
Averages	1.35	0.35	1.80	0.80	1.5 : 1 *

Notes: * Shows how much T/Cd exceeds T/C; on average it is
              1½ times as high.

The study involved eleven companies making synthetic resins, knitwear, electric cables, spun and woven textiles, bicycles, footwear, cement mixers, brake blocks, aluminium extensions, stainless steel welded equipment, glassware, water valves, beehives, electric hoists, and citrus fruit crates. The companies were situated in two countries, Israel and the USA. The investigation illustrates how total earnings can be used to compare the productivity of different companies and across countries.

Of course, it can be argued that this is only valid if similar product mixes are produced; even so the potential is still great.

Potential output analysis is concerned with measuring the effectiveness of an organisation. As stated in the previous chapter, basic measurements of potential productivity can never exceed unity; productive work costs cannot be greater than total conversion costs, and neither can processing costs. While the analysis made has used costs, utilisation productivity can also be measured in time units; eg in the ratio Cd/C, C would be the total feasible time available and Cd the total time when resources are occupied on productive and ancillary work. These basic measurements of utilisation productivity can be used at three levels of the organisations:

1   For the organisation as a whole, that is:

$$\frac{\text{Total of all times/costs on processing work}}{\text{Total conversion costs}}$$

2   At individual department or section levels.
3   For specific items of plant, work groups or for individuals.

The indicators for these levels should be connected into the comprehensive family of ratios previously mentioned. In chapter 7 simple techniques for obtaining information on this division of work are described.

CAPACITY, UTILISATION AND EFFICIENCY

These three terms have been used in this and previous chapters. But as they are important aspects of productivity measurement and are often used synonymously, their definitions are summarised below:

Capacity: the agreed total hours when people and physical resources (eg plant, equipment, tools, buildings, space etc,) are available for use. As stated earlier, the theoretical maximum is 365 days a year, 24 hours a day. The more realistic figure needs to be agreed, with a published statement of lost-time deductions, that is, allowances for breaks and late and early finishing, some organisations include equipment breakdowns.

Utilisation: this is the time when resources are occupied on productive and ancillary work compared to the capacity available. Two utilisation figures are therefore possible:

1 $\dfrac{\text{Productive} + \text{ancillary work}}{\text{Feasible capacity}}$ can be in cost or time terms $= \dfrac{Cd}{C}$

2 $\dfrac{\text{Productive work}}{\text{Feasible capacity}}$ or $\dfrac{Ce}{C}$

Both ratios assume that idle or slack capacity costs should be isolated, with the second being more theoretical, when resources are wholly used on productive work.

Efficiency: even when a resource is seen to be utilised on productive work, this does not necessarily mean the work is being performed efficiently. For example, if a task has a standard time of two hours and it actually takes three hours, the efficiency would be $\frac{2}{3}$ or 66 per cent. Measurements of efficiency are therefore often associated with standard times. These are usually determined by industrial engineers and cover a wide range of activities such as operation times for making products, typing rates, times to prepare meals in hospitals and so on. The relationship between times and costs is just another view of the physical/financial or engineering/accounting facets of productivity measurement. At its most basic the planning of the effective use of resources in any organisation must be based upon agreed standards of times. Equally the cost of the times incurred has to be included. The T/C and Cd/C concepts recognise this interrelationship.

The economic use of equipment also should be added to plant efficiency. If for instance, an item will process materials up to 2″ in diameter and on average only 1″ is processed, its economic efficiency is 50 per cent.

Capacity, utilisation and efficiency are therefore three related but differing aspects of resource productivity.

SUMMARY OF MEASUREMENTS

An integrated framework for measuring productivity has now been described. The primary measurement is total earnings productivity, with a number of secondary measurements each having some influence on it. A summary of what these are and how they relate to each other is shown in Figure 4.3. Each of these measure-

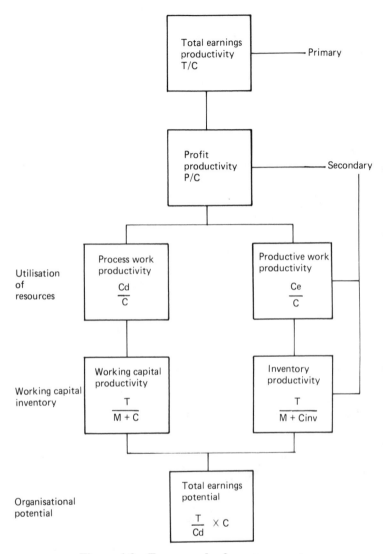

Figure 4.3   Framework of measurements

ments and the macro type measurements stated in Chapter 1
involve some of the following criteria of measurements.

1   Level, ie macro or micro
2   Complexity, ie simple or compound

3   Order, 1st or 2nd
4   Five aims: objectives, efficiency, effectiveness, comparisons
    and trends.

All of the measurements used so far are analysed against these
four criteria in Figure 4.4.

There are many more productivity ratios in use. Mali (6) lists
120 and suggests that there are an endless variety of ratios. He
categorises his productivity indicators as overall indexes, objectives, work standards and time standards. Mali's work is useful for
his attention to productivity measurement in such contrasting
organisations as business, government, education, and health and
human services. An interesting survey of international productivity measurement is provided by Bailey and Hubert (7). Not
only is this a good cross-section of measurement systems from such
countries as Austria, Canada, England, Israel, South Africa, and
the USA, but it is also a practical reference book to the world
network of agencies interested in productivity. An expanded
version of this network is provided at the end of this book.

PRODUCTIVITY COSTING

Productivity measurement is influenced in varying degrees by
accountants, economists, and engineers. This is why there is a
large number of ratios in use and unfortunately in some cases they
are unrelated; they may even conflict with each other. In this
section the aim has been to present a framework which can be used
in any organisation. The measurement system presented has been
used in practice. But, providing the cautions previously stated are
observed, there are other measurements that may be just as
effective.

Whichever methods are used the measurements must be unified
into some form of interlocking system. The approach developed
by Martin (3) to achieve this aim is called Productivity Costing and
Control.

Productivity costing is based upon the total earnings concept
and is also a combination of absorption, marginal and capacity
costing. The most prevalent costing system in industry is the
absorption method. This is the system where overheads (or the
fixed portions of purchased services and wages and salaries) are
apportioned generally in direct relation to the amount of direct
labour used. Because the apportionment percentage is based upon
last year's sales and product mix its deficiencies are under- and
over-recovery of overheads, and it is based upon the notion of the

No	Measure	Level		Complexity		Order		Five basic aims				
		Macro	Micro	Simple	Compound	1st	2nd	1 Objective	2 Efficiency	3 Effectiveness	4 Comparison	5 Trend
1	GNP per capita — GNP/PC	✓			✓	✓		✓	✓			
2	$GNP/PC \div GNP/PC$ of others	✓			✓		✓	✓	✓	✓	✓	
3	Added value per worker — AV/PW	✓			✓	✓		✓	✓			
4	Total earnings productivity — T/C		✓	✓		✓		✓	✓			
5	$T/C \div T/C$ of others		✓	✓			✓		✓		✓	
6	Profit productivity — P/C		✓	✓		✓		✓	✓			
7	Total earnings potential — $T/Cd \times C$		✓	✓		✓		✓		✓		
8	Sales per employee — S/TE — over 3 years		✓		✓	✓			✓			✓
9	Profit per employee — P/TE — over 3 years		✓		✓	✓			✓			✓
10	$P/TE \div P/TE$ of others		✓		✓		✓	✓	✓	✓		
11	Utilisation productivity — Cd/C		✓	✓		✓			✓	✓		
12	$Cd/C \div Cd/C$ of others		✓	✓			✓				✓	
13	Utilisation productivity — Ce/C		✓	✓		✓			✓			
14	Working capital productivity — $T/(M+C)$		✓	✓		✓			✓			
15	Inventory productivity — $T/(M+Cinv)$		✓	✓		✓			✓			
16	Output per hour — O/H		✓		✓	✓			✓			

Figure 4.4 Comparison of productivity measures

88

ability of the company to sell rather than its potential to produce.

Marginal or direct costing overcomes the apportionment problem by only costing the indisputable direct cost of materials and direct labour consumed in making the product. These variable costs are deducted from sales to give contribution margin, as shown in Figure 2.8 in Chapter 2. But the marginal costing method assumes that the rate at which contribution margin is generated is the same for all production facilities used.

Productivity Costing was developed to overcome these difficulties. At the same time the aim was to have a productivity control system that integrated the accounting and physical engineering measurements of productivity into one system. In productivity costing products only absorb material conversion costs at a rate based on the facilities capacity (ie people and equipment) to produce rather than on the ability to sell products. This is a subtle but significant point for productivity control in any commercial undertaking. Alternatively it can be considered as a marginal costing system in which due proportions of overheads are absorbed by products according to their usage of facilities at a costing rate based on their maximum feasible availability. The hourly costing rate for operating facilities (eg heating, lighting, rents and indirect wages and salaries) is allocated in proportion to their relative present-day purchase value divided by the agreed maximum feasible hours. An example of the allocation of expenses on this basis is shown in Table 4.2. This shows a processing costing rate (ie productive plus ancillary work costs) 'Cd' for each facility. Products bear costs at this rate, but when facilities are not in use idle capacity costs are incurred at the same rate.

The extensive research carried out by Martin in enterprises in America, England, Israel and Italy is reported in 'Productivity Costing and Control' (3). The principal attributes of the technique are as follows:

1 It is simple and uses information which exists in most organisations, or can easily and cheaply be obtained.
2 It makes use of a comprehensive family of ratios which all relate to one basic objective.
3 The concept of productive work which is carried out at the grass roots of an organisation plays an important part in the measurements used.
4 Products only bear costs when they are occupied on processing work.
5 The processing costs are based on maximum feasible capacity or the ability of the available resources to produce.
6 The potential total earnings can be obtained.

Table 4.2   Development of facilities costing rates for productivity costing

Item No.	Item description		Manufacturing information (for one week)			
1	Manufacturing departments		Fabrication		Assembly	Totals
2	Facility no.		10	12	14	
3	Type of facility		Machine tool	Welding machine	Labour and equipment	
4	Nominal working hours		40	80	80	200
5	Maximum feasible hours		34	66	70	170
6	Present-day values		60,000	90,000	30,000	£180,000
7	Percentage of total value	7a) By dept	40	60	100	
		7b) Whole system	33.3	50	16.6	100
8	Weekly operating expenses apportioned as % of items 7a) and 7b)	Total expenses	4000		1000	£5000
		8a) Dept. expenses	1600	2400	1000	
		8b) General expenses	1332	2000	668	£4000
		8c) Totals — 8a + 8b	2932	4400	1668	£9000
9	Facilities costing rates per hour - 8c ÷ 5		85.23	66.67	23.82	£175. 72
10	Direct labour costs	10a) Per week	140	280	300	£7. 20
		10b) Per hour	4.12	4.24	4.29	£12. 65
11	Processing costing rates - Cd, per hour - 9 + 10b		89.35	70.91	28.11	£188. 37

7   Idle capacity costs are segregated for management decision making. For example, how should they be absorbed and how

can the wasteful use of resources they represent be directed to productive work?

8 The strength of absorption, marginal and capacity costing are combined into one system.

9 It can be used for a more effective pricing policy.

SUMMARY

In this and the previous two chapters the groundwork for analysing and measuring productivity has been covered. This has included dealing with the question: 'What is productivity not?' as well as 'What is it?' For many organisations, levels of activity eg sales, products made or passengers carried, are seen as a kind of productivity measurement. Financial indicators also exert a strong influence, with profitability being a powerful yardstick for judging organisational performance. While for many commercial enterprises the size of the cash balance or bank overdraft tells management the state of their economic health, at the more physical end of enterprises industrial engineers compare outputs to the time consumed.

Sales, profit, money in the bank and the use of time are all important parts of the productivity measurement task. Total earnings productivity and the associated concept of productivity have been described as a method for linking the accounting and physical aspects of assessing performance. While the total earnings concept has been used in many practical situations, we acknowledge there are other equally good systems in use. But whatever the method used, it should take account of the following factors.

1 Allowance must be made for the effects of price changes and varying output/input mixes in the periods being compared.

2 The information required to do the measuring can be obtained; it is one thing to devise good measurements but for many smaller enterprises the information may not exist.

3 The system should have the five basic aims described, that is:

   a) *Objectives*: reveals to what degree agreed organisational objectives are being met.

   b) *Efficiency*: deals with the question posed in Chapter 1 Where are we now? or 'How efficiently are available resources currently being used?'

   c) *Effectiveness*: a measure of what is possible if resources were used more effectively. It is also a measure of the potential within the organisation. This deals with the last two questions in Chapter 1 'How much better could we be?' and 'What else could we be doing?'

d) *Comparisons*: how do we compare with others in current efficiency levels?
e) *Trends*: is our performance improving, remaining the same or getting worse?

In the next chapter a practical scheme of productivity measurement is described. It is called Productivity Audits and has now been used in some 100 small to large manufacturing and retailing companies in England.

REFERENCES

1   *Common Crisis North–South Co-operation For World Recovery: The Brandt Commission, 1983*, Pan, 1983
2   Martin, Professor Harold W. and Bahiri, Simcha, *Effective Management Through Productivity Costing*, Industrial and Commercial Techniques Ltd, London 1968
3   Martin, Professor Harold W., 'Productivity Costing and Control', *Productivity Measurement Review*, No. 37, OECD, Paris, May 1964
4   Davis, Hiram S., *Productivity Accounting*, University of Pennsylvania Press, Philadelphia, 1955
5   Martin, Professor Harold W., *Management Development and Productivity in Developing Countries*, The Operations Research Society of America, Santa Monica, California, 18 May 1966
6   Mali, Paul, *Improving Total Productivity*, John Wiley & Sons, 1978
7   Bailey, David and Hubert, Tony (eds), *Productivity Measurement*, Gower, 1980

Part III
Improving Productivity

Introduction to Part III:

The Practicalities of Productivity Improvement

Effective productivity information is an essential part of the overall task of improving the performance of organisations. But improvement in essence is a continuous change process. As we saw in Chapter 1, it is not just that we are involved in profound economic, social and technical changes but the pace at which such changes are taking place. This means that though information is an important prerequisite, there is also the equally significant need to gain full human commitment to the changes; it is one thing to measure productivity but something quite different to get increases in it. The experience of the American Productivity Center, as illustrated in Chapter 2, shows quite clearly that piecemeal approaches are not successful. If there is an all-pervading factor, it is top management commitment and the involvement of everyone. The purpose of Part III is to show how to get this commitment to action.

Productivity improvement is therefore concerned with getting good information and overcoming the human resistances in the way of it. Our work over the last five years has been directed to developing these two factors of measurement and gaining people involvement in the changes. It is our experience that bringing about the necessary changes to get lasting and continuing increases in productivity is a four-stage process:

1 *Recognition*: we have to recognise the need for change and improvement. The productivity audit including the interfirm comparison aspect is a device for doing this.
2 *Decision*: Once we have convinced ourselves that we should improve, a decision must be made to act. Initially, top management must make this decision.
3 *Permission*: even though decisions have been made to do something, there is the important human requirement of getting the permission to actually do it. For some, their 'internal permission' is strong enough, but for others external influences are necessary; comparison with the performance of other organisations has been shown to be a powerful force to get this permission.
4 *Action*: actually implementing plans for improving productivity must be the ultimate objective. But for this action to become a continuing part of the change process for the better, support is necessary. Real changes in habitual ways of doing things are not easy to start, let alone to sustain as a natural part of behaviour; productivity as a continuing process, therefore, needs careful nurturing.

These four stages are the human part of increasing productivity. The approach that best fits all these needs is action learning. It was pioneered by Professor Reg Revans, the founder of the action learning movement, (1) and has now been used all over the world in such diverse organisations as banks, factories, hospitals, mines and retail shops. We have developed the original concept of action learning into an approach which is ideally suited for productivity improvement programmes, its principal attributes being:

1 The setting up of mutually supportive groups of people at all levels of the organisation or externally between organisations. These groups jointly attack the productivity problems of the organisation. This critical mass of people is the key to real lasting improvements.
2 The existing way of doing things is challenged in the critical climate of the action learning groups. Skill is developed in posing entirely new questions, 'Q', which stimulate the fresh thinking so important to productivity improvement. In this way, what is called existing, and possibly outdated, pre-programmed experience, 'P', is challenged; nothing can be

more obstructive to effective change than using yesterday's experience to solve tomorrow's problems.

Part III has three objectives:

1 To consider the problems involved in improving productivity.
2 To describe the action learning method in more detail: what it is, how it can be used for productivity improvement, and some selected applications.
3 To explain how action learning was used within one large electronics company to improve performance.
4 To show how an interfirm productivity audit was combined with action learning to improve the productivity of 24 garden centres in various parts of the UK.

REFERENCE

1 Revans, Reginald W., *The ABC of Action Learning*, Chartwell Bratt, 2nd edition, 1983

5 Performance improvement programmes

The effectiveness of any method for measuring productivity should be judged against the simple question 'Is it used?' If it is to be of practical value to busy managers any system adopted must be understood by them: they need to know what they need and how to use it, and be able to obtain easily the information to measure.

Some ten years' experience with action learning groups has confirmed that managerial performance is closely related to information about what is being managed. Action learning is described in some detail in Chapter 8. Briefly, it was pioneered by Professor Reg Revans and consists of groups of people, generally managers, who support each other in tackling real problems in their own and someone else's, organisation. The activities of around 40 such groups (some idea of their diversity is shown in Figure 5.1) has revealed information as a common problem with some combination of the following factors:

- an ignorance of the key information that should be available – the 'what do I need?' problem

● a confusion about how to select and use information which
    is available – the 'how do I use it?' problem.

Size of participating organisations
1 to 5,000

Job levels of participants
– Shop floor workers
– Nursing staff
– Retail shop assistants
– Supervision
– Functional specialists, eg accountants, industrial engineers,
    designers and sales staff
– Middle   managers   eg   district   librarians,   departmental
    managers, sales managers, police superintendents, ward sisters
    and works managers
– Top managers eg general managers and managing directors.

Countries
The countries which have taken part in action learning include
Australia, Belgium, India, Irish Republic, Northern Ireland,
Saudi Arabia, Scandinavia, the United Kingdom, and the United
States of America.

Types of organisation
Banks, coal mines, defence equipment manufacturers, forging and
casting companies, garden centres, hardware stores, hospitals,
libraries and retail chemists.

Kinds of improvement
Better communication in 10 hospitals, increased rate of stock turn,
improved productivity, lowering scrap costs, marketing strategy
for a bank and reduced factory throughput times.

Figure 5.1   Range of action learning activities 1965–83

It was this recurring information problem that led to the development of what we call Performance Improvement Programmes
(PIP). They are a combination of productivity measurement,
interfirm comparisons and action learning. The aim was to introduce practical productivity audits of companies, interfirm comparisons to act as a spur to change and action learning to use the
resulting information to bring about improvement in performance.

About 100 companies have now taken part in PIP schemes. They have ranged in size from 2 employees to 5000 and included a variety of manufacturers and retailers. Some idea of the scope covered is shown in Figure 5.2. The first experimental programme was started in 1978, involving eight small to medium manufacturers in the West Midlands region of England. It was sponsored by the Engineering Industry Training Board and lasted for twelve months. A similar scheme was launched in 1979 for 17 retailers with funding from the Distributive Industry Training Board and again a twelve-month programme. Both programmes reinforced the earlier action learning experience, that is:

1 information must be easily obtainable;
2 targets have to be set when information is to be supplied, eg two weeks after the end of the month;
3 there has to be a stimulant to maintain the supply of information and to use the resulting measurements. The interfirm comparisons and action learning meetings do this.

Products made	No of employees
Chemists	15
Clothiers (3)	12–18
Defence equipment (4)	2000–5000
Electrical switchgear	460
Electrical switches	330
Electrical wholesalers	18
Electroplating	80
Fancy brassware (2)	114
Hardware merchants (4)	8–12
Heat exchangers	180
Heavy fabrications (2)	3–60
Newsagents (4)	10–20
Needles	50
Photographic equipment	17
Presswork	250
Wireworkers (2)	52–420
Electronics (2)	1000-1500
Garden centres (31) *	2–42

Figures in brackets indicate number of companies involved
* current MSC project

Figure 5.2   List of types of company involved

Since 1979 the Manpower Services Commission in the UK have provided further support for the development of the PIP approach. Twelve manufacturers took part in 1980 and in 1983 24 garden centres. The garden centre programme is described in Chapter 9. The principal purpose of this chapter is to examine the Primary Productivity Audit part of the PIP scheme; the action learning aspect is dealt with in Chapter 8. But first an overview of the complete PIP scheme.

THE AIMS OF PERFORMANCE IMPROVEMENT PROGRAMMES (PIP)

PIP schemes have been developed to provide a link between the establishment of an effective productivity measurement system and the more human task of improving it. The four stages of the scheme are illustrated in Figure 5.3. The primary productivity audit in stage 1 is the principal concern in this chapter, with secondary audits and how to analyse the audits being the subjects of the next chapter. The 'How to Improve Productivity' aspects of stages 3 and 4 form the content of Chapters 8 and 9.

The broad objective of the PIP approach is to enable organisations to improve their performance through a continuing performance improvement programme. More specific objectives are as follows:

1 to set up an effective productivity information system at the primary and secondary levels. The system should meet the five aims of productivity measurement, ie objectives, efficiency, effectiveness, comparisons and trends.
2 to organise a network of organisations interested in setting standards of performance.
3 to set up in-house productivity programmes.
4 to take part in external action learning group meetings with other organisations, the aim being mutual support in actually bringing about organisational improvement and to develop fresh thinking.

A concerted total approach of this kind to productivity improvement is almost certain to prove beneficial. The experience with the PIP scheme has generally been successful, with the common benefits being:

● increased awareness of the factors affecting productivity;
● a linking of existing accounting procedures with pro-

ductivity measurement and the need to establish a regular monitoring of performance;
● setting new standards to remain competitive;
● gaining the commitment of everyone to the need for continuing attention to productivity improvement;
● making use of productivity improvement techniques.

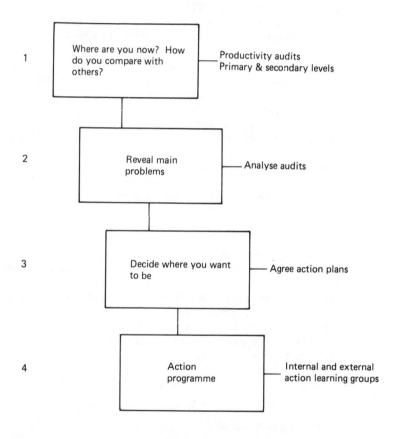

Productivity improvement means working smarter, not harder at old ways.

Figure 5.3   The main stages of the performance improvement programme

These all lead to increased productivity and profits. Real improvements come from adopting wholly new approaches rather than working harder at old methods.

WHAT IS A PRODUCTIVITY AUDIT?

Productivity Audits are the measurement part of the performance improvement programmes. They are intended as low-cost practical methods of increasing awareness of the need for productivity information on the current position. Answers to the question 'Where are you now?' are therefore given. At the same time, managers learn by active involvement the kind of information they need and, of equal importance, how to use it to improve the performance of their organisations. The productivity audit approach described here consists of an overall primary audit and a secondary audit at the grass roots level. As stated elsewhere, the measurement of productivity will depend on the use of available information or information which can be obtained with a minimum of time and cost. This is a particularly important requirement for the smaller enterprise. For these reasons the primary audit takes account of the following factors. Secondary audits are explained in the next chapter.

1 To stimulate initial interest in the question 'Where are you now?' a quick cursory appraisal of current performance is used.
2 Agreement must be reached on the information required and how it is to be obtained.
3 The audit system must be simple and low-cost.
4 It should increase productivity awareness and provide quick management information.
5 It highlights the areas for improvement.

THE AUDIT PROCESS

Whether a productivity audit is used within an individual company or involves several, on an interfirm comparison basis, careful preparation is essential. The people who will be supplying the information and using it must understand it and the basic routine. A brief guidance manual which describes the procedure and includes the information used should form part of the preparation. At the time of writing the Manpower Services Commission have given sponsorship to the development of a self-help manual to enable smaller enterprises to start PIP schemes. If the contents of the manual and the elements of productivity measurement are explained at a meeting, this should ensure understanding and commitment. Typical contents for a productivity guidance manual developed by the author for a manufacturing audit are shown below.

THE CASE FOR IMPROVING PRODUCTIVITY

In order that there is strong positive initial interest in the audit, those taking part have to be convinced that their productivity situation needs attention. Gaining this early recognition that present performance could be better can be done in three ways. Firstly, reminders of the more common ways of judging performance are stated. These are generally a combination of intuition, flair and some facts and figures. This can include

- levels of activity like sales, products made, patients seen and so on;
- the amount of incoming work and the present load of work;
- the size of the bank overdraft or more optimistically the bank balance;
- obvious changes in stocks, costs, delivery times of some supplies or adverse alterations in taxes.

All of these day-to-day occurrences will leave managers and workers feeling that things seem better or worse. Clearly instinct and flair are highly important attributes for management. However, additional, more objective, information may reveal unknown problems.

Secondly, therefore, those who take part in productivity audits are asked to do an audit of their existing information systems. Examples of this method for evaluating the availability of information were provided in Figures 3.4 and 3.5 (pages 66 and 68). It is emphasised here that information is what is published on a routine basis, and is used for managing the business and not just when there is pressure for it.

Thirdly, what are called 'Quick Productivity Audits' are used to achieve the recognition that there is room for improvement. Figure 5.4 is an example of one used for manufacturers. The questionnaire in Figure 1.6 (page 25) is another example.

Below are two easy-to-calculate popular productivity indicators.
So that you can compare your performance, the productivity
of other manufacturers is given.

Productivity indicator	Your company	UK manufacturers *		Other countries highest
		Lowest	Highest	
Sales per employee		14,890	34,300	44,000
Rate of stock turn		3.9	7.5	76

* The types of manufacturer included are ceramics, footwear,
   electronics, metals, furniture, food, plastics, engineering
   equipment, printing and packaging.

Explanation of measurements

1   Sales per employee: total annual sales net of VAT
     divided by average total full-time equivalent employees.

2   Rate of stock turn: total annual sales net of VAT
     divided by average stock carried at sales value net
     of VAT.

Figure 5.4 Quick productivity audit for manufacturers

While these are more cursory appraisals of the current position,
experience shows that they do create awareness. But it is the
continuing monitoring of productivity that gives the detailed information which is the main thrust of productivity audits.

DEFINING AND COLLECTING INFORMATION

A significant part of the preparatory process is defining the information that will be needed. This is particularly necessary if the
productivity audit is to include an interfirm comparison. When the
definitions are understood and agreed, a routine form for collecting the regular information required can be produced. One used
for manufacturers and based upon the definitions of information
included in Figure 3.1 is illustrated in Figure 5.5. This requires 10
items of data to be completed on a monthly basis, with one only
requiring additions and the other two subtractions. All of the
information required already exists in most manufacturing companies, thus satisfying the criterion that information must be easily
obtained. It will be seen that this form includes the percentage of

costs to sales. In this way significant cost areas are revealed and can then be monitored for any adverse changes.

Notes:	1 Ensure all information is included for period reported and it agrees with 'Definitions of Information'
	2 Use form for 3 periods (i.e. 3 months - 1 quarter)
	3 % columns are % of sales

Company code no

Item no.	Item definition	Period no. From: To:	%	Period no. From: To:	%	Period no. From: To:	%	One quarter totals	
1	Sales value - less VAT and credits								
2	Materials and bought outparts		%		%		%		
3	Total earnings - item 1 less item 2		%		%		%		
4	Total employees - adjust for part-timers								
5	Total wages and salaries		%		%		%		
6	Total purchased services		%		%		%		
7	Depreciation		%		%		%		
8	Total cost items 5 + 6 + 7		%		%		%		
9	Average inventory		%		%		%		
10	Net profit item 3 less item 8		%		%		%		

Figure 5.5   Basic information sheet (BIS): manufacturers

MEASUREMENTS USED

The measurements used are largely influenced by the information collected. They should also:

- be simple and easy to understand
- not be too many, to avoid the problems of information overload and the consequent tendency to lapse into non-use.
- cover the principle resources

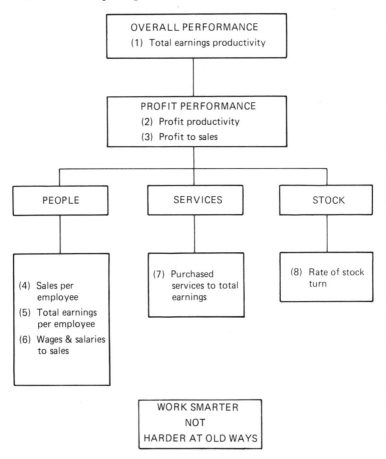

Note: Numbers in brackets refer to index number on period analysis sheet (Figure 5.

Figure 5.6 Main productivity areas: manufacturers

MANUFACTURERS

Company Code No 1

Period No 16

From 27.6 To 1.8 Year 1980

Index no	Productivity index	Your company	Company comparisons		
			Average	Lowest	Highest
1	Total earnings productivity $\frac{\text{Item 3 *}}{\text{Item 8 *}}$	1.21	1.14	1.06	1.21
2	Profit productivity $\frac{\text{Item 10 *}}{\text{Item 8 *}}$	0.12	0.07	0.03	0.12
3	Profit to sales as % $\frac{\text{Item 10 *}}{\text{Item 1 *}} \times 100$	5.8	3.9	2.1	5.8
4	Sales per employee $\frac{\text{Item 1 *}}{\text{Item 4 *}}$	£1921	£1437	£953	£1921
5	Total earnings per employee $\frac{\text{Item 3 *}}{\text{Item 4 *}}$	£1073	£916	£799	£1073
6	Wages & salaries to sales as % $\frac{\text{Item 5 *}}{\text{Item 1 *}} \times 100$	31.6	37.5	31.6	43.4
7	Purchased services to total earnings $\frac{\text{Item 6 *}}{\text{Item 3*}}$	0.18	0.32	0.18	0.48
8	Rate of stock turn $\frac{\text{Item 1 *}}{\text{Item 9 *}}$	0.2	0.18	0.1	0.4

Notes: * refers to items on basic information sheet, Figure 5.5.

Figure 5.7 Period analysis sheet: manufacturers

A mixture of measurements based upon total earnings and the more widely known indicators are used. The areas included and their related eight indicators are shown in Figure 5.6. Total earnings are included in items 1, 2, 5 and 7, with the remainder finding fairly common use in many countries. Further explanation of the measurements is shown next under interpretation. The monthly routine also includes a period analysis form which records achievements against each of the eight measurements. In 1982 twelve manufacturers in the UK took part in an audit. A period analysis sheet for one of these companies, a medium-sized producer of heat exchangers, is shown in Figure 5.7. This provides four items of information for each of the eight indicators, that is:

a)   the performance for the individual company
b)   average for all companies
c)   lowest companies
d)   highest company. It can be seen that this company, at a
        total earnings productivity 1.21, was the highest, as it was
        for profit.

Companies who are not involved in the interfirm comparison only get item (a) above.

INTERPRETING THE AUDIT

Each month a company receives the eight indicators of its own performance shown in Figure 5.7. If they have taken part in an interfirm comparison the stimulus of a league table effect is also evident. The actual results in Figure 5.7 reveal that the company used in the example is at the top of the league table on the first five measurements, is lowest for items 6 and 7. Only in its use of stock is it about average.

Four of the measurements use total earnings. The other four, viz.

3   Profit to sales as a percentage of sales
4   Sales per employee
6   Wages and salaries to sales as a percentage
8   Rate of stock turn

are included because of their widespread use. As they are frequently published, companies can judge their performance against other similar organisations. In this way even if interfirm comparisons are not used individual companies can get some idea of how they stand with others. Total earnings, though a well tested method of measuring productivity, is not so well known, but the spread of productivity audits may change this.

To assist companies in the interpretation of their monthly results the guidance manual also includes a more detailed examination of each of the eight measurements. Figure 5.8 is another example from the manual provided to manufacturing companies who have participated in audits. The same kind of explanatory information should be published for in-house productivity improvement programmes. Guidance material of this kind is essential but can be even more useful if combined with introductory meetings.

Remember the measurements tell you where you are now. They therefore include varying levels of productivity.

Index no	Productivity index	What they tell you
1	Total earnings productivity (TPE) Expressed in £	An overall indication of productivity. Also a measure of conversion efficiency. Your aim is to increase the rate at which you generate total earnings. Reveals total earnings for every £1 of total cost, eg 1.25 means £1.25 total earnings for every £1 of cost, or 25p net profit.
2	Profit productivity (PP) expressed in £	Shows the ratio of profit to total cost. Is closely linked to total earnings productivity, if you improve this you also improve profit. Shows profit for every £1 of cost, eg 0.25 is 25p net profit for every £1. Can also be obtained by deducting 1 from total earnings productivity eg $1.25 - 1 = 0.25$.
3	Profit to sales (P/S) expressed as %	A common indicator in industry, so watch for published figures. Shown as a percentage, eg 5% is £5 of net profit for every £100 of sales, or £1 of sales generates 5p profit.

Figure 5.8   What the measurements tell you – manufacturers

Index no	Productivity index	What they tell you
4	Sales per employee (SPE) expressed in £	Another much published productivity indicator. Because SPE includes varying material content (item 2 of definitions), compare yourself with a similar type of company. Most published SPE figures are annual, so multiply yours by 12 to get a comparable figure, with the caution that the monthly figures chosen could be maintained for a year – better still take your annual sales.
5	Total earnings per employee (TEPE) expressed in £	Similar to SPE but the influence of mark ups is removed. A more reliable figure than SPE but not published.
6	Wages and salaries to sales (W/S) expressed as %	Shows what employees cost to get sales. For example 15% means every £100 of sales costs £15 in wages and salaries.
7	Purchased services to total earnings (PS/TE) expressed in £	Indicates how much purchased services cost you for every £1 of total earnings, eg .3 means purchased services cost 30p for every £1 of total earnings.
8	Rate of stock turn expressed as a ratio	Shows how many times you turn your inventory over per month, eg .5 is half your stock per month or at a rate of 6 times per year (ie .5 × 12). A widely published figure always on annual basis. 52 divided by ROST gives number of weeks' stock eg 52 ± 6 = 8.6 weeks' stock.

Figure 5.8 (concluded)

It is evident from Figure 5.6 that the 'people' measurements receive a lot of attention. This is understandable when it is realised that it is managers, nurses, operators, sales assistants, typists and so on who influence productivity. The way customers and the public are treated, the quality of the service and the availability of products are all in the hands of people. Therefore, information on the use of an organisation's most precious resource that is believed and used, combined with effective teamwork, are the keys to success.

The experience with the PIP approach has shown that the usefulness of audit returns can be considerably enhanced by group discussion, especially if an experienced adviser is present. These are the action learning meetings presented in Chapter 8. But individual organisations can make the figures work simply by going through the routine of studying them at the end of each period. The following further points have been found helpful in making practical use of the audit information:

1 *Deferment*: Avoid putting off looking at the audit return. A senior member of the organisation must ensure a regular time is reserved for reviewing the information. Interest is soon lost if it is not used.

2 *Understanding*: This will take time and patience but is well worth the perseverance. People who use productivity information must get a working understanding of what each ratio means and their relationship to each other. When this is achieved they will have the confidence to use them.

3 *Comparisons*: Even where interfirm comparisons are not used individual companies can monitor any significant changes between periods.

4 *Cost changes*: The percentage costs on the basic information sheet, Figure 5.5, provide a basis for assessing any upward movement in costs relative to such outputs as sales.

MAINTENANCE OF THE AUDIT PROCESS

Once a routine has been established to measure productivity on a regular basis the last part of the process is to ensure it is maintained. To prevent what may have been started with enthusiasm lapsing into disuse someone with known responsibility for the whole PIP idea should keep in mind the following objectives:

1 Agreed productivity information (eg the forms shown in Figures 5.5 and 5.7) must be available on a routine basis and within an agreed time after the end of the period being evaluated.

2   The information must reach the people who can use it to
      improve upon the current position. If it does not, the in-
      formation or attitudes or both need changing.
3   The audit must be regularly evaluated against these objec-
      tives and changes made as the need arises.

Several years' experience with the PIP has shown that these
objectives can be attained when the following rules are
observed:

1   Involve people in the audit; elicit their suggestions on
      how it might be improved. This participative approach
      will result in the all-important commitment and hence
      increases its effectiveness.
2   Integrate the existing accounting-type systems with the audit
      process. To be sustainable the audit needs to be a natural
      part of day-to-day management.
3   Eliminate any information that ceases to be useful.
4   Change the presentation of some information and introduce
      new measurements where required, for example, total earn-
      ings productivity for specific products in addition to the
      overall figure previously described.

The first two or three months of an audit usually involve clearing
up various queries on information collection, establishing the
routine and becoming aware of what the measurements really
mean. When this stage is reached an analysis of possible trends in
figures can begin. The tracking of trends can be done in three
ways:

1   Deflating for price increases: sales and costs should be com-
      pared with previous periods to ascertain any movements up
      or down or if a state of calm exists. This kind of analysis is
      best done when a year's figures are available. However, to
      reveal any real changes the actual figures need to be deflated
      to remove the distortions of price and cost increases.
      Methods for doing this have been explained previously, but
      if a guidance manual is used this should include advice on
      how to adjust for changes of this kind.
2   Smoothing for short-term fluctuations: output and input
      figures will give a 'dragon's teeth' effect when examined on a
      monthly basis. Peaks in the figures may be due to known
      seasonal effects and where this is so adjustments can be
      made similarly to the price adjustment method. The two
      other ways in popular use are:

a) Moving Quarterly Averages (MQA): This is a useful method because it can be started as soon as three months' figures become available. The technique simply involves getting the arithmetical average for three

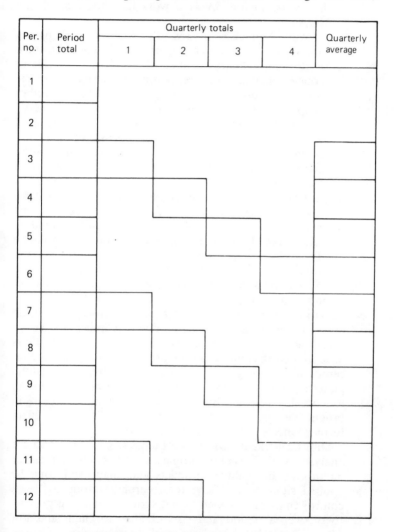

Notes:
  i) Obtain quarterly total by completing appropriate box
     eg first quarter is the total of periods 1 + 2 + 3

  ii) Obtain quarterly average by dividing quarterly total by three

Figure 5.9 Moving quarterly averages

months, moving forward a month to calculate the next average, and so on. For example, add the sales figures for January, February and March and divide by three; then add February, March and April and continue on this basis. Figure 5.9 is a worksheet for maintaining MQAs.

b) Moving Annual Totals (MAT): When a year's figures are available the monitoring of annual trends can start. Performance figures over a 12-month period will, of course, give a more representative insight into the operating position. A moving annual total is another simple technique for revealing annual trends. A MAT consists of obtaining a year's figures (eg sales, total earnings, costs etc) called the base year and then comparing the monthly figures in the current year with the corresponding month in the base year. The annual total for the base year is then adjusted by the difference. For instance if the total earnings for the year were £1,500,000 and the difference between January this year and last year (the base year) was + £5,000, the MAT would be £1,505,000. If February was + £1,500 the Mat would be £1, 506,500. The method smooths out monthly fluctuations and shows if any trend is taking place. For both MQA and MAT it may be necessary to take account of any seasonal effects.

3 Variations in performance: One of the problems of using figures of any kind, including productivity indicators, lies in revealing meaningful patterns. Indeed Beer (1) and others have argued that this is an important task for anyone concerned with helping busy managers to spot the change in the pattern. Trends analysis, previously described, is a useful tool in this respect. But the monitoring of variations in productivity performance is an added tool that can fill in further aspects of the performance picture.

Statistical quality control techniques is one method for analysing variations in performance. As it would be used for monitoring the quality of products being made, so it could be applied similarly for, say, total earnings productivity. A control chart of this kind would show the average productivity over a period and control lines for high and low achievements for 65 per cent levels of probability. An even simpler method used in productivity audits is to calculate average productivity, with control lines being based on the highest and lowest actual figures achieved. The chart is then used to record current performance figures. The intention is to create awareness of variations and possible patterns of performance and to stimulate discussions, with the recurring plea that must be used for practical purposes. An example of such a chart for a small retailing company is illustrated in Figure 5.10. This not only exposes the productivity performance of the company but is a vivid example of the seasonal effects on productivity. It can be seen that productivity varies about an average of 1.32 between a low of 0.67 and a high of 2.31, or a range of nearly 3∂ to 1. But even in the months of May to October when productivity is positive, ie above 1, it ranges from 1.09 to 2.31, or about 2 to 1. This

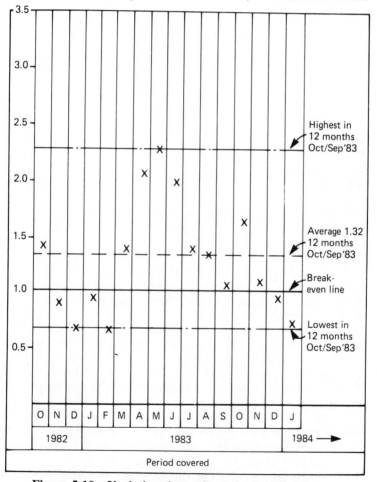

Figure 5.10   Variations in total earnings productivity

example has been taken from a large performance improvement programme for 24 UK garden centres, which is examined in greater depth in Chapter 8.

Although sales, costs and total earnings have been used to illustrate the use of trends analysis and variance monitoring, the techniques can be used for any aspect of organisational activity. Combinations of performance figures can also be a valuable aid in getting the most out of the information. Plotting MAT figures for sales and total costs on the same graph will reveal if there is any tendency for costs to rise faster than sales.

INTERFIRM COMPARISONS

The interfirm comparison approach to productivity measurement has been in use now for many years. In the UK the Centre for Interfirm Comparison (IFC) has been in existence for over twenty years. Similar schemes are reported by the European Association of National Productivity Centres (2) and by Bailey and Hubert (3) in their international survey of productivity. IFCs fulfil the fourth of the aims of a productivity measurement system mentioned earlier. Indeed, Carl Thor (4) of the American Productivity Center in Houston suggests that without account being taken of levels (ie comparisons) and the tracking of trends, productivity measurement is not much use. From our experience working with many types and sizes of organisation, companies do need to be aware of the external standards of performance that are being achieved. Equally, an internal analysis of potential total earnings using the Cd/C concept will also expose what is possible.

The use of IFCs indicates that they can be a powerful stimulant for companies to want to improve upon their productivity. Even so, experience also reveals two problems. Firstly, the managers of organisations have mixed views about comparisons with other organisations. It is commonly argued that 'the other enterprise is not the same as ours', 'the figures are suspect', and so on. While some of the claims are valid these reactions may be the understandable human defensive mechanism at work; if I rationalise the figures as not applying to me then I do not need to change! Secondly, even well-presented IFC reports can often be looked at with interest and then put on one side for attention later. This is partially because of the first problem or because the report is not part of an active programme of improvement.

The comparison aspect of productivity audits described here was designed to overcome these difficulties. To fulfil the now monotonous plea that information must be used, attention is given to:

1   ensuring the information provided is understood, clearly defined, and returned by agreed dates;
2   arranging action learning meetings to provide opportunities for studying the audit returns, that is, to enable the participating companies to get 'underneath the figures' and agree where action is necessary.
3   Giving each participating company a code number, so that they are assured of confidentiality. The procedure for an interfirm comparison is based upon the following three forms described earlier.

   a)   Definitions of information Figure 3.1 required. To ensure understanding and commitment these definitions should be agreed at a meeting with the participating companies.
   b)   Basic Information Sheet (BIS), Figure 5.5, contains the information which needs to be sent to a central processing source by an agreed date. For the MSC PIP schemes mentioned at the beginning of this chapter Action Learning Associates, as the project leaders, acted as the base for converting basic information into productivity indicators. But for most industrial and commercial companies trade associations and productivity centres are ideally suited for this role.
   c)   Period analysis sheet (PAS): an example of this is shown in Figure 5.7. This analysis is returned to each company within a week of the processing base receiving the 'BIS'.

Additionally, companies have found it useful to have comparisons of the actual sales and costs for each period. Such information acts as a reinforcement for the productivity indicators shown on the 'PAS' form. When company code number 17 saw in Figure 5.11 that number 11 was getting more sales than he was, and with virtually the same number of people, he was motivated to start taking action.

The stages in a productivity audit including interfirm comparisons are summarised below:

1   Gain commitment at an introductory meeting;
2   Complete Basic Information Sheet and send to the processing source;

3   Period Analysis Sheet completed and returned to each
     company;
4   Interpret results of analysis;
5   Maintain procedure;
6   Take part in external action learning meetings. Some

Month	August						Year 1983
Arranged in rank order of sales Lowest sales = 1							
Code no.	Rank	Sales £	Total employees no.	Sales area sq. feet	Total wages & salaries £	Overheads £	Tot. earn[s] prod'y.
13	1	1532	2.5	11,844	582	853	0.567
23	2	2930	1.5	2,500	360	681	0.844
21	3	8224	6	5,200	2,559	1,279	1.1
12	4	9531	4.5	21,237	2,631	1,715	0.67
7	5	10,873	2.5	2,200	1,215	1,512	0.8
17	6	15,095	8.3	23,237	2,694	1,941	1.27
4	7	17,212	6	22,869	2,407	1,204	1.4
3	8	17,289	8.7	23,000	6,547	1,731	0.9
8	9	18,398	7	11,000	2,442	9,244	0.55
24	10	23,404	8	18,500	5,025	1,760	1.138
22	11	23,637	14	15,000	5,952	1,935	1.24
6	12	24,344	10	15,000	3,784	7,585	0.75
11	13	34,194	8.5	39,090	4,104	4,996	1.3
10	14	48,929	23	20,000	9,424	3,604	1.2
9	15	90,042	35	25,000	17,262	8,545	1.27
15	16	101,980	47	86,871	19,914	22,088	0.85

**Figure 5.11   Garden centre productivity audit: monthly sales,
area, costs and productivity**

companies may decide to set up internal meetings in place of or in addition to the external activities.

These six stages are a more detailed version of the diagram in Figure 5.3.

SOME LESSONS AND CHALLENGES

The productivity audit described is a primary or overall evaluation of an organisation. It measures where the enterprise is now and consequently, as noted elsewhere, is bound to embrace both acceptable levels of efficiency and areas where improvements seem necessary. In the period from 1978 the companies taking part have all been manufacturers and retailers ranging in size from 1 to 5,000. However, the fundamental concept of taking agreed measurements of performance and sharing the results through interfirm comparisons and action learning meetings is just as appropriate to any kind of organisation. While the meetings are an important part of the change-for-the-better process, improvements have taken place even for those companies which were only able to participate on a postal basis.

As a vehicle for arousing awareness this practical and personal form of productivity audits has proved its worth. There are also a number of cases where productivity has been improved. But at the same time there are some lessons and challenges, listed below, which are pertinent to the general question of how to improve productivity.

1 The primary productivity audit is based on the idea of only using what information is known from experience to exist already or be easily obtainable. However, to get to the kernel of productivity new information is necessary and companies have to recognise this for themselves.
2 To begin with many smaller enterprises maintain very little productivity information.
3 The larger organisations suffer from an overload of information, which leads to it being ignored or misunderstood.
4 The productivity audit procedure needs to be sustained, until it becomes a natural part of the company. It must not be allowed to go by default.
5 If a practical and used interfirm comparison system is necessary, the problem is who will get it started and then maintain it.
6 How can the productivity audit idea be introduced into

public organisations? As the American Productivity Center and the Israel Institute of Productivity have suggested, the answer to the above problem is to create a national awareness of the productivity issue. At the local level senior managers can get programmes started and by skilful leadership retain the interest and commitment of grass roots personnel.

The next two chapters continue this look at the technical aspects of productivity improvement. They deal with secondary audits, which are the types of measurement necessary at the lower levels of organisations, and reveal in more detail how resources are currently being used, thus providing some answers to the earlier question 'How much better could I be?' The information for secondary measurements frequently does not exist, so low-cost techniques for obtaining it are also presented. Before making a start on the next chapter you might like to consider the six points made above.

REFERENCES

1   Beer, Stafford, *Brain of the Firm*, John Wiley, 2nd Edition, 1982
2   *The Changing Concept of Productivity and Action Consequences*, European Association of National Productivity Centres, Brussels, 1982
3   Bailey, David and Hubert, Tony (eds.), *Productivity Measurement*, Gower, 1980
4   Thor, Carl, *Productivity Measurement, Corporate Controller's Manual*, Warren, Gorman & Lament, New York, 1982 update

6 How much better could you be?

The primary productivity audit just described will reveal the present position within the organisation. But to answer the question 'How much better could you be?' more detailed information is required. While longer-term survival will require radical changes in many aspects of organisations, in the short term any enterprise can improve upon its present performance by making more effective use of its existing human and physical resources. What is required is secondary audit information on the productivity of resources at the lower levels of the organisation. But before examining these secondary measurements the influence of grass roots personnel on productivity needs attention.

ORGANISATIONAL FUNDAMENTALS

To be able to improve the productivity of any type of organisation it is first necessary to understand its socio-economic aspects. The term socio-economic as distinct from just economic is used to highlight the primarily social nature of all economic systems. Martin (1) defined such systems as: 'An integrated assemblage of people into interrelated and interdependent groups each using and managing energy consuming or facilitating devices and related resources for purposes of achieving satisfaction of human needs'. This definition suggests that people at the grass roots of all organisations have a managerial function in the sense that they alone manage the resources and time at their disposal. Martin confirms this in his division of management with a small (m) and nominative management with a capital (M). In the purely functional sense, management with a small (m) are the people who, through the control of their own efforts at the point where work is done, contribute to organisational productivity. The task of management with a capital (M), ie people who probably have manager in their official title, is to create the conditions where those at the lower levels are motivated to give of their best. These conditions will include a human climate which encourages people,

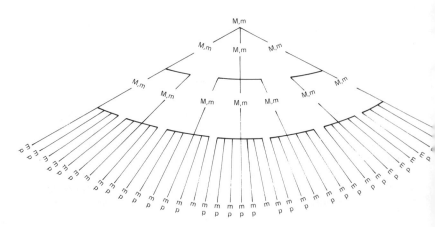

(M = nominative or positional Management, m = functional management, p = potentially productive-work-accomplishing functional management person)

Figure 6.1   Conical concept of a socio-economic system's personnel hierarchy

With acknowlegment to Professor Harold Martin, Socio-Economic Systems Productivity Analysis and Control Methods, New York, 1976 (unpublished paper).

an effective measurement system which feeds back information on their efforts, and appropriate physical resources. The success of (M)-type managers is wholly dependent on their skill in inducing people in subordinate positions to so manage themselves that they get the most out of their potentially productive resources. As Martin also states, nominative or official managers also have a functional (m) part in the way they manage themselves.

In the context of secondary audits, the concept of (m) and (M) is very relevant, bearing in mind that most productive work 'Ce' is done at the lower levels of organisations. Figure 6.1, as originally suggested by Martin, illustrates 'M', 'm' and 'p' for productive work aspects and how they relate to each other in a hierarchical structure. It will be seen that not all people with a small (m) are shown as doing productive work. This is in keeping with the fact that some personnel will be engaged solely in ancillary work, eg administrative work, cleaning, and moving materials. The conical shape of the organisation structure is used to show that communications need to flow around the hierarchy to promote a highly productive work climate.

There is considerable practical research evidence to show that there is a high positive relationship between Management's (M) attitudes to subordinates (m) and levels of productivity. Notable amongst these research methods is that developed by Revans and Hussain. (2) Dr Hussain, a Pakistani mechanical engineer, interviewed about 800 workpeople and obtained some 10,000 statements in a number of Manchester firms in the UK to test out people's attitudes to innovation and change. The same method was used by Martin in a study of five Nigerian coalmines to test the hypothesis that Management's treatment of subordinates and productivity are interdependent. Figure 6.2 summarises the results of interviews with 400 Nigerian mineworkers. An extract from the questionnaire used is shown in Figure 6.3. These series of statements originally developed by Hussain provide evidence of workers' views about management and their attitudes to innovation. The response method ranging over Strongly Agree to Strongly Disagree makes replies less time-consuming and also facilitates scoring for the eventual correlation analysis between attitudes and productivity. It is a technique worth including as a method of collecting information on the people aspect of productivity. The statistically determined correlation between workers' attitudes and productivity (total earnings productivity) shows that productivity increases as attitudes towards management become more favourable.

The *In Search of Excellence* study mentioned in Chapter 1 is further evidence of the connection between above-average

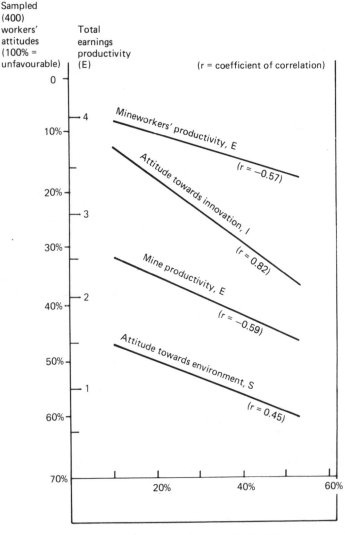

(M) Degree management unfavourable toward workers
(as scored by sampled workers) (100% = unfavourable)

**Figure 6.2   Relationships between workers' perceptions of
management is workers' attitudes and productivity.**

With acknowledgement to Professor Harold Martin, Socio-
Economic Systems Productivity Analysis and Centre Methods,
New York, 1976 (unpublished paper).

Response instructions: respondents are merely asked to put a ring around one of five responses to a number of statements. Each response can be:

SA = strongly agree
A = agree
U = uncertain
DA = disagree
SDA = strongly disagree

Example statements

Statements about works information system:

No 11 In this firm the management clearly explains to all its employees the purpose of what they are doing.
SA A U DA SDA

No 85 The higher management here rarely runs into difficulty through being out of touch with shop floor problems.
SA A U DA SDA

Statements about satisfaction with the supervisory task

No 25 A foreman in this company is easily able to get any help from other departments he needs to do his own job.
SA A U DA SDA

No 90 In our firm, the management attends to the foreman's problems so promptly that he has no cause for complaint.
SA A U DA SDA

Figure 6.3 Attitudes to management and innovation

Extracts from a questionnaire survey method developed by Professor R. W. Revans and Dr Hussain.
With acknowledgement to R. W. Revans, *Studies In Institutional Learning*, European Association of Management Training Centres, Brussels, 1967

performance and people involvement. But perhaps the outstanding proof of the power of participative management in improving productivity is the acknowledged success of the 90-year-old American Lincoln Electric Company. The company's policy of guaranteed employment described by Robert Zager (3) is one of the factors which has contributed to their unique commercial and social achievements. Their results include a counter-inflationary policy leading to lower-priced products than over the previous 10 years, above-average earnings for employees, profit sharing and manufacturing productivity increasing by an average of 7.3 per cent a year (compounded) between 1934 and 1971. Zager shows that by 1979 the success of the company was continuing. The principal factors in their above-average performance are:

1   Management has stuck to the products and services in which its expertise is greatest.

2   Economy is designed into products: manufacturing and design get together to reduce production costs.

3   There are no unnecessary frills, so overhead costs are low.

4   Employees know that their higher productivity will not affect their annual income; they also have the security of guaranteed employment.

5   New methods including good old-fashioned workstudy, the latest machines and innovative organisation structures (eg factories within the factory) are continually introduced.

Peter Drucker (4) in 1984 was also saying that it is still the simple things that produce higher-than-average results. He cites the example of a highly profitable chain of barbershops in the Southwest of the USA. The two young men who started the business just applied basic techniques to the question 'What are the key elements in the performance of a barbershop?' The answers were full utilisation of barbers and barber chairs (ie minimum downtime), high quality work and no customer waiting. They pay above-average wages and are so confident of their operation that a sign in their shops states 'If you don't sit in a barber chair within twelve minutes after you enter our shop, your haircut is on us!'

The lessons seem to be, involve people and use simple measurement methods for the productive work activities of the enterprise, be it mining coal in Nigeria, making welding electrodes at Lincoln or cutting hair. The question is 'where to start?'

WHERE TO START

Primary productivity audits carried out over a 3 to 4 month period, especially if interfirm comparisons have been included, should have revealed areas for improvement. Assuming that the audit has included the support of top management, a more detailed study of organisational productivity can now begin, commencing with a secondary audit.

There are no hard-and-fast rules where to start secondary audits. However, variations on one or both of the following methods have proved effective in practice.

1. Arrange a study meeting of managers representing a cross-section of the organisation to discuss the results of the primary audit. The questionnaire presented in Figure 1.6 can also be used to focus attention. Experience shows that meetings of this kind benefit from being residential, with agreed inputs and outputs at the outset, the inputs being the primary audits and the organisational questionnaire and the output a plan of action to carry out an in-depth secondary audit.

2. Probably as the result of a meeting of the kind described above, agree upon the area, function, department, process, product and so on to be called the subsystem which is to be investigated. The following steps should then be followed.

   a) Agree with the senior manager concerned and other representatives the basic objective of the subsystem.

   b) Identify and define the productive work of the subsystem.

   c) Determine the maximum feasible capacity for the subsystem.

   d) Take secondary audit measurements as described below.

   e) Collect information on the personnel, organisation structure, attitudes, equipment and work layout in the subsystem.

As the results of steps (a) to (e) above, agreement should be possible on the actions to improve productivity. This will form the basis of the in-company action learning and interfirm comparison programmes described in Chapter 9.

SECONDARY AUDITS

There should be two principal objectives in carrying out a secondary audit. These are:

1   To agree upon the key factors which are influencing overall productivity revealed in the primary audit;
2   To implement action plans to actually improve productivity.

Secondary audits embrace one of the central themes running through the book, that is, you cannot improve productivity without first measuring the current position, and any measurements made must be put to practical use.

The procedure for conducting a secondary audit will depend upon the kind of organisation, ie manufacturers, retailers, service, hospital, government and so on. A method for a manufacturing firm is described below, though many aspects are just as relevant to any kind of enterprise.

INITIAL STEPS

1   Get a consensus agreement of main functions (eg accounts, design, planning, production and sales) on maximum feasible capacity.
2   Obtain information on the percentage of time people and equipment are engaged on purely productive work. This should include both blue collar and the more difficult to define professional white collar workers. This form of information may not be available but can be easily obtained by the activity sampling technique described in Chapter 7.
3   Detemine processing costs for all equipment on the basis of maximum feasible hours and only costs for the time when people and equipment are engaged in processing work 'Cd' (ie productive plus ancillary work). The method for doing this was discussed under productivity costing in Chapter 4.
4   Carry out a trends analysis using the Period Analysis Sheet and Basic Information Sheets. This should be done for at least 12 months, but two to three years' historical data will provide even more reliable evidence. This should reveal longer-term percentage changes as shown in Figure 6.4.
5   Do a preliminary estimate of where delays occur in main functions. This should also include the average percentage of time the functions account for the total manufacturing cycle time and whether the times are preplanned. The planning task

No	Item	% change + or −
1	Sales	
2	Materials	
3	Total earnings	
4	Total employees	
5	Total wages and salaries	
6	Purchased services	
7	Total costs	
8	Total earnings productivity	
9	Profit productivity	
10	Wages to sales	
11	Purchased services productivity	
12	Rate of stock turn	
13	Product mix - analyse for significant changes in products and the likely effects on processes	
14	Set up costs (ie changing over from making one product to another)	
15	Batch sizes (ie quantity made at each set up)	
16	Quality costs (ie scrap and rectification work)	

Figure 6.4   Secondary audit trends analysis

(ie deciding in advance how long jobs or operations should take) is known to have a significant bearing on manufacturing efficiency. The influence of production planning on productivity is examined in more depth by the author in *Works Organisation*. (5) Figure 6.5 is a method for analysing delays, percentage of manufacturing cycle time and whether functions are planned or not. These are subjective estimates of these three factors which should be followed up by more objective studies, eg activity sampling.

No	Function	Delays			% of total manufacturing cycle time	Pre-planned	
		L	M	H		Yes	No
1	Design						
2	Material procurement						
3	Production planning						
4	Manufacturing, state key processes						
5	Subcontracting						
6	Assembly						
7	Despatch						

Notes:

L = low, M = medium and H = high delays.
More objective information should be
obtained by activity sampling

Figure 6.5   Secondary audit functions analysis

6 Carry out a comprehensive secondary audit under the four principal areas listed below:

Technical: design time, product productivity, plant productivity, technical competitiveness, plant economics, plant replacement, quality and maintenance productivity.

Flow: delivery performance, planned time achievement, delays, work layout.

People: productive work achievements, customer acknowledgement, telephone image, good housekeeping and absenteeism.

Materials: rate of stock turn for specific items, stock outs, working capital productivity and material yield.

ANALYSIS

Figure 6.6 is an analysis form for secondary audits, to cover the above four areas together with guidance on sources of information. This is a more detailed version of the secondary audits described in Chapter 4 and illustrated in Figure 4.3. It will be seen that productive work productivity forms part of the audit for plant and people. In addition a number of new measurements are introduced; these are briefly described in Figure 6.6. but some are further explained below:

Design time: manufacturers will need to give increasing attention to how quickly they can get new ideas into a saleable form. White collar productivity which designers are a part of is now regarded as a sufficiently significant subject to be dealt with under this heading in the last chapter.

Product productivity: specific products do require evaluation for total earnings productivity using processing cost 'Cd' as the cost input. Those that rank low should be studied to see how their productivity could be improved.

Technical competitiveness: as mentioned elsewhere, technology is under constant change with consequent, at times dramatic, effects on processing times. Therefore, current manufacturing times need regular reviews against the best known times. There is the additional dilemma of the possibly higher cost of the new technology to provide the more competitive time.

Plant economics: Bahiri (6) has made an extensive study of how much the 'size' capacity of individual items of plant are actually used. His findings show that only a proportion of the maximum capacity is utilised. This has two important implications for plant productivity: i) more expensive capital is tied up than is necessary; and ii) the running costs are higher than they need to be. Two examples are automatic lathes which can take up to 2″ diameter

No	Item	Your position	Sources of information
1	**TECHNICAL** **DESIGN TIME** How long in weeks to: i) get new designs into production ——— ii) get existing designs into production ———		If this information does not exist obtain in three ways: 1 Estimates 2 From records 3 Keep a check on new orders
2	**PLANT PRODUCTIVITY** $\dfrac{\text{Productive work time Ce}}{\text{Maximum feasible time}} \times 100$ ———		Either available records or activity sampling. Take key items of plant first
3	**PRODUCT PRODUCTIVITY** $\dfrac{\text{Product total earnings}}{\text{Processing cost Cd}}$ ———		Use available records or start to collect for key products. Use Pareto Analysis to reveal product groups with highest profit
4	**TECHNICAL COMPETITIVENESS** $\dfrac{\text{Best world time}}{\text{Your time}}$ ———		Take 2 to 3 key processes, get current actual times for making products and compare to the world's best. Not easy information to get but should be known
5	**PLANT ECONOMICS** $\dfrac{\text{Capacity used}}{\text{Maximum size possible}}$ ———		Take 2 to 3 key items of plant, assess their maximum capacity (eg maximum sized material) and compare with average amount of capacity used
6	**PLANT REPLACEMENT** Replacement cost of plant with current technology % increase in price ——— % decrease in price ———	% Age	An assessment of the cost of current technology, it may be increasing or decreasing. Select 2 or 3 items of key plant. Compare also to age of plant.
7	**QUALITY PRODUCTIVITY** Quality costs trend Costs of all rework and scrap as a % of costs on a moving quarterly average ———		If these costs do not exist records may be a source. Failing this start collecting them
8	**MAINTENANCE PRODUCTIVITY** $\dfrac{\text{Total breakdown time}}{\text{Maximum feasible time}} \times 100$ ———		Use a combination of records and activity sampling

Figure 6.6 Secondary audit: manufacturers

No	Item	Your position	Sources of information
	FLOW		
9	DELIVERY PERFORMANCE $\dfrac{\text{Actual delivery time}}{\text{Planned delivery time}}$	———	Take some orders at random and compare actual delivery with the planned or promised delivery. How precise are delivery promises eg 6/8 weeks or 4.4.1984?
10	STAGNATION FACTOR $\dfrac{\text{Actual total time to get through factory}}{\text{Total of planned operation times}}$	———	Select a typical batch, total the planned times for all operations and compare with the actual time. Should always be greater than 1
11	DELAYS Length and location of longest delays Length ——— Where ———	——— ———	The extent and whereabouts of significant delays needs to be monitored eg. design, suppliers, production. Figure 6.5 is a method for doing this
12	WORK LAYOUT $\dfrac{\text{Actual distance travelled}}{\text{Ideal distance}}$	———	Select one or two popular products, measure the actual distance travelled from start to completion and compare with what it could be under ideal conditions
	PEOPLE		
13	PRODUCTIVE WORK ACHIEVEMENT $\dfrac{\text{Productive work time Ce}}{\text{Maximum feasible time}} \times 100$	———	Will probably involve activity sampling
14	CUSTOMER ACKNOWLEDGEMENT $\dfrac{\text{How long, in days, to acknowledge orders/letters}}{\text{Target time in days}}$	———	The speed and quality of customer response is important. Should be monitored on a regular basis
15	TELEPHONE IMAGE Good (G) Mediocre (M) or Bad (B)	———	The company image to the outside world. May have to be a subjective judgement but still requires some evaluation
16	GOOD HOUSEKEEPING Tidiness of factory, offices and stores Good (G) Mediocre (M) or Bad (B)	———	General tidiness is some guide to company efficiency. Produce a Good Housekeeping form for all depts. and assess monthly

Figure 6.6 (continued)

No	Item	Your position	Sources of information
17	PEOPLE (continued) ABSENTEEISM $$\frac{\text{Total hours absenteeism}}{\text{Maximum feasible hours}} \times 100$$	———	Reveals lost potential productive hours and may also indicate low morale. Personnel records are a source of this type of information
18	MATERIALS RATE OF STOCK TURN FOR SPECIFIC ITEMS $$\frac{\text{Sales of item}}{\text{Average stock of item}}$$	———	ROST in primary audit only shows average ROST for all stock. Information is required on slow and fast moving items. Do a ROST for raw materials, w.i.p. and finished stock. Use Pareto analysis to make selections
19	STOCK OUTS The number of times per month orders cannot be completed because of stock shortages	———	ROST reveals if stock is too high. Stock outs is an indication that some stocks are insufficient. Store records should be a source; if not start keeping them
20	WORKING CAPITAL PRODUCTIVITY $$\frac{\text{Total earnings}}{\text{Material costs (M)} + \text{Total costs (C)}}$$	———	An indication of total inventory costs (M + C) in relation to total earnings (T). Use also T/M + Cinv to cover carrying charges. See also Chapter 4 and Figure 4.3
21	MATERIAL YIELD Material as a % in final product $$\frac{\text{Material in final product}}{\text{Total material issued}} \times 100$$	———	Select products with known high value materials. Also reveals waste. Existing cost records may be a source; if not start collecting for some items

Figure 6.6   (concluded)

material but on which $1\frac{1}{4}''$ diameter is the largest ever machined, and large electro-plating vats which are never more than half full.

Plant replacement: relates to technical competitiveness above. It raises two issues: for strategic management, i) can the higher cost of the latest more competitive plant be absorbed in prices? The answer lies in avoiding low plant economics and ensuring the plant productivity is high. ii) In some cases the latest electronically controlled plant could be cheaper with consequent effects on pricing policy.

Quality productivity: quality productivity can be measured in a number of ways, the one shown in Figure 6.6 being a relatively easy method. The costs of quality are influenced by the design specification coupled with how well people and plant conform to the specification. This interaction between design and conformity results in two opposing costs. There are the preventative costs, that is, inspectors and quality control staff, and the indirect costs such as returns from customers, rework and scrap. There is little doubt that quality is an important factor in competitiveness but quality can cost a lot of money unless it is managed effectively; it is pointless to design in more quality than is required or quality specifications that people and equipment cannot conform to. A lot of the confusion and unnecessary cost arise from ambiguous design specifications and varying standards of conformity in the manufacturing areas. For instance, 'must have a smooth finish' on a drawing is open to considerable interpretation. Furthermore, if production personnel form the impression that quality varies with the pressure for output or the status of the customers, they too will have varying standards of conformity.

Maintenance productivity: as with quality there are the complementary costs of prevention (eg stocking spares and employing maintenance staff) and downtime or indirect costs. It is clearly uneconomical to stock no spares if downtime costs are very expensive, and the reverse is also true.

Flow: the whole aspect of flow through any system requires routine assessment. The four measurements chosen highlight the significant factors. Delivery is often not monitored on a regular basis; moreover even 'a delivery' lacks precision. It is, for example, difficult to plan production and the necessary material supplies on the basis of a 6 to 8 weeks delivery. In these circumstances, if the purchasing function assumes 8 weeks and production 6 weeks, chaos is bound to occur. What has been called the stagnation factor is a good indication of flow efficiency. When actual times are compared to planned times, ratios of the order of 3 to 1 are not uncommon. This means that it takes three times longer than planned to get work through the system. The reasons for this have been examined by the author (5) in detail but are likely to be a combination of batch sizes, set up times, the amount of work in progress, rectifications, poor production planning and the work layout.

People: the idea of productive work for people and plant is significant but the simple but overlooked items 14 to 17 also need further treatment. Improving the response time to customers' letters not only enhances goodwill but will also have an indirect effect on improving the planning process; delays in acknowledging orders may signify indifference and inadequate planning information. The productivity of the telephone exchange requires measuring just as much as production processes. Robert Townsend in his highly amusing book *Up the Organisation* (7) relates his method for assessing the quality of their exchange: he simply used an outside telephone and asked for himself!

Good housekeeping is another indication of people's attitudes, untidy and dirty surroundings probably revealing an inefficient organisation. Though an evaluation method is suggested, lasting improvements will necessitate looking at a number of factors including attitudes, planning and work layouts.

Item 17, absenteeism, is an aspect of organisational performance that can go unnoticed. It is known to be as high as 15 per cent in some companies, especially if late starting and early finishing is included. Absenteeism is a drain on possibly productive work but may also be what Fox (8) describes as unorganised conflict; people show their dissatisfaction through absenteeism.

Materials: apart from working capital productivity discussed earlier, items 18, 19 and 21 are good guides to materials productivity. Item 18 is a specific measurement of ROST for products or divisions of stock (eg raw materials, work-in-progress and finished stock). The overall ROST in the primary audit may for example give a figure of 3 times per year. But this average obscures some items that may not have moved at all and others that have a ROST of 50. This more detailed analysis isolates the slow movers and the fast ones.

Stock out (SO), item 19, is the other aspect of stock control when production is held up because there is no stock, with all the consequent costs. It is unlikely that stocks can ever be just right. Even so it is necessary to know whether ROST and SOs are changing in the wrong direction.

Finally, item 21 provides information on the yield obtained from materials purchased. Some materials, such as paint, are particularly low, giving figures which can be as low as 18 per cent.

Although this lower-level audit is directed to manufacturers the general principle is pertinent to any enterprise. The specific measurements will need to suit particular circumstances, but attention will still be necessary in the four areas of Technical, Flow, People and Materials.

The use of such techniques as activity sampling will lessen the time and cost to get information of the kind described. Even so, if none of it exists, it should still be regarded as an important part of the total performance improvement programme. Each area should be a project with an agreed plan of action. However, once the information is available a regular routine, similar to the primary audit, can be established. In this way, a total measurement system will have been introduced into the company. How the five basic aims, the primary audit and the secondary audit relate to each other are shown in Figure 6.7.

CONCLUSIONS

Although many enterprises in all parts of the world will be suffering from reduced demand and cuts in budgets, they could still make better use of existing resources. To discover how much better they can be more detailed information is required than that provided by a primary audit. The system for obtaining it has been described as secondary or grass roots audits. It is at this level that a significant proportion of productive work, in its many forms, takes place. It has to be understood that people at these lower levels have a great personal influence on the way they manage time and resources. Evidence has been presented to support the view that there is a positive relationship between above-average productivity and how functional management (m) are treated. These people-oriented aspects of productivity improvement are dealt with at greater length in Chapter 8. In this chapter, for purposes of continuity, the link has been described, but the main aim was to examine methods for carrying out secondary audit-type measurements. A general approach has been taken and, while the specific example is directed to manufacturers, the principles can be adapted to any kind of organisation. The answers to the two questions 'Where are you now?' and 'How much better could you be?' depend upon sound information at the primary and secondary levels. This and the previous chapter have shown how this can be done.

In the next chapter, techniques for collecting productivity information are described. A participative approach is proposed. If

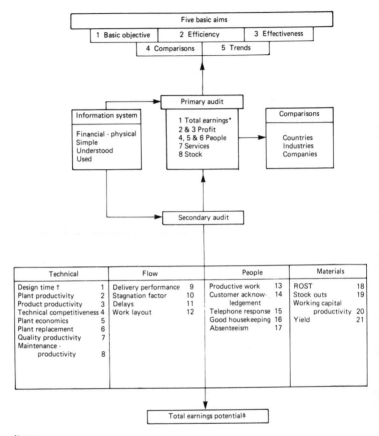

Notes:
* item numbers from period analysis sheet, Figure 5.7
† item numbers from secondary audit, Figure 6.6
‡ see Figure 4.3

Figure 6.7   Total measurement system for manufacturers

those at the grass roots are involved in carrying out their own studies of productivity they will be more willing to use the results to improve it.

REFERENCES

1. Martin, Professor Harold W., 'Socio-Economic Systems Productivity Analysis and Control Methods: Vital indicators of changes in socio-economic phenomena', unpublished paper, New York 1976
2. Revans, R. W., 'Managers, Men and the Art of Listening', *New Society* 4 February 1965
3. Zager, Robert, 'Managing guaranteed employment', *Harvard Business Review*, May/June 1978
4. Drucker, Peter F., 'Our entrepreneurial economy', *Harvard Business Review*, January/February 1984
5. Lawlor, Alan, *Works Organisation*, Macmillan, 1974
6. Bahiri, Smicha, 'How to measure Productivity', *Management Today*, July 1970
7. Townsend, Robert, *Up the Organisation*, London, 1970
8. Fox, Alan, *Industrial Sociology and Industrial Relations*, Research Paper no. 3, HMSO London, 1966

7 Productivity improvement techniques

There are many productivity techniques and research methods to aid the collection of information about productivity, all with the ultimate aim of improving it. But can the data collection process, the analysis of the resulting information and actually using it to increase performance be combined? If those who do investigative work are also already actually involved in what is being studied, they may be more committed to implementing action plans for improvement.

It has long been argued in action learning circles that effective diagnosis of problems by people who are part of them produces its own remedies. If those involved also learn from the experience, that much-prized situation of self-generating improvement will have been achieved, what Ashmawy and Revans (1) describe as autonomous learning. There is extensive experience to support the view that a participative approach to studying work activity is more successful in increasing organisational performance. It has been used in such widely differing situations as improving communication in hospitals (2) and getting better services for the mentally handicapped; (3) to increasing productivity in a large warehouse supplying a national chain of retailers. (4) Baquer (5) developed the approach further in a project to better co-ordinate the providers and receivers of services for one-parent families. A multiprofessional group of people were soon able to learn the skills of social survey methods to study this highly emotional area and at the same time to gain support for improved services. The warehouse project also confirmed that middle-aged women supervisors were, much to their surprise, able to master and apply method study and activity sampling techniques to the work of their sections. A consequence of their investigations was the revelation that productive work only occupied 14 per cent of total time, with an eventual campaign to lessen ancillary work and reduce idle time.

In the light of the above the techniques and study methods that follow are presented in the belief that they will be far more effective if used on a participative basis. Furthermore, investigation, taking action and learning should be regarded as one interrelated process.

QUANTITY AND QUALITY

There are a number of techniques in use for collecting information about productivity and related matters. They also aim to use the information as a means of changing and improving upon the current position. Some of the techniques are quantitative, that is, they lean towards technical and numerical assessments, while others are more qualitative, with a bias towards the subjective. While they are difficult to measure, we do need to ascertain people's feelings about efficiency. An understanding of productivity requires a blend of both quantitative and qualitative information on productivity. The other important general point about established techniques for collecting information is their systematic approach to observing and recording actual activities.

From the many techniques available, 17 have been selected as being of practical use in productivity investigations. For ease of reference, these are summarised in Figure 7.1. The first 14 fall under the general heading of quantitative, while the last three are qualitative methods.

No	Technique	Applications
1	Flow process charts	Study of flow and sequencing of people and materials. Reveals how unnecessary activities can be reduced.

Figure 7.1 Productivity technique applications

No	Technique	Applications
2	Flow diagrams	Routing and sequencing of people and materials.
3	String diagrams	Reveals degree of complexity of movement and hence how to remove congestion.
4	Man/machine activity charts	Used for finding a better balance between people and equipment.
5	Two-handed operator charts	Reveals how individual operations can be improved.
6	Micro motion study	A technique for improving the minute aspects of individual operations.
7	Value analysis	Especially useful for analysing the functional and cost effectiveness of products, materials and services.
8	Estimating	Useful for providing quick estimates of time, generally subjective and therefore inaccurate.
9	Time study	A method for obtaining objective time standards, most suitable for repetitive operations.
10	Synthetics	Cheaper than time study for providing accurate time standards. Can be developed internally or bought out.
11	Analytical estimating	A relatively quick and accurate method for obtaining estimates of complete jobs. Will find increasing use with the advent of customised products and services.
12	Activity sampling	Particularly useful in productivity studies for percentage of time spent on productive/ancillary work and idle time.
13	Pareto analysis	Useful for identifying areas which incur the greatest cost, time and scrap. Main applications are purchases, stock and scrap.
14	Work simplification	A participative use of method study. A form of quality circles effective for releasing creative potential.
15	Critical incident analysis	An open-ended approach to revealing productivity problems.

Figure 7.1   (continued)

No	Technique	Applications
16	Illuminative incident analysis	A team and pictorial method for gaining understanding of human problems affecting group effectiveness.
17	Questionnaire	Used for studying the attitudes affecting productivity.

Figure 7.1 (concluded)

METHOD STUDY

Work study is still the most practical tool for studying productivity. The Lincoln Electric and the barber shop business mentioned previously are good examples of the use of simple work study techniques leading to above-average results. It embraces the three main areas affecting the performance of any organisation, which are shown in Figure 7.2. Our main attention here is to the method

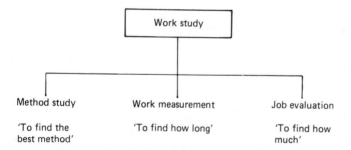

Figure 7.2 The main divisions of work study

study and work measurement aspects. Method study is described as a systematic application of common sense. It seeks to observe and then record how equipment, materials, people and space are currently being used. How this relates to productivity, and possible areas of waste, are shown in Figure 7.3. The specific method study techniques to obtain information in each of these areas now follow.

The procedure for using method study generally involves the following eight stages:

1. Problem selection – the problems chosen for study can arise in two ways. Firstly, problems are brought to the notice of supervision or management, a reactive policy. Secondly, management can adopt a proactive approach and seek out

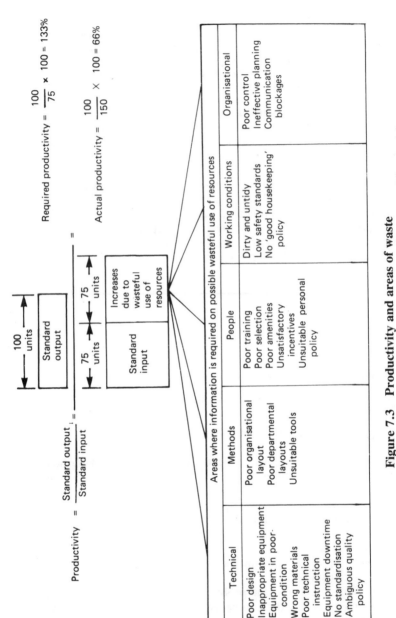

Figure 7.3 Productivity and areas of waste
With acknowledgement of Alan Lawlor, *Technical Aspects of Supervision*
Pergamon, 1970

areas where improvements should be made. The primary and secondary audits described previously are examples of not waiting for problems to require attention but discovering opportunities for increasing productivity.

2   Preliminary stage – involves preparations for making the study and will include getting a cursory appreciation of the problem, getting to know the people involved with it, the terms of reference and the specific method study techniques to be used. The terms of reference are especially important at this initial stage and should clarify the amount of time and money that can be allowed and what can and cannot be done.

3   Specific technique to be used – if the study will involve the coarse movement of men and materials, what we call '6″ rule' techniques can be used, that is, the finer measurements of distance and time are not necessary. On the other hand, if the study involves the more minute movements of hands and eyes, 'micrometer' or micro motion study techniques will need to be used.

4   Recording phase – no improvement in the present method is possible until information is collected and recorded in a form that makes for quick and easy analysis. This supports the general requirement of productivity improvement – you cannot improve it until you first measure the present position.

5   The questioning phase – every aspect of the record of the present method should be critically examined with regard to Purpose, Place, Sequence, Person and Method. These involve the critical method study questions of 'What is done?', 'Why is it done?', 'Who does it?', 'Where is it done?', 'When is it done?' and 'How is the work done?'

6   Development phase – examine possible alternative means and test the one that will improve productivity.

7   Implementation phase – involves training people in the new method and the best way of introducing it into the department.

8   Control phase – regular monitoring of the new method, to clear up any difficulties and ensure it becomes a normal part of work activity in the department. This procedure is summarised in Figure 7.4.

The method study techniques developed by Frank Gilbreth and described by Barnes, (6) which have been refined over many years, are essentially methods for facilitating observation and easing the analysis of the facts collected. As shown in Figure 7.3 the techniques are divided into '6″ rule' and

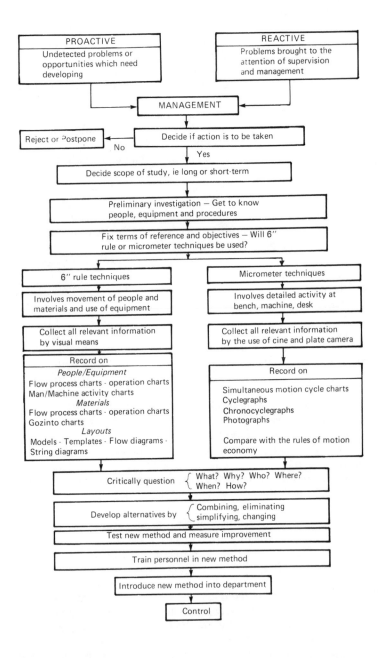

Figure 7.4   Method study procedure flow diagram

Standard language		Productive work language	
Description	Symbol	Description	Symbol
Operation	◯	Productive work operation	 ⊖ PW
		Ancillary work operation	 ⊖ AW
Transport	T	Transport: ancillary work	T
Delay/Storage	D	Delay: idle time	D
Inspection Quantity/Quality*	□	Inspection: ancillary work	□

Note: * to distinguish between quantity and quality inspections
□ can represent quality and ◇ quantity

Figure 7.5   Method study language

'micrometer' methods. It is the former which finds the greatest use and will therefore receive the most attention here.

6" RULE TECHNIQUES

So that the information collected by method study techniques can be easily interpreted, a basic language has been developed. The standard method study language, which is appropriate to equipment, materials and people, is shown in Figure 7.5. The activity Operation shown with the symbol O includes some productive work and ancillary work, with further ancillary work being included in transport and inspection, ie T and □. Delays, D, are the

equivalent of idle time. For the purposes of revealing purely productive work the symbol for Operation can be divided thus, ⓟⓦ
for productive work operations and ⓐⓦ for ancillary work. The
five modified symbols are shown on the right-hand side of Figure
7.5.

Within the framework of the basic method study language there
are a number of ways of recording and analysing information. The
main ones are:

Flow process charts

These charts can be used to study the activities of people, eg
workers carrying out manufacturing operations, the flow of customers in retail shops, or nurses in hospitals. This kind of recording analysis form can therefore be used for investigating the flow of
materials in factories, goods in a warehouse or linen in a hospital.
The usefulness and conciseness of the standard basic language is
shown in Figure 7.6. This shows the first twelve of a total of 27
activities for packers working in a despatch department. The chart
isolates operations, ie those activities that really add value, from
ancillary work (ie transport and inspection) and idle time (delays).
As previously noted, operations can be subdivided into productive
and ancillary work. This analytical recording method, through
directing attention to productive activities, reveals ways of improving upon current methods. As previously stated a good diagnosis
produces its own remedies.

When using processing charts and their supporting language the
symbols for activities will depend upon what is being studied (eg
equipment, materials or people). For instance, delivering parts is
an operation for a delivery vehicle, that is, the vehicle is doing the
job it was acquired for. If it were empty returning to its base, that
would be a transport activity. The materials are in transit and
therefore would be recorded as a transport. The driver of the
vehicle is engaged in productive work when driving his vehicle
loaded with materials, so operation is an appropriate description.
But this study does not necessarily tell us to what extent the
resources of equipment (the vehicle) and people (the driver) are
utilised, eg, is the vehicle carrying a full load? The activity
sampling technique described later on will help to do this. Figure
7.7 is a practical exercise to promote discussion on a wide range of

Subject charted	Parcel packing despatch dept.			Page No. 1 of 2			
Chart begins	Packing bench		Chart ends Packing bench		Date started 13. 4. 1984		

Summary				Critical questions			
Items	Present	Proposed	Difference	Why? What? When? Where? Who? How?			
O : Operation	5			Alternatives			
T : Transport	6						
D : Delay/Storage				Eliminate	Combine	Change the sequence	Simplify
□ : Inspection Quantity/Quality	1						
Total times	29 mins						
Total distance	80 feet						

Present method						Date:	Proposed method						Date:
Distance feet	Time mins	O	T	D	□	Sequence	Distance	Time mins	O	T	D	□	Sequence
	4				●	Packer checks goods with instructions							
10	2		●			Take instructions to supervisor's desk							
	3	●				Collect advice note							
10	2		●			Return to loading bench							
11	4	●				Collect goods							
11	2		●			Take to packing bench							
	1	●				Deposit on packing bench							
6	2		●			Fetch roll of corrugated paper							
	3	●				Cut off piece							
6	2		●			Return to packing bench							
	1	●				Deposit corrugated paper							
26	3		●			Go to carton rack							

Figure 7.6 Flow process chart. Part of a study of a parcel packing operation (one of two sheets).

work activities (ie operations, transport, delay/storage and inspections). The adding value column is intended to promote discussion on what is pure productive work.

Flow diagrams

This technique is often used to supplement flow process charts and is a means of illustrating diagrammatically the actual path of movement of materials and people around an organisation or department. They reveal in pictorial form the distance travelled and the degree of complexity of movement. A scale drawing of the area being studied is necessary and then coloured pencils or

	Activity	Sym*	Adds value		Activity	Sym*	Adds value
1	Workman painting door			12	Designer working on a drawing		
2	Customer checking change			13	Ship being unloaded		
3	Students awaiting tutor's arrival in class (he is late)			14	Nurse sorting dirty linen		
4	Workman walking to a store			15	Customer waiting at check-out in supermarket		
5	Lorry carrying sacks of coal to point of delivery'			16	Finished parts in a store		
6	Housewife mixing pastry			17	Machine awaiting repair		
7	Tutor lecturing to class			18	Using telephone		
8	Parts awaiting processing in a factory			19	Aeroplane in 'stack' awaiting landing		
9	Inspector checking incoming materials			20	Items in supermarket warehouse		
10	Operator assembling part of a television set			21	Partly processed parts being moved to next operation		
11	Designer thinking about his work			22	Electricity inspector reading domestic meter		

Figure 7.7   Method study practical exercise

Note: Against each of the above activities mark in the appropriate box what you consider to be the correct process chart symbol.* Also indicate with a tick in the column provided if the activity 'adds value', ie it is pure productive work.

coloured thread stretched around pins are used to plot the movement. In the latter case they are called string diagrams and include the facility that the string can be removed to measure the total distance travelled. Templates and three-dimensional models can also be employed as an aid. They are particularly useful in developing methods due to their flexibility for experimenting with various positions for equipment and so on. Figure 7.8 is a flow diagram for the packing department shown on the flow process chart, Figure 7.6.

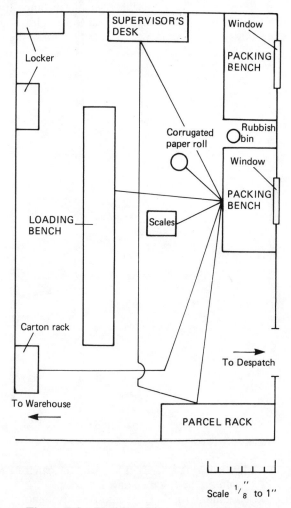

Figure 7.8   Packing shop – present layout

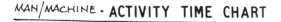

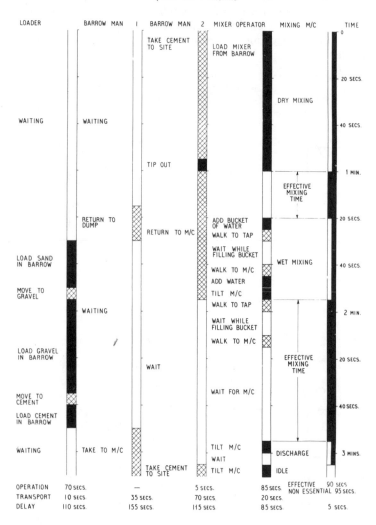

**Figure 7.9   Man/machine activity time chart for concrete mixing
(old method) 4 men and 1 machine**

With acknowledgement to BTH Method Study School, Rugby,
England

Man/machine activity charts

When the relationship between people, equipment and materials is to be studied, this kind of study device can be applied. Each activity on the chart (eg operation, transport, delay and inspection) is represented on the chart by a vertical column drawn to a time scale. This reveals the activity/time relationship for the people, equipment and materials, which can then be critically analysed. An example of this chart for concrete mixing is illustrated in Figure 7.9.

Two-handed operation charts

These are often used to examine in more detail the operations contained on flow process charts. An example of such a chart for assembling a switch is illustrated in Figure 7.10.

'Gozinto' or assembly charts

These provide a useful means of analysing what materials, parts and subassemblies go into making a complete product. Assembly charts, which are a form of flow process chart, give information on the flow of parts and will reveal areas for more intensive study.

MICROMETER TECHNIQUES

The study in great detail of the minute movements of hand and eye is not possible by purely visual observation. Micro motion study as developed by its founder Frank Gilbreth (Barnes, (6)) makes use of the camera, delayed action photography and other devices to record movement. As the movements or elements are of a very small time duration a special language or set of symbols are used, called THERBLIGS, which is Gilbreth's name spelled backwards. The technique is not described in more detail because it is not in widespread use, but it is mentioned here for possible reference. However, his six original rules of motion economy are still of general relevance. They are:

1　Minimum movements
2　Symmetrical movements
3　Simultaneous movements
4　Rhythmic movements
5　Natural movements
6　Habitual movements.

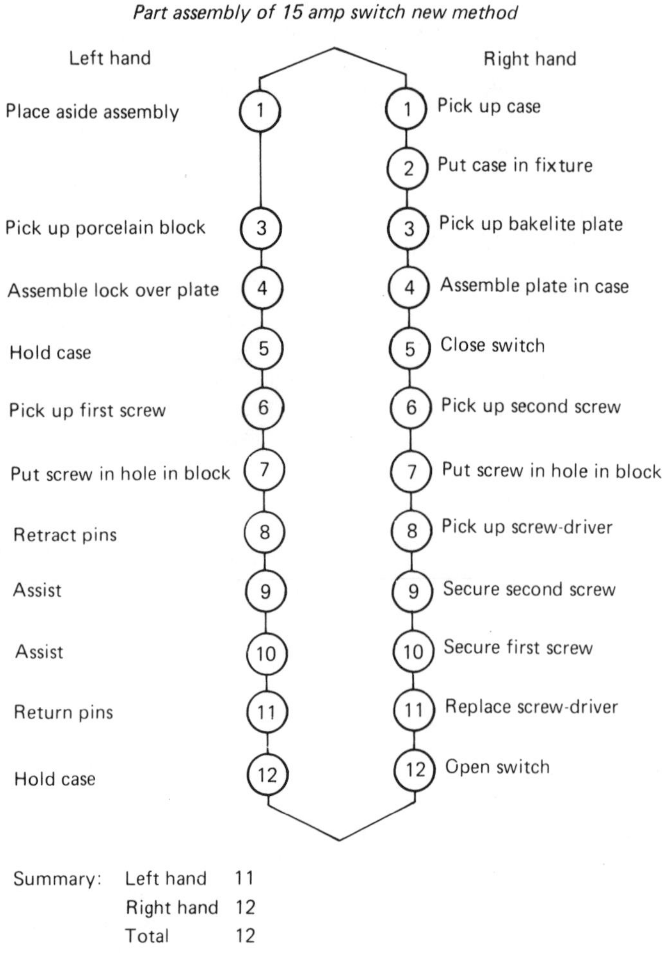

Part assembly of 15 amp switch new method

Left hand			Right hand
Place aside assembly	①	①	Pick up case
		②	Put case in fixture
Pick up porcelain block	③	③	Pick up bakelite plate
Assemble lock over plate	④	④	Assemble plate in case
Hold case	⑤	⑤	Close switch
Pick up first screw	⑥	⑥	Pick up second screw
Put screw in hole in block	⑦	⑦	Put screw in hole in block
Retract pins	⑧	⑧	Pick up screw-driver
Assist	⑨	⑨	Secure second screw
Assist	⑩	⑩	Secure first screw
Return pins	⑪	⑪	Replace screw-driver
Hold case	⑫	⑫	Open switch

Summary: Left hand   11
           Right hand   12
           Total   12

Figure 7.10   Two-handed operator chart
With acknowledgement to J. Walker Morris, University of Aston,
Birmingham, England

In general changes of direction of movement should be avoided.

These rules of motion economy, which are principally concerned with laying out a workplace, are rules 1, 2 and 3 combined
with the areas of reach as shown in Figure 7.11.

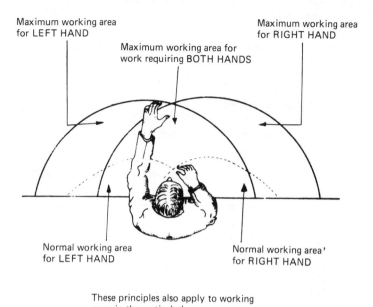

Maximum working area for LEFT HAND

Maximum working area for RIGHT HAND

Maximum working area for work requiring BOTH HANDS

Normal working area for LEFT HAND

Normal working area' for RIGHT HAND

These principles also apply to working areas in the vertical plane

Figure 7.11   Efficient workplace layout and the laws of motion economy

ANALYSIS AND CRITICAL QUESTIONING

The two principal objectives of method study are simple and systematic means for recording the present method, the 'Where are you now?' question and a procedure for critically questioning every aspect of what is being studied. A basic questioning procedure for any activity is shown in Figure 7.12. This is based on the timeless advice of Rudyard Kipling: 'I keep six honest serving men (They taught me all I knew); Their names are What and Why and When And How and Where and Who' (*Just-So Stories*).

VALUE ANALYSIS

This technique is really a modified form of method study. It is particularly directed to cost reduction in products and materials while maintaining or even improving quality and reliability. The

Primary questions
1   Purpose
    What is achieved, is it necessary and *why*?
2   Place
    Where is it done and *why* there?
3   Sequence
    When is it done and *why* then?
4   Person
    Who does it and *why* that person?
5   Means
    How is it done and *why* that way?
Secondary questions, necessary to develop a new method
1   Purpose
    What else could be done and *what* else should be done?
2   Place
    Where else could it be done and *where* else should it be done?
3   Sequence
    When else could it be done and *when* else should it be done?
4   Person
    Who else could do it and *who* else should do it?
5   Means
    How else could it be done and *how* else should it be done?

Figure 7.12   A basic analysis and questioning procedure
With acknowledgement to Alan Lawlor, *Technical Aspects of Supervision*, Pergamon, 1970.

approach has also been used for reducing the costs of such services as gas and electricity.

Value analysis generally proceeds through seven stages:

Stage 1 Introduction: What is to be studied, objectives and who will be involved.

Stage 2 Information collection: Obtaining all relevant information, eg usage, costs, expected demand, quality standards, specifications and so on.

Stage 3 Speculation: Brainstorming sessions to explore all ideas.

Stage 4 Analysis: Produce cost estimates of ideas and select those with the greatest promise.

Stage 5 Detailed study: Each idea selected is explored in detail.

Stage 6 Recommendations: Proposals are made to senior management for a decision.

WORK MEASUREMENT

Amongst the various facets of productivity improvement is the task of setting expected standards of performance. Some of these standards concern the amount of material to be consumed in the conversion process, while the other important area is time standards. Work measurement is the generic term to embrace the techniques for measuring how long various work tasks should take. At the outset it is emphasised that an important prerequisite to work measurement is the establishment of an appropriate method. There are four principal methods in use which are now briefly described:

1 ESTIMATING

Estimating is generally based upon past experience. It tends to be subjective, with consequent errors unless experience is refined in some way by actual results.

2 TIME STUDY

This involves continuous study by trained time study engineers. Operations are divided into suboperations or elements and stopwatches are used to observe and record the actual time for each operation. At the same time through a process called *Effort rating* the observer also assesses the pace at which the operator is working. The actual pace is compared to a standard rate of working and is defined as 'the average rate at which qualified workers will naturally work, at a job, using standard methods and applying average motivation'. Some still argue that it is a subjective method, but the observers are trained to recognise a standard rate. In the British Standard scale a standard rating is equal to 100. The formula for obtaining a basic time from actual observed time is

$$\text{Basic time} = \text{Observed time} \times \frac{\text{Rating}}{\text{Standard rating}}$$

If an observed time were 0.75 minutes and the rating was 80, the basic time would be

$$\frac{0.75 \times 80}{100} = 0.6 \text{ minutes}$$

Time study is useful where accurate information is required on highly repetitive operations.

3 SYNTHETICS

For most work that takes place in organisations, even the one-off type of job, there are common elements that repeat themselves. It is therefore a waste of human resources to continually estimate or time study operations when some of the data already exist. Synthetic information is therefore used for this reason. It can take two forms, i) home-made synthetics and ii) bought out synthetics. In the former cases the times for performing various operations are suitably classified and filed, with the caution that they should be regularly reviewed for any changes. This kind of data can be used to build up times in such work areas as manufacturing, design, retailing, maintenance, hospitals and government departments. Bought out synthetics are now available for a variety of uses, Predetermined Motion Time Systems (PMTS) and Methods Time Measurement (MTM) being two examples.

4 ANALYTICAL ESTIMATING

For the large one-off project or where quick information is required on methods and times, analytical estimating is a useful technique. It can provide reasonably accurate estimates of projects and jobs. The main steps are listed below:

1   Form a small group, say 3 or 4, who have an interest in and a good knowledge of the work to be estimated.
2   Break down the job into suitable suboperations and place them in an agreed sequence.
3   Apply times to each suboperation. These times may already exist within the organisation; if not it reveals the case for setting up a routine for collecting and storing them. It is also possible, as previously mentioned, to purchase standard data for calculating the times for basic operations, eg Methods Time Measurement (MTM). Figure 7.13 shows an example of using the method for decorating a works canteen. With the spread of more customised products and services the use of analytical estimating is likely to increase.

ACTIVITY SAMPLING

One of the important items of information required in productivity

Estimating worksheet			
Project/work to be done	People involved	Date	Estimate no.
Decorate canteen	Maintenance, canteen personnel	16.4.1984	35

Op. No.	Description of operation	Standard time	Total time mins
1	Remove furniture, 30 tables, 120 chairs	3 mins per item	150
2	Place dust sheets		15
3	Fetch trestles, boards, steps and decorating materials		24
4	Erect trestles and boards		5
5	Apply two coats of emulsion to ceiling, area 900 square feet using 6'' brush	.2 mins per sq. foot	360
6	Move trestles for operation 5, 12 times per coat	1.5 mins per move	36
7	Apply two coats to four walls, total area 1080 square feet, using roller	.15 mins per sq. foot	324
8	Move trestles for operation 7, 24 times per coat	1.5 mins per move	72
9	Paint 120 feet of pipework, 3 coats	0.5 mins per foot	180
10	Steps movement for operation 9, 20 times	1.0 min per move	60
11	Paint three doors total 50 square feet, 2 coats	1.0 min per sq. foot	100
12	Filling in around light fittings (6) 120 feet	0.25 mins per foot	30
13	Remove dust sheets and trestles etc.		10
14	Replace furniture		150
	Total		1516
	Contingency 10%		151.6
	Fatigue/Relaxation allowance 10%		151.6
	Total allowed time in hours		30.32

Figure 7.13   Analytical estimating

analysis is how customers, employees, equipment, materials and space are being utilised. More specifically, the proportions of time on productive and ancillary work and idle time are needed. The simple low cost/time technique for getting information of this kind is called activity sampling. As implied in the title it is a technique for obtaining samples of activities, rather than making continuous observations. Swann (7) defines activity sampling as:

> A technique for making a large number of instantaneous observations over random periods of time of equipment, materials and people. Each observation records what is happening at the instant of the observation. The total of observations for each activity studied can then be expressed as a percentage of all observations, thus giving a picture of the proportions of time on each activity.

It will not provide the same accuracy as the continuous method. Even so it will provide sufficiently accurate results to give a good idea of the situation being studied.

The technique is based upon statistical principles, so it is possible to predetermine the amount of error. If the main variables remain unchanged (eg new equipment or people are not employed), by increasing the number of observations the accuracy of the results also increases. For example, if it is necessary to take a sample of the downtime of an item of equipment that is estimated at 20 per cent and study results are required to be accurate to plus or minus 5 per cent, the number of observations can be found from the following formula:

$$N = \frac{4P\,(100 - P)}{L^2}$$

where N = required number of observations
P = percentage occurrence of activity, and
L = percentage accuracy

Therefore, in the above example

$$N = \frac{4 \times 20\,(100 - 20)}{5^2}$$

$$= \frac{80 \times 80}{25} = 256 \text{ observations}$$

An assessment of the accuracy of a study from a known number of observations and percentage occurrence of the activity can be obtained as follows:

$$L = \pm 2 \times \sqrt{\frac{P(100-P)}{N}}$$

If, again, the downtime is 20 per ent and the number of observations is 500, the limits of accuracy would be

$$L = \pm 2 \times \sqrt{\frac{20(100-20)}{50}}$$

$$= \pm 2 \times \sqrt{\frac{1600}{500}}$$

$$= \pm 2 \times \sqrt{3.2}$$

$$= \pm 1.79\%$$

While it is useful to have an understanding of these technical principles, references on the subject contain tables of N for various values of P and L.

HOW TO USE THE METHOD

Activity sampling methods need to meet specific circumstances. The overall requirement is to involve the people engaged in the activity to be studied in both the design and conduct of the investigation. In this way commitment is obtained. People see for themselves how matters could be improved as well as collecting information. It thus has inherent personal development characteristics. There are three main stages in carrying out an activity sample:

1 Design an appropriate study form to suit the particular circumstances. This will generally include:

    a) details of when and where the observations take place, eg date, time, department and possibly weather conditions.

    b) observer's name.

c) frequency of observations – this may range from every few minutes to every hour.

d) description of the subject or subjects to be studied. This could be people (staff or customers), equipment, displays, space, products or materials.

e) headings for the activities to be observed, eg productive work, ancillary work and idle time.

2   Make observations; momentarily observe (ie at the instant you see what is happening) and record in the appropriate column. Record one observation as 1 and five observations thus, ⊞; this will facilitate the eventual totalling of results. So as to prevent any bias, tables of random numbers are used to indicate the exact time of the next observation. For example, if observations are to be made every hour, from the extract below from a random number tables, observations would be made at 09, 25, 33, 53, 01, 35, 34, 35 and 48 minutes past the hour (numbers greater than 60 being ignored). If random numbers are not readily available the last two digits from a telephone directory can be used.

Extracts from a table of random numbers: 09, 73, 25, 33, 76, 53, 01, 35, 34, 67, 35, 48

3   At the end of the study period total columns to obtain the total observations for each activity. If, for instance, the total observations made are 1,000, with 250 being made for productive work, 600 ancillary work and 150 idle time, this signifies 25 per cent, 60 per cent and 15 per cent respectively.

Activity sampling can be used in a large variety of ways, self-reporting diaries being a form of activity sampling for studying personal activities. A sample daily diary for a supervisor is shown in Figure 7.14. The main headings (ie location, information used and activities) would need to be determined by the people using the diary and will probably have to be modified by trial and error. It has been found useful to increase awareness in the job of supervision.

Activity sampling has been used extensively in the general field of productivity analysis. We used it in one of the first applications of productivity audits in a UK national chain of motor accessory retail shops. The company has some 300 outlets spread over a wide geographic area. In 1974 an audit was carried out for a representative sample of 40 shops. This initial assessment, as illustrated in Figure 7.15, showed a variation in total earnings productivity of

Location	OBS*	Information used	OBS*	Activities	OBS*
Own office		Internal memos		Grievance handling	
Boss's office		Letters		Dealing with queries	
Buying office		Schedules		Assessing priorities	
Planning office		Purchase orders		Progressing	
Drawing office		Tool orders		Using telephone	
Maintenance		Works orders		Travelling/walking	
Customer's premises		Budgets		Planning ahead	
Supplier's premises				Monitoring performance	

* Observations: place a tick against the appropriate sub category, if possible hourly but at least twice a day.

Figure 7.14   Self-reporting diary for supervision

the order of 2 to 1. As a result of this spread of performance the company decided to make a more intensive, secondary audit, study of 15 shops, five low performers, five in the medium range and five high performers. One of the aims of the study was to obtain information on staff activities during periods when customers were present in the shop and when there were no customers at all. During the customer present times (it is only during these periods that staff can be productive, remembering the earlier definition of productive work in retailing), information was also sought on productive work.

Activity sampling was used, with cashiers, sales staff and shop managers all taking part. Two-hour training sessions were conducted in each of the 15 shops. The study lasted for four weeks, with a sample being taken every hour for six days, every week. There were thus many hundreds of observations and a consequent impressive amount of data on staff and customers. The project conducted by Bahiri and described earlier also involved many foremen studying the utilisation of equipment and people in their own departments.

Although senior managers were doubtful that the initial interest would be sustained, the observation forms were returned for analysis on a regular basis with very few omissions or mistakes. Figure 7.16 is an example of the study form used, with Figure 7.17 showing diagrammatically the average results for the whole study. Much to the surprise of the company, productive work activity was much lower than they had thought.

Activity sampling can also include an effort rating aspect. Performance ratings can be made at the time of the observation.

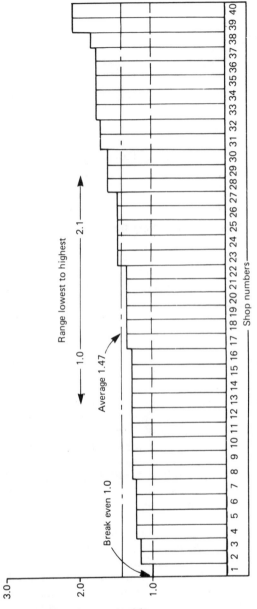

Figure 7.15 Productivity audit of 40 shops in a UK national retail chain business, automotive and ancillary spares, arranged in ascending order of total earnings productivity

164

PARETO ANALYSIS

Time is a precious asset in all organisations and therefore anything that can help make more effective use of it deserves consideration. We need to have our attention directed to those aspects which, if left unattended, could harm the organisation, in other words, management by exception. For example, a small number of faults cause the largest amount of scrap, a large part of stocking costs is contained in a few items and a low proportion of managerial decisions have the most significant impact on the enterprise. The technique for revealing the significant few is called Pareto analysis, after the Italian economist who developed the idea. It is sometimes called the 80/20 rule because in general terms 80 per cent of the results come from 20 per cent of the effort. It is another useful and simple tool for productivity analysis because it concentrates the mind and helps us see things in perspective. The technique is used in stock analysis, the study of purchases, sales analysis and investigations of scrap problems.

The basic steps in doing a Pareto analysis are listed below:

1   List the items to be analysed in ascending order of usage, cost or occurrence.

2   Total usage, cost or occurrence.

3   Express the individual usage etc as a percentage of the total (ie step 2).

4   Produce a cumulative percentage column for step 3.

5   Divide cumulative percentage column into three groups say, 70 per cent, 20 per cent and 10 per cent. For this reason Pareto analysis is sometimes called 'ABC' analysis, 'A' being the expensive 70 per cent, 'B' the moderate ones and 10 per cent the low cost/occurrence items.

6   Repeat steps 1 to 4 for items. The previous steps have all related to cost etc. We now need to relate the 'ABC' aspects to the percentage of items contained in each category.

7   Compare cumulative percentage usage/cost/occurrence column with cumulative percentage item column.

BRANCH NO *162*

LOCATION *GLOUCESTER.*

DATE *5/3/9-* DAY *SATURDAY* TIME *10·42.* PERIOD NO *2*

CONDITIONS: DRY ⟋   WET   SNOW   COLD/ICE   SUNNY

OBSERVER: *W.*

Code	Activity	Customer present		Customer absent	Totals		Remarks
	Description	Customer	Staff	Staff	Cust.	Staff	
A	Selecting goods for purchase or sales talk (productive work)						
B	Closing sale (taking cash)	II	IIII		*2*	*4*	
C	Prepg/Repg cycles		I			*I*	
D	Walking (with or without goods)	JHT JHT	III		*10*	*3*	
E	Looking for goods						
F	Looking at goods	JHT JHT JHT JHT JHT JHT JHT JHT			*40*		
G	Examining goods						
H	Conversation cust/staff	JHT II	III		*7*	*3*	
J	Conversation staff/staff		II			*2*	
K	Telephone						
L	Clerical		II			*2*	
M	Filling Fixt.Put.Stk.Aw.						
N	Unloading goods						
O	Marking off Stk and Pricg						
P	Window dressing						
Q	Interior display						
R	Cleaning & tidying		I			*I*	
S	Waiting	JHT JHT	IIII		*10*	*4*	
T	Misc. personal/absent		III			*3*	
	Totals	*69*	*23*				

Total customer till roll count for day   *1819*

General observations:

Figure 7.16 Customer–sales activity study observation record

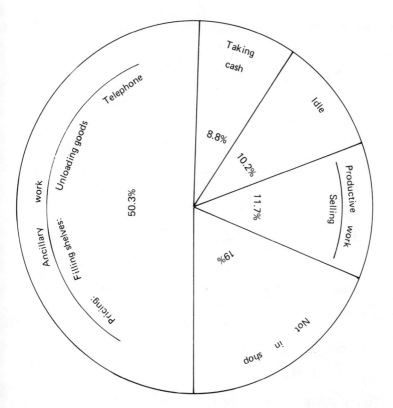

Figure 7.17   How shop staff spend their time

Source: A study of 15 branches of a national retail chain.

An example for stock analysis is shown in Table 7.1. To simplify the task the stock has been arranged into 10 groups.

Table 7.1
Pareto analysis of stock

Item no	Stock group	Usage		Cum%	Items	
		Cost £	%		%	Cum%
1	A	60,000	40	40	10	10
2	A	44,000	29.4	69.4	10	20
3	B	22,000	14.7	84.1	10	30
4	B	15,000	10	94.1	10	40
5	C	5,000	3.4	97.5	10	50
6	C	2,000	1.3	98.8	10	60
7	C	1,000	0.7	99.5	10	70
8	C	500	0.3	99.8	10	80
9	C	250	0.1	99.9	10	90
10	C	250	0.1	100	10	100
Totals		150,000	100	100		100

Summary:

Stock group	% of cost	% of items
A	69.4	20
B	24.7	20
C	5.9	60
Totals	100.0	100

WORK SIMPLIFICATION (W/S)

Work simplification has been described by M. Scott Myers (8) as the most potent management system for encouraging creativity. Work simplification makes use of the method study techniques previously described and is based upon the following assumptions:

1 Most people have creative potential for improving their own jobs, and
2 Self-initiated change is positive change, while imposed change by an authority figure (eg method study engineers) is likely to evoke fear and hostility.

The necessary skills (eg process charting, flow diagrams and so on) can be acquired in simple training programmes – at the most about two days. The warehouse project previously mentioned is a good example of how enthusiastically people with no work study experience soon learnt to use it. As Myers says '. . . an assembler ceases to be just a pair of hands . . . instead the individual has a new outlet for personal creativity – involving work planning . . . earning recognition, growing professionally and in general identifying more with the company'.

W/S involves a somewhat similar approach to method study in the following five steps:

1   Select the job to improve.
2   Get the facts and make a chart.
3   Challenge the facts using the six honest serving men approach, ie who and what etc.
4   Develop a better method.
5   Install the improvement.

Texas Instruments in the USA and the UK have made extensive use of the approach and so have many other companies. The currently widespread quality circles are another application of the same concept. While most of the applications of W/S have been to manufacturing enterprises, the philosophy is just as appropriate to any work activity. (9)

CRITICAL INCIDENTS

A more open-ended way of seeking information on organisational problems is to use the critical incident technique. We describe it as open-ended because those taking part are completely free to express their views in any way they wish. Furthermore, the questions asked are also open-ended. Warr (10) describes the use of the technique for studying supervisors in a UK steelworks. A sample critical incident questionnaire for a selected day is shown in Figure 7.18. It was used on a daily basis for several days in a study of maintenance problems.

Another variation of the use of critical incidents is suggested by Revans (11) in his study of a large engineering factory in the North West Region of the UK. Every week five managers selected at random from a total of 50 are asked to report upon the incident that has given them the greatest embarrassment or satisfaction. The five meet to review the five incidents and select one for more intensive study. Through this method no individual feels

Day 3
_____

What was the most difficult job or situation that you had to deal
with today?

Every Thursday I have to get out a work programme for the men
in my section who come in at the weekend when production stops.
It isn't hard to decide what needs doing. The problem is co-
ordinating our work with the jobs that other maintenance gangs
will be doing. If we don't do this we usually finish up getting in
each other's way. But it is never easy to find out what the other
maintenance people will be doing and this makes planning our
work difficult. This is how it was today.

Approximately how often do you have to deal with a difficulty of
this kind?
Tick one of the following:
     a)   Once a day
     b)   Once a week __
     c)   Once a month
     d)   Once every three months
     e)   Once a year.

**Figure 7.18   Critical incident questionnaire: extract from a study
of maintenance problems**

deliberately selected to reveal his merits or deficiencies and in the
course of three months all 50 managers would probably have
reported and discussed some critical incident.

ILLUMINATIVE INCIDENT ANALYSIS

This is a unique team approach to problem solving. It was
developed by Diana Cortazzi (12) and, while it was originally used
in hospital situations, we have applied the method in manufacturing and retailing organisations. Involving those who are part of the
problem forms a central part of the method. But its unique nature
lies in the way problems are described. So as to overcome the
usual difficulties of describing problems either verbally or in writing, pictures are drawn instead. The problem staters do not have
to be artists; indeed 'matchstick' drawings can vividly portray the
essence of a problem.
    Figure 7.19 illustrates an actual incident of a complaint of

negligence made against a ward sister by four sons following the death of their 86-year-old mother. The first drawing depicts how the nurse was seen by the four sons when their mother was admitted; the second when the sister was accused of negligence; and the third how the sons saw their mother. Finally, we see the view the nurse had of the doctors. In the words of the nurse: 'I felt completely abandoned.'

Figure 7.19 Illuminative incident analysis
With acknowledgement to Diana Cortazzi, *Illuminative Incident Analysis*, ACP International Publications, 1973

Through a group examination of incidents in this way, insights are gained into how they occur but also, like a ray of light, the analysis reveals the human factors behind the incident. Every organisation has 'four sons'-type horror stories. Illuminative incident analysis is a powerful method for dealing with the deep human problems of how everyone concerned perceives their role in the situation.

QUESTIONNAIRES

Whether used as a basis for more structured interviews or completed by respondents and returned, questionnaires are a very effective way of collecting information. To facilitate getting as reliable information as possible the following factors should be considered.

1   Consider the alternative advantages of an open-ended un-
    structured approach or a closed-ended structured design. In
    the former case people have an opportunity to express them-
    selves, unimpeded by possibly constraining questions. How-
    ever, the eventual analysis will be a difficult task. A
    structured interview on the other hand is easy to analyse, but
    unless careful thought is given to the questions important
    information could be overlooked or may not be obtained.
    The critical incident technique uses an open-ended
    approach, with the questionnaire in Chapter 1 being a
    closed-ended multiple choice example, ie each answer can
    range over a scale 1 to 10. A combination of both methods
    can be used with, say, most of the questions being structural
    and an open-ended one at the end. Whichever view is taken,
    careful preparation is essential, together with an overall
    objective of what is required.

2   Avoid leading questions, eg 'Why do you consider pro-
    ductivity is low?' as opposed to 'What do you consider is the
    current level of productivity?' with a response scale of say
    low, medium or high.

3   Make use of common language. Questions about pro-
    ductivity may require explanation; see also the next point
    and point 9 on participative research.

4   If necessary educate the respondent with simple explana-
    tions at the beginning of the questionnaire.

5   Avoid multiple questions, eg 'Are the principal factors
    affecting productivity equipment, management and people,
    reply YES or NO'. If the reply were yes, does it mean yes to
    all three or just one? Rule, only one idea per question.

6   Keep the number of questions to a minimum.

7   So as to reduce the amount of time needed to complete the
    questionnaire, limit the amount of writing to a minimum.
    Multiple choice replies which only require circling of
    numbers or ticking should be used. See the questionnaire
    designed by Hussain in Figure 6.3 (page 125) for an example.
    This method of response, which ranges from Strongly Agree
    to Strongly Disagree, can also be scored, eg $+ 2$ to $- 2$, to
    facilitate statistical analysis.

8   Questionnaire layout or structure of interviews is important.
    The aim is to elicit support and gain confidence. It is best to
    start with non-controversial issues and leave possibly difficult
    areas till the end.

9   Participative research. It has been stressed throughout this
    chapter that the people involved in productivity studies
    should be actively involved in the investigative aspects. This

is just as necessary for questionnaire/interview surveys. The Hussain/Revans method outlined in the previous chapter adopts a two-stage approach. Initially informal, open-ended interviews are conducted to uncover the real issues and to obtain the actual 'shop floor' language for eventual use in the final questionnaire. The second stage is a questionnaire survey with its content and language based on stage one. In this way people's feelings are reflected back to them in a way that they can understand and feel a part of.

CONCLUSIONS

It is unlikely that sufficient information will be available in a total approach to productivity improvement. Therefore methods for obtaining new data will be necessary. Whichever techniques are employed they should make minimum demands on time and produce reliable data. But the real objective should be to integrate information collection with a commitment to action. The participative research philosophy suggested in this chapter will do this. It will take time and patience to achieve but is well worth the effort.

Seventeen productivity techniques have been described. Though there are more, these cover the main areas where productivity studies are made. Fourteen are concerned with such technical aspects as flow, departmental layout, and measurement. But, as we have noted in a number of places, productivity needs to be approached as a total problem. Information is therefore required on the qualitative and subjective areas. People's attitudes and the differing ways in which they each see their roles are clearly important. They are not easy to measure but even so they must be understood.

Critical incident analysis is a well-tried method for getting information on how technical and human factors affect productivity. But any technique should be creatively used to suit particular situations. The sampling method used by Revans is one example. The pictorial team approach developed by Cortazzi is another one. Questionnaires and interviewing are widely used for seeking data of a qualitative and quantitative kind. Similarly to the use of any other technique the information obtained by this method will lead to improved performance if those concerned with the study have played a part in its design and conduct.

Before you proceed any further you may wish to pause and consider the following questions:

1   In the light of what has been said about productivity
    measurement, how would you rate the quality of your cur-
    rent measurement system?
2   What are the factors which are currently limiting produc-
    tivity and helping to improve it?
3   Do you foresee any obstacles in introducing a participative
    research approach, either of a personal kind or to the
    organisation?

REFERENCES

1   Ashmawy, Professor Saud and Revans, Professor R. W.,
    The Nile Project: an exercise in educational autotherapy,
    ALP International, 1976
2   Revans R. W., *Action Learning in Hospitals*, McGraw-Hill,
    1975
3   Baquer, Ali and Revans, R. W., *'But Surely, That is Their
    Job'*, ALP International, 1973
4   Lawlor, Alan, *Improving Productivity in Retailing*, Action
    Learning Trust, London, August 1975
5   Baquer, Ali, *Innovation in Participation* (Greenwich Lone
    Parent Survey – a Local Response to a National Problem),
    private publication, September 1975
6   Barnes, Ralph, *Motion and Time Study*, John Wiley, 1951
7   Swann, Ken, *Techniques for Production Efficiency*,
    Macmillan, 1973
8   Scott Myers, M., 'Conditions for Manager Motivation',
    Harvard Business Review, January/February 1966
9   Clement, Zinc W., *Dynamic Work Simplification*, Reinhold
    Publishing Corporation, 1962
10 Warr, Peter and Bird, Michael W., *Identifying Supervisory
    Training Needs*, HMSO, 1968
11 Revans, Professor R. W., *Studies in Factory Communica-
    tion*, ALP International, Brussels, August 1973
12 Cortazzi, Diana, *Illuminative Incident Analysis: A technique
    For Team Building*, ALP International, 1973

8 Action learning

In the previous chapters methods for measuring the performance of enterprises both in the UK and in other parts of the world have been examined. The aim now is to show that, although an effective measurement system is an important prerequisite for bringing about lasting improvement in performance, the human factors of change also require attention. As a first step we need to appreciate that the types of problem encountered in increasing productivity require quite new initiatives. These are notably the involvement of people in both the identification and the solution of the problems they face. Action learning has been found to meet these needs and is therefore described fully in this chapter. But before we do this let us examine the nature of productivity problems.

CLOSED- AND OPEN-ENDED PROBLEMS

The problems that prevent organisations improving their productivity tend to fall into two broad categories. Those that are easiest to deal with are the closed-ended problems. They can be treated rationally and have a limited number of known solutions.

Moreover this class of problem is unaffected by the people who study them. Revans (1) aptly calls them puzzles. On the other hand open-ended problems are very much affected by the attitudes of the people who try and solve them: indeed the problem solvers are quite often part of the problem. For this reason there will be no known solutions partly because they are judged in the minds of people and also because each problem is unique. In Revans' terms they are problems as distinct from puzzles. To even understand open-ended problems requires the asking of totally new questions, 'Q', and will involve many people across different organisational boundaries. Their effective treatment will also require commitment by those concerned and an acceptance that they need to own the problem. Open-ended problems seem to be intractable and unfortunately are of a kind to stand in the way of real improvements in productivity at national levels and for organisations. Introducing a new marketing strategy and improving customer service are examples of open-ended problems that require the attention of a number of people just to reach agreement on what is a marketing strategy or how we shall know when service to customers is better. How to convert industry to an information age is a national problem of this kind.

In contrast, closed-ended problems are relatively easy to deal with. They can mostly be resolved by using existing knowledge and experience, what was previously described as 'P' for programmed. But if 'P' is used to resolve open-ended difficulties, at best it will be inappropriate and at worst harmful – the solving of tomorrow's problems with yesterday's experience syndrome. Examples of closed-ended problems are, at the simplest, how to start the car up to how to manage the building of a new factory. In the first case the relevant technique is a fault finding procedure and in the second, critical path analysis.

Closed-ended problems therefore require a logical approach for their solution and exhibit the following characteristics:

- They respond to the use of standard problem solving techniques.
- The solution of problems is not affected by the problem solver.
- Known definitive answers exist.
- One person, or a small group of people, can solve the problem.
- Once the solution is selected and implemented, that is the end of the problem.

The factors which distinguish open-ended problems are:

- There are no right answers; what the problem is and how it should be dealt with, if at all, will be seen in different, sometimes conflicting, ways.
- They can be perceived in three ways: i) through the eyes of individuals – the assumptions; ii) the reality of the problem – the extant position; and iii) what should be done about the problem to suit the actual circumstances – the requisite solution. It is most likely that the problem will be seen in the first way and if 10 people are involved, initially, there could be 10 different assumptions.
- They are affected by the values, attitudes and beliefs of the people concerned. The standards by which one person will judge a successful outcome will be different from another person.
- The scope is large and multi-faceted and generally involves many people.

For these reasons the solving of open-ended problems differs markedly from all the methods used to tackle closed-ended ones in these respects.

Firstly, the only part of the procedure which is under the control of the problem solvers is the setting up of the problem solving process to identify the problem and the required action. What would be considered the solution of a closed-ended problem is only the first tentative step for open-ended problems.

Secondly, the successful solution of open-ended problems requires the commitment and involvement of large numbers of people. This is what Revans (1) calls the client group. They are defined as those who know, who care, and who can, that is, they have information about the problems, could be motivated to do something about it and have the power to change it if they wished to. It is the active participation of the client group and the posing of new questions that exposes false assumptions about problems, reveals the realities and leads to requisite solutions.

All this means that the successful solution of open-ended problems takes considerable time, cost and patience. Management are understandably tempted to go for quick closed-ended-type solutions, but productivity problems necessitate genuine involvement of people and the time for the real underlying problems to be understood. Furthermore, the situations where open-ended problems are found are uncertain and consequently those concerned really have no idea what to do next. For example, an in-plant action learning programme (2) takes at least six months to achieve the first results. Moreover, the majority of the management team need to participate in the diagnosis and action on the problems.

Indeed, it is possible that through this involvement of different people and an orientation to fresh questions 'Q' the problem may be dissolved rather than solved, as suggested by Beer. (3)

Boddy, (4) describing an in-plant scheme in one of Motorola's UK Scottish factories, said 24 supervisors gave over 1000 hours, mostly in their own time, over a three-month period. Likewise, over a six-month period, 120 people were directly involved in a Bowater plant on the North East coast of the UK. (5)

Thirdly, because the process of necessity involves many people across the enterprise there is a much higher risk for management than in closed-ended problem solving. Things which some managers would rather hide will be exposed, and experience shows that some of the problems have been traced back to senior management incompetence. Once the process has started this cannot be avoided without destroying total management credibility.

A summary of the characteristics of closed- and open-ended problems appears in Figure 8.1.

Closed-ended	Open-ended
Unaffected by people	Affected by values, beliefs, attitudes
Known answers	Answers unknown
Logical procedure	Process
Analyse facts	Analyse situation
Consider alternative solutions	Consider alternative approaches, eg in-plant action learning
Choose solution	Choose approach
Implement	Set-up process
End of procedure	Start of problem solving process
	Result?

Figure 8.1   Characteristics of closed- and open-ended problems

The need to recognise the difference between the two types of problem is particularly important as the most intractable productivity problems in many enterprises fall into the open-ended category. Yet while most organisations have well-developed ways of solving closed-ended problems and are reasonably good at it, few have any structured systems for tackling the open-ended ones. The obvious exceptions are the Japanese, who have ably demonstrated the use of the quality circles philosophy, with similar approaches in other parts of the world, for example Rolls Royce and Jaguar Cars in the UK and Texas Instruments in the USA. In Sandnes, in Norway, Jonas Ogleand have been using a productivity group approach (6) for the last nine years in their bicycle manufacturing plant with very impressive results.

These are just a few examples and there are obviously more organisations using these techniques than the few quoted here, but the number is still very small in comparison to the size of the problem, certainly in Europe.

The Japanese have demonstrated to other countries the practicality of what the social scientists have been saying for years, that real productivity in modern complex enterprises can only be achieved through the involvement and participation of the employees in the decision making processes. This involvement goes hand in hand with technical excellence and technological development to create successful organisations. The current productivity problems facing most enterprises are not new, particularly in Britain. The UK is no worse today than it was 30 years ago, in fact it might be marginally better in statistical terms, but with the price of something like a quarter of the working population unemployed; it is not that the older economies are any worse, it is just that the others are better.

Why should this be? When it can be clearly demonstrated that open problem solving techniques are essential to the successful management of modern complex enterprises, why have they not been much more widely adopted?

THE PEOPLE PART OF PRODUCTIVITY PROBLEMS

CARROT, STICK OR TRUST

Douglas McGregor in his book *The Human Side of Enterprise* (7) asserts that as man has a natural resistance to being controlled, any effective form of control over man in the long term must be self control. He suggests that behind every managerial decision or action lie certain assumptions about human nature and human behaviour. One of these sets of assumptions holds that the average human being has an inherent dislike of work, must be coerced into making an effort through either reward or punishment, prefers to be directed, has little ambition and wishes to avoid responsibility. This traditional set of assumptions is what McGregor called Theory X and has been the basis of management thinking in many enterprises worldwide. In contrast McGregor went on to outline a very different view of man based on researches in behavioural science. This view, which he labelled Theory Y, assumes that the expenditure of physical and mental effort in work is as natural as in play. If man is committed to an objective he will exercise self-direction and self-control to achieve it. The average human being learns under proper conditions to accept and even seek responsibility. The capacity to apply a relatively high degree of initiative and creativity in the solution of organisational problems is widely, not narrowly, distributed in the population, and in modern industrial life the intellectual potential of the average worker is only partly used – some put it as low as 10 per cent. These views, first aired over 50 years ago, are still as true today as they were then. Yet most enterprises continue to manage with a Theory X style. Some managers may adopt a benevolent autocratic style as a softer form of Theory X. Others have tried Theory Y and been met with indifference, not realising that it takes time for people to use their inherent potential to behave responsibly when for years their real capacities have not been used. We still have not accepted that if the human being does not wish to control him/herself, then there is little chance that all our systems, be they paperwork in a factory or policemen on the streets, can achieve it. If we wish to improve performance in organisations we must first measure it, then manage the improvement through the people. We have to decide whether we manage on the principle of the carrot and stick or whether we trust people by treating them responsibly.

CHANGE OR DECLINE

So why hasn't it happened? Why has competition closed whole industries which might have survived had they been more responsive? Why haven't McGregor and many like him been listened to? Why, when it is demonstrably obvious from the results achieved by the Japanese that open problem solving techniques are an essential management tool in modern complex industries, have these not been adopted in other parts of the industrialised world?

The reason is probably the unwillingness/inability of both individuals and organisations to change. People and enterprises behave as a function of their personal history and their current environment. So whilst what McGregor is saying in his theory may be demonstrably true and managers may in fact personally agree that a change in style is necessary, the individual is him/herself constrained by the values of the enterprise itself. The enterprises in turn are influenced by the social systems in which they operate and these social systems are increasingly influenced by the world at large and particularly by the industrial competitiveness of other nations. The interrelationships of these factors are shown in Figure 8.2.

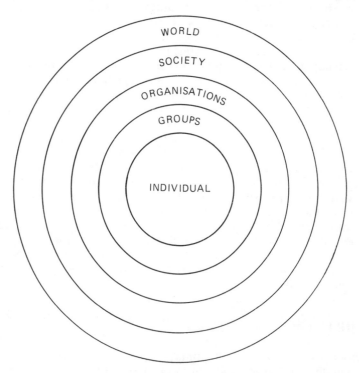

Figure 8.2   Influencing factors

It is particularly important to appreciate the effect of these factors when considering the introduction of open-ended problem solving techniques into traditional organisations. It is quite easy to *say* that we can produce more effective solutions to certain types of problem by using open-ended techniques, that indeed this type of problem can only be effectively solved by using these methods. But it is quite a different matter to have the approach accepted. In most cases even where managers individually accept the philosophy it remains unacceptable because it conflicts with the historical value systems within the enterprise and most likely within the social structure. In traditional enterprises the value systems are extremely strong and consequently there is a strong resistance to change. Many would, sadly, rather not survive than accept change in the old way of doing things. Considerable numbers of organisations have already made this choice. It is those managers and enterprises which have the courage to take risk and change that survive, but these seem to be in the minority. Hayes and Abernathy (8) noted in their study of the senior executives of America's top 100 companies that over 70 per cent of top executives are from legal/accounting backgrounds. Their conclusion was that these appointments reflect a need for stability and minimum risk in the appointing enterprises. This obviously, as they point out, bodes ill for the development and growth – change – within these organisations. Some organisations however, are prepared to change; in fact they seem to be designed to accept change as a fundamental part of their structure, as shown by Peters and Waterman in the book, *In Search of Excellence.* (9) Their researches, which covered some 200 companies in the USA and Europe, demonstrate quite clearly that in the best-run companies employee involvement is part of the basic philosophy and open-ended problem solving techniques are standard practice. In fact, one of the eight criteria they identify for success in the most effective companies is 'Productivity improvement via people'. The book suggests that the openness of the 'excellent' companies acts like a built-in survival kit. This is quite the opposite with traditional companies, whose very closed attitudes are a recipe for eventual demise.

THE ELEMENTS OF CHANGE

Productivity improvement primarily concerns change, and this generally involves the solution of open-ended problems. As previously stated, whilst enterprises are currently used to working with closed-ended problem solving systems, most do not have any systems in place for solving open-ended problems. The first step therefore is to have these systems adopted and the second is to get them used. This means influencing current management attitudes toward the process of problem solving before the problems can actually be tackled, and creating an awareness and acceptance amongst management that the fundamental productivity problems facing enterprises cannot be solved by 'more of the same'. The problems themselves are different and need to be treated differently. The real difficulty is that managers in traditional organ-

isations using Theory X behavioural values do not, quite reasonably, readily recognise the need for change and certainly the
necessity for an open approach to problem solving. Such concepts
are an anathema particularly in Britain, where in 1975 the Bullock
Committee's recommendations (10) for a very limited introduction
of industrial participation – an open-ended problem solving technique – met with strong resistance from the traditional lobby.
Autocracy is still safe even if it is wrong. Even if/when managers
do realise that the old ways are not succeeding, change is fraught
with potential risk and to be avoided if at all possible. People are
more secure with their existing situations, warts and all; it is much
safer to keep it the way it is than to risk changing it.

Why? It is all to do with security. Human beings have 'models'
in their minds of a whole range of different behaviours, views of
the world from particular perspectives: as husbands, wives,
mothers, fathers, sweethearts, lovers, shopstewards and
managers. These 'models' are triggered by environment and we
use them as the basis for our actions. As long as we try to satisfy
the values incorporated in the model, even if we fail we have done
our best. For example, as long as a manager with a traditional
value system – Theory X – tells his subordinates what to do, even if
they fail to do it because the task was impossible he is not personally at fault because he told them what to do. There is a 'model' of
managerial behaviour which dictates how managers should
operate in managerial situations. Unfortunately the traditional
manager model only carries messages about solving closed-ended
problems, nothing about open-ended ones. Enabling managers to
use open-ended techniques not only requires change in the individual management model but, because the individual's 'model'
is triggered and reinforced by the environment – the organisation,
it is also necessary to change the value systems in the enterprise.
This can only be done if the majority of managers in any organisation are committed to the process. The management team are
collectively the custodians of the value systems of the enterprise
and only the majority of them working together can actually bring
about the sort of changes necessary in traditional organisations for
their long-term survival.

The approach proposed here and developed over the last five
years for bringing about this change uses the four-step process of
Recognition, Decision, Permission, and Action first discussed in
an article on the subject in 1981. (11)

As previously stated, to enable organisations both to accept and
to use open-ended problem solving techniques it is necessary to
bring about change in individual and organisational values. To do
this the process outlined in Figure 8.3 is used. Whilst in this book

the emphasis is on organisational productivity improvement, the model is equally applicable to, and has been extensively used in, the area of individual development.

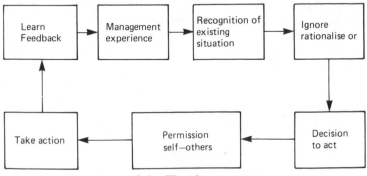

Figure 8.3   The change process

The first step in the process is to persuade the enterprise/individual to recognise that a problem exists. To do this the existing situation is used, eg current performance data. This can either be done with groups, in the case of general productivity problems, or with individuals if the problem is one of personal performance. It is important to encourage those concerned not to ignore or rationalise the problem, but to face it, ie the quality problem really does exist and there is no single right answer – and persuade them to recognise it for what it is.

Having obtained recognition, the next stage is to encourage a decision to act. It is one thing to recognise a problem but quite another to be committed to do something about it.

Once this has been achieved the next step involves the permission to go ahead. This feeling of permission is important in human problem solving. Some of us have sufficient inner strength to overcome the insecurity which goes with the risk of doing something new. Others need to acquire the confidence to act from those who have already done something similar, for example, to talk with someone who has successfully implemented a full-scale quality circles programme, like Rooney of Rolls Royce. (12) If the interest is in in-plant action learning programmes considerable successful experience is available in the literature: eg Precious of Bowater Hills (13) gives at least some assurance to the potential user that these programmes do work. Permission helps to rationalise risk.

The final step in the process is the action itself and this, as stated earlier, is really just the beginning of the problem solving process. Certainly as much support as possible is needed through the whole process of change, remembering Revans' (1) principle of insufficient mandate: we cannot expect others to change unless we too are prepared to change.

There are a number of action options at this stage, the best known being Japanese quality circles or small group improvement activities. The approach described here, and called in-plant action learning, is based upon Revans' action learning philosophy. It is perhaps not so well-known as quality circles, but its origins and its many applications go back some 40 years. Indeed Professor Sasaki (14) confirmed that action learning had a message for Japan. Five large-scale programmes have been conducted since the first one in Motorola Semiconductors in the UK during 1978. Both quality circles and in-plant action learning aim to solve open-ended problems. But quality circles concentrate on quality and related problems and are strongest at shop floor level. However, in-plant action learning is more concerned with tackling total productivity problems and involves the complete management team, including supervisors.

To summarise, action learning is particularly suited to dealing with the open-ended problems which predominate in the task of improving total productivity. In more detail what is action learning?

WHAT IS ACTION LEARNING?

Traditional action learning as pioneered by Revans (1) over the last 40 years is primarily concerned with helping individuals to solve open-ended problems. Revans' basic hypothesis is that in conditions of rapid change traditional learning systems cannot effectively provide for the training needs of line managers. He argues that, as the knowledge has to be written down and learnt by academics before it can be taught, with the current rate of change it is out of date by the time it is used. For managers to survive in conditions of rapid change it is therefore more important that they learn how to learn than that they acquire knowledge from the past. He suggests that this can most effectively be done by practising line managers using their real problems and working with other managers to solve them. Through this process they learn with and from each other in their treatment of here-and-now problems, and in the process develop themselves.

There are probably as many views about what action learning is as there are about religion. It is as simple as it is demanding and should be seen more as a philosophy than a technique. It is an extremely effective way of bringing about change and its main strengths lie in the fact that it tackles real problems and provides support to individuals or groups while they solve them. The main reason for the success of action learning as a change agent and the reason for using it for productivity improvement is that it has the built-in ability to achieve the four steps necessary in the change process, ie recognition, decision, permission and action.

The main elements of any action learning programme are:

NOMINATOR

This is the person who authorises and pays for the programme. In the case of individual development programmes this could be anyone of the senior line managers and even, in the case of very small organisations, the participant himself. However, where this type of programme is mainly used as part of a company's management development policy the nominator is much more likely to be the personnel or training manager.

For in-plant programmes the nominator must be the senior line manager in the enterprise, normally the managing director. This is essential with this type of programme because of the resources involved and the potential long-term impact on management in the organisation.

PROBLEM

In any action learning programme the problem is the vehicle for development and change. The type of problem chosen and the method of choice will obviously vary according to circumstances, but there are some basic rules which must be observed if the problem is to serve the required purpose:

● The problem must be a real one. It is pointless creating problems especially for the programme.

● It should ideally have a blend of human and technical aspects. Closed-ended problems of a purely technical kind are to be avoided. Problems selected for action learning activities should be open-ended and the answers should not be known in advance.

● There must be ownership of the problem and commitment to solving it. Without this there will be no implementation.

The following are some examples of the types of objective which can be aimed at:

● Achieving cost, quality and delivery performance as good as the best of the international competition.
● Motivating everyone to achieve high standards of performance in conditions of low order book and manpower reductions.
● Creating new products, processes and markets and innovating new forms of organisation to cope with the change.
● Achieving required levels of productivity to support investment in new technology.
● Creating a climate for the acceptance of change at all levels in the organisation.
● Finding ways of improving the service provided by public enterprises, eg local government, health services etc., without increasing costs.
● Reducing levels of labour turnover amongst salesmen.

These are a few examples of the type of open-ended problems currently affecting the performance of many organisations which readily respond to solution by action learning.

Problem selection can be made in a number of ways but generally takes one of the following forms:

● The problem is suggested by a member of senior management. Unless the participants have had some say in the decision there could be a feeling of imposition. This method is therefore not recommended.
● It is determined by the members of action learning groups with some agreement by senior management. This participative approach will ensure commitment to the ultimate solution of the problem. This method is described more fully in the second case study in the next chapter.
● Productivity audits at the primary and secondary levels have been found to be an effective means of identifying the problems that are restricting performance.

CLIENT

This is the individual or group who actually owns the problem. It is the one Who Knows – what the problem is, Who Cares – about its solution, and Who Can – has the authority to implement solutions. In the case of individual development programmes this may be anyone in the organisation or externally who has a real problem they want solved. With in-plant programmes it will certainly be the senior line manager, the senior client, who actually owns the problem. For the kind of open-ended productivity problem facing most organisations the client groups will be a large and mixed group of people. They will cross functional boundaries and could easily involve other organisations. A typical diverse group could include operators, line managers, functional specialists (eg accountants and production engineers), trade unionists, customers and suppliers.

In the early stages of a programme the senior client's role is to specify the problem and to help as required with clarification. He can give overall direction but should not interfere. However, once the person or, in the case of an in-plant programme, the group has presented their recommendations on solutions the role changes. The client decides and agrees with the group which of the proposed solutions to action. Now in the implementation phase the client role moves from supportive encouraging to supportive direction. There is a job to be done, a system to be put in place, new plant to be ordered, etc. Now the client operates like a project manager laying down budgets, time scales and measuring performance. The individual fellow or group becomes his project team and carries out the implementation on his behalf. It is in this second phase that most action learning programmes run into difficulty. This is usually because the client was never really committed to the project in the first place. It was a nice idea at the time and whilst it was in the investigation phase it had little effect on anyone, but when the project reaches the implementation phase it is different. At this stage it needs change. Unfortunately, particularly in the case of individual development programmes, the client commitment is often not forthcoming. This is not really a problem with in-plant programmes where all the senior managers are involved together including the managing director.

There is also the larger client role involving all those who will be affected by the solution to the problem. The maintenance men in the Bowater Hills project were clients for the new working practices which the project group introduced. The nurses in Revans' HIC project (15) were clients to the proposed changes in patient care. This informal client role is an area which is often overlooked, yet the involvement and the commitment of this group are essential to success. Without them the best solutions in the world will not work.

FELLOW

This is the individual, sometimes also called participant, or in the case of in-plant programmes the group who actually works on the problem. The primary selection objectives in the case of the individual fellow will be to satisfy specific management development needs. However, this is not the case with the in-plant approach where the problem solving groups are deliberately chosen from across the organisation on the basis of what their involvement can contribute to the project. These groups need to be representative of all sections of the organisation which are or could be affected by the problem and its solution. For example, in quality problems the group members could come from quality, accounts, purchasing, engineering, sales and production.

GROUP OR SET

The set is the forum in which the participants meet to learn with and from each other. This is achieved by all the group members reporting on their own projects and helping the others by listening to and questioning their reports.

Typically these groups have four to six members – up to ten for in-plant programmes – and meet once every one to two weeks for half a day. Each individual member presents a report on the current state of his project, where he is now, what problems have been experienced since the past meeting and his view of why these have occurred. Other group members ask searching questions to try to develop their own understanding of what is happening, which forces the individual presenting the project to face up to the reality of his problems. The set is the place where truth can be spoken and illusions shattered and where support, often critical, is provided. It is the group's home, its safe ground; it is somewhere to go, a place to find what Revans has called 'comrades in adversity'. It is the core of any action learning programme.

Once the actual position on a particular project has been agreed the fellow defines what he will try to achieve before the next meeting. When this has been done and agreed it is someone else's turn to present.

With in-plant programmes, even though the group is tackling a common problem, the actual tasks are usually subdivided with members working in small groups of two or three on particular aspects of the problem. These subgroups report back to the set in exactly the same manner as the fellow on the individual project.

It is emphasised that action learning groups are concerned with action and not interesting discussions, therefore work in between meetings is essential.

GROUP ADVISER

The adviser role is a key activity at least in the early stages of any action learning programme. The basic objective of the traditional adviser is to help the group to function in the process sense. This means helping them to understand what is happening in the group, their personal strengths and weaknesses and the ways in which they contribute to their own problems. This can most effectively be done by the adviser acting as a mirror, asking searching questions and playing back what is happening to group members.

The group adviser is: a challenger of beliefs; a difficulty knocker; a catalyst; an opportunity promoter; a developer of skills – listening, questioning, giving and receiving critical feedback etc; a resource suggester; and in the early stages of the programme a kind of project manager.

The group adviser is not a: teacher, director, father figure, problem solver, or presenter.

The traditional adviser's role has been well documented by a number of people. Probably the best description of the activity is given in David Cassey's paper, 'The Emerging Role of Set Advisers in Action Learning Progammes.' (16) In this paper he outlines the tasks of the adviser through the life of a set. For those who are interested in actually becoming involved in set advising the booklet *Management Groups: A Guide to Set Advisers* (17) is recommended. This covers a range of behavioural 'tools' and is invaluable to anyone tackling the role of set adviser for the first time.

The traditional view of the set adviser as someone who helps the group with its process problems is fine as far as it goes. But experience suggests that it does not go far enough. Where no one in a group knows about some particular aspect of a problem the group cannot proceed any further along that particular avenue. This means that vitally important technical aspects of a problem can be left out of the solution because of lack of knowledge in the problem solving group. The traditional argument is that if the group does not have particular specialist knowledge within itself it should ask for it. Unfortunately, however, a group which doesn't have the knowledge doesn't know it is missing and cannot therefore seek to obtain it. This is a particularly important problem with in-plant programmes, where the solution of the problems is of vital importance to the sponsoring enterprise.

The easy answer on in-plant programmes would be to attach a technical expert in the project subject matter to each group. However, experience shows that the expert finds it difficult not to take over and the group itself easily becomes overawed by the professional. Some current in-plant programmes are experimentally using two advisers in a group, one responsible for the traditional process role and the other as technical adviser, for assisting the group in developing specific technical skill. For example, if a group wishes to find out more about materials flow in a production area, it may well not know what techniques are available. Equally a group investigating quality problems may well need guidance on how to measure workers' attitudes to interpret the results. The technical adviser is normally chosen for his/her knowledge of the systems and procedures pertinent to the group project. They function in exactly the same way as the process adviser, the only difference being that their role is to develop the group's technical rather than process skills.

In conventional action learning programmes the adviser role is normally taken by the programme organiser or a paid professional. However, in in-plant programmes middle managers from within the host enterprise are used as both process and technical advisers. This has several very important advantages because i) it involves all middle managers in the programme in what they see as a legitimate role. This is particularly important as their commitment to the solutions arrived at by the group is essential for successful implementaton; ii) it provides an ideal management development opportunity. Large numbers of middle managers have never really developed the skills of working with groups. The adviser role is an ideal training vehicle; and iii) it enables attitude change. As the manager is an adviser to a project group working in an area that he is not familiar with, eg the quality manager may be adviser to an employee attitudes project, he has the chance to see the organisation from a different perspective. In addition he is exposed through the mix of people in his project group to different attitudes within the enterprise.

For in-plant programmes involving a number of groups it is useful to have an external adviser to the internal advisers' group.

TYPES OF PROGRAMME

In traditional action learning, there are four principal types of programme available, as illustrated in the windows numbered 1 to 4 in Figure 8.4.

JOB COMPANY		PARTICIPANT'S JOB	
		FAMILIAR	UNFAMILIAR
F A M I L I A R		Same department Same company	Different job in the same company
		Development of existing job 1	Gaining understanding of other functions 2
U N F A M I L I A R		Same job in a different company	Different job in a different company
		Improving skill in existing job 3	For managers destined for senior positions 4

Other options:

* Part-time or full time
* External groups of mixed companies
  or in-plant
* Individual problems for each participant
  or common problems for group

Figure 8.4   Programme options

1   THE OWN JOB MODEL

The own job model provides management development through
the participant tackling a familiar task in a familiar environment.
This approach, called management clinics and the forerunner of
the own job type of action learning, was developed in the UK
largely by the author in conjunction with The Institution of Works
Management. (18) In this version the managers stay in their current jobs and tackle problems related to their everyday work.
They meet in small, locally organised groups with participants
from different companies about every two weeks with an adviser,
usually the organiser. Such programmes normally run for six

months and are a useful and cost-effective means of providing low-level management development. This has been a particularly popular approach to management training amongst small companies. The company not only get a manager trained, but usually there is the added bonus of having a real problem solved.

This approach was combined with a series of in-plant programmes in the Performance Improvement Programme which was launched with support from the Manpower Services Commission in 1981. The programme was designed to improve productivity within participating organisations. Each business provided basic audit data which were used to identify the main productivity problems within the enterprise. They also nominated a senior manager to be responsible, with external help, for setting up and running his own in-plant programme to tackle the issues identified by the audit. These managers meet externally on a monthly basis to learn with and from each other about the experience. This programme will be covered in more depth in Chapter 9.

The main strengths of this approach are: Firstly, the fellow stays in his own job and continues to function as a manager within his own enterprise throughout the programme. He thus learns as he works. For this reason this kind of programme is called part-time action learning. Secondly, the fellow solves actual, job related problems. For example a programme run in the UK Sperry Gyroscope Company in 1982 focused on a participant's personal performance improvement problems as highlighted during annual appraisals. Finally, a cross-fertilisation of ideas takes place because participants come from different backgrounds and companies, hence the name: external action learning. It also includes the multiplier effect of dealing with the problem solving and development needs of a number of companies.

This approach does not create the high level of promotion expectation often resulting from conventional management development programmes. However, the programme has been used for managing directors as well as managers and supervisors. Figure 8.5 illustrates the structure of the model.

2   THE GEC MODEL

The unfamiliar task in a familiar environment is sometimes called the GEC programme, because the first programme of the type was run in GEC in the UK in 1974. (19) The participants were mainly potential senior managers recruited from the various businesses in GEC. They were taken out of their current jobs and given projects in other companies within GEC. The programme ran for six months and began with an initial three-week introductory session at Dunchurch Lodge, the GEC training establishment.

Programme stages:

1 Initiation: gaining commitment of nominator
2 Planning: selecting participants and problems, agreeing programme design
3 Introductory workshop
4 Action phase: diagnose and take action on problems
5 Evaluation: review whole programme

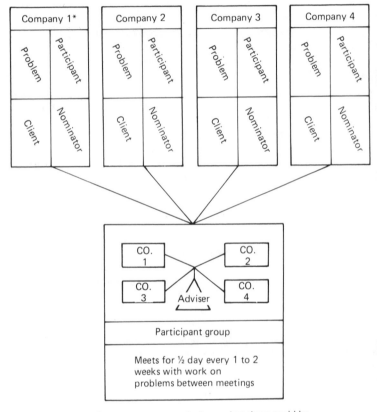

* A four-company group is shown, but there could be up to 6 companies involved

Figure 8.5 Structure of part-time 'own job' external model

After this delegates worked for the rest of the time in the host companies on their projects, meeting fortnightly in project groups. Another programme using this approach was Revans' Hospitals Project (15) in which hospital staff from a group of London hospitals carried out a large-scale study looking into methods of improving patient care in each other's hospitals. The approach is applicable particularly in the large organisation. Apart from its obvious value as a management development tool its particular strengths are: the cross fertilisation of ideas across diverse businesses within groups; as a vehicle for defusing corporate policies and philosophies; and exposure of budding executive talent to senior corporate management.

3 NCB MODEL

The familiar task in an unfamiliar environment is called the NCB model because it was used by Revans in his early work in the National Coal Board. (20) In this model the participant does the same job in another place. Revans exchanged the mine managers between mines, creating a situation where, although the task was the same, the conditions under which it was carried out were unfamiliar. This meant that the manager saw the job in a different light, which enabled the project to become a learning opportunity. As with all the other programmes the transferred managers met regularly in small groups to focus their learning. Many large companies actually use this temporary 'expert' transfer approach but unfortunately do not take advantage of the learning potential.

The other advantages of the approach, apart from the management development aspects, are that: it uses the manager's task expertise to do an actual job, and is therefore very cost-effective; the project is real and therefore success or failure is easily measurable; there is little risk of losing managers who have been developed in this way. They just become better managers.

4 THE BELGIUM MODEL

This particular type of programme derives from Revans' first significant public application of action learning to management development. (21) This was in Belgium, hence the name, in 1969. Here the manager is developed through doing an unfamiliar job in an unfamiliar place. Each participating organisation nominates one potential senior manager whom they wish developed and a serious problem they need solved. The participants are then allocated projects in unfamiliar organisations and different disciplines to their own. For example a chemist from a large metal processing plant carried out a project in a main bank in Brussels to increase the bank's investment in small businesses. The bank's nominee carried out a project in a steelworks.

As with all the other types of programme the fellows worked in the host enterprise most of the time, in this case four days a week, and on the fifth met together in the set to focus the learning. It is therefore a full-time programme and consequently expensive. This is without doubt the most powerful type of programme in management development terms and it is by far the most challenging. This approach: develops a high level of self-confidence, interpersonal skills and the strategic level of thinking necessary for senior managers; broadens understanding of organisations and how they function; identifies those with ambition and provides a focus for it; and enables the visiting fellow to bring entirely fresh thinking to bear in the host organisation.

A TYPICAL ACTION LEARNING PROGRAMME

A typical action learning programme consists of six main stages and normally lasts for six months. However, with in-plant programmes where the philosophy is adopted as a basic approach to open-ended problem solving the approach should continue to be used.

The stages are as follows:

Stage 1   Programme introduction. Form groups, choose projects, choose advisers. The length of this stage will depend on the introductory workshop and could range from a minimum of one day up to three weeks.

Stage 2   Investigation. Get information, develop solutions, choose and test. Three months.

Stage 3   Presentation of findings to clients. Fellows present their findings and recommendations formally backed by written project documentation. The length of this stage will obviously depend on the number of projects to be presented but it will usually be less than a day.

Stage 4   Clients present response to recommendations and agree formal action plans for implementation, timescales, budgets etc., with individuals/groups. This normally takes about one day and is done in plenary session. It should take place within two to three weeks of Stage 3.

Stage 5   Implementation. This stage lasts nominally for three months. Obviously the time necessary to implement different solutions will be different for different projects. If solutions require the installation of a new system to monitor quality across the plant this will obviously take very much longer to achieve than a project concerned with improving the standards of the existing company newspaper. For this reason it is obviously necessary to set some arbitrary end date for the programme.

Stage 6   Final review. This is an opportunity for all those who have been involved in the programme, clients, advisers, fellows and the nominator, to meet together to share their experience. It is normal practice for the fellows to organise this session, which normally lasts about half a day.

IN-PLANT ACTION LEARNING

In-plant action learning is a further development by Boulden (2) of Revans' original work, focusing primarily on organisational development. The chief differences between this approach and the action learning models previously described are:

- It focuses within one organisation.
- It involves the whole management team, with senior managers as clients, middle managers as advisers and the first line group as fellows. Shop floor groups have been used, but this has normally occurred after the first programme, when the approach has been adopted as a means of solving open-ended problems.
- It uses crossfunctional groups working on one common problem. For example, one group in the Bowater Hills programme (13) had the job of finding ways of improving customer service, while another was charged with improving cash flow. One of the groups in the electronics company – case study Chapter 9 – was asked to reorganise the company's technical training procedures.
- It is principally concerned with solving complex cross-functional problems, especially in the area of productivity improvement.
- It has a highly committed nominator, usually the chief executive, who has a strong vested interest in the success of the programme.
- There is within the organisation a co-ordinator who monitors the programme and helps overcome any difficulties of a personal or technical nature. He/she is a kind of sheet anchor who tries to ensure the smooth running of the

whole programme. While the first scheme will probably be designed and conducted by an outsider who has experience in running in-plant action learning programmes, the co-ordinator should eventually take over this role.

● It is the equivalent of setting up a number of external action learning type groups with the same organisation. At one stage the Bowater programme previously mentioned involved 12 such groups.

Since Revans first introduced the brilliant idea of using real problems as the basis for developing people and their organisations there have been many applications of this simple principle. What has now been described as specifically suited to the human and technical problems of productivity improvement is in-plant action learning. The characteristics of this approach are highlighted below:

1   Those at the lower levels of the organisation participate in deciding the problems that are inhibiting performance.
2   A critical mass of people at the upper, middle, and supervisory levels are actively involved in the identification and solution of pressing problems. In this way these three levels see the problems, their jobs and how the organisation really functions through different eyes; they appreciate the differing perceptions of problems – assumptions, their realities and what should be done about them.
3   The 'no preconceptions' philosophy make it ideally suited to open-ended problems.
4   An introductory team building workshop is used to enable the fellows to become a cohesive group. A learning simulation is also included for recreating the actual conditions in the organisation.

The in-plant action learning programme is summarised in Figure 8.6.

CONCLUSIONS

In this chapter it has been suggested that organisational productivity problems fall into the two categories of closed- and open-ended. The former have known, rational answers while the latter do not. We can go further and say that to even understand open-ended problems we need to pose entirely new questions.

Probably without realising it many organisations have become accustomed to using a closed-ended problem solving style. It is

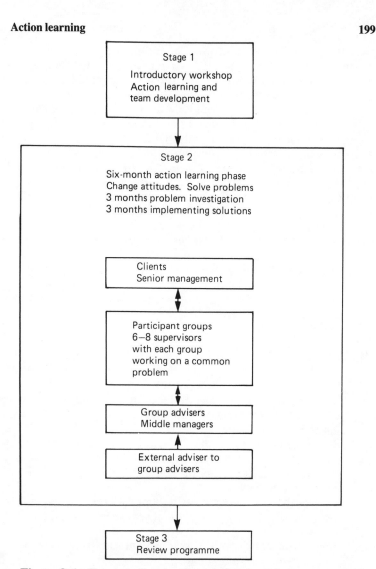

Figure 8.6   Format of an in-plant action learning programme

assumed that the answers exist and the need to involve the client group in the problem identification/solving process is not appreciated – or accepted. The available experience shows that many enterprises are good at dealing with closed-ended problems but not with the more intractable open-ended problem. The likely reasons for this are firstly that open-ended problems are not recognised for what they are and secondly that managers are reluctant to enter the risky and uncertain climate of open-ended problem solving. It involves challenging what may be longstanding and cherished beliefs. However, in conditions of such rapid change our assumptions need to be subjected to the critical debate found in an action learning group. This will help us to recognise problems as they really are, not as we believe them to be. But even this is not enough. We may have to change the actuality to a position more in keeping with the altered circumstances. The in-plant action learning approach, with its multifunctional, three-managerial level approach reconciles differing perceptions and gains the commitment to requisite changes. This open-ended attack on open-ended problem solving and a good measurement system are a powerful combination for improving productivity.

Reduced then to its elements, action learning aims to:

1 bring together those who can (and should) do something about organisational problems;
2 enable groups of people to learn with and from each other as they tackle problems that concern them and which they need to treat, whether they have heard of action learning or not;
3 widen managerial horizons and bring fresh insights into problems by exposing them to the critical inquiry of people from quite different functions and backgrounds. Personal inhibitions, even some overtones of organisational resistance to new ideas, are quickly overcome in the open and challenging climate of an action learning group;
4 discourage recommendations for others to act upon. Action learning accepts from the outset that each participant, no matter how difficult his or her problem may be, will be committed to action;
5 enable the participants to reappraise their existing experience to cope with current and new problems and to learn how to learn;
6 help all those involved to take a significant step forward in their personal development;
7 help participants to manage their time more effectively, that is, to learn to persist with underlying problems and to resist being diverted by day-to-day difficulties. Personal development, problem solving and work are recognised as the same process and time as the most precious of managerial assets.

In the next chapter the practical application of action learning and productivity audits is described in three case studies. The first was an experimental performance improvement programme for twelve manufacturing companies. Secondly an in-plant action earning programme conducted in a large electronics company is described. Lastly a project involving 24 companies in a single industry is examined. Before you pass on to the next chapter you might reflect on the kind of open-ended problems you are currently facing and how you deal with them.

REFERENCES

1   Revans, Reginald W., *The ABC of Action Learning*, Chartwell Bratt, 2nd edition, 1983
2   Boulden, George, 'How Action Learning Can Teach Firms', *Management Today*, February 1981
3   Beer, Stafford, *Decision and Control*, John Wiley, 1966.
4   Boddy, David, 'An Action Learning Programme for Supervisors', *Leadership and Organisation Development Journal*, Vol 4, No 3, 1983
5   Lawlor, A., Boulden, George and Steel, David, 'Company Revival: Two Firms Take a Fresh Approach', *Works Management*, July 1981
6   Arbrose, J., Assoc., ed., 'Listening to Workers Produces Results', *International Management*, February 1980
7   McGregor, D., *The Human Side of Enterprise*, McGraw-Hill, 1960
8   Hayes, Robert H., and Abernathy, William J., 'Managing Our Way to Economic Decline', *Harvard Business Review*, July/August 1980
9   Peter, Thomas J., and Waters, Robert H., *In Search of Excellence,* Harper and Row, 1982
10 *The Bullock Report,* HMSO 1975
11 Boulden, G. P., and Lawlor, A., 'Surviving in a Changing World', *Leadership and Organisation Development Journal*, Vol. 3, No 5, 1982
12 Arbrose, J., 'Quality Circles: The West Adopts a Japanese Concept', *International Management*, December 1980
13 Precious, W., 'Flush Doors in the 80's', *MEAD*, vol 13, Pt 2, Summer 1982
14 Sasaki, Professor Naoto, *Management and Industrial Structure in Japan*, Pergamon Press, Oxford, 1981
15 Revans, R. W., *Action Learning in Hospitals: Diagnosis and Therapy,* McGraw-Hill 1976
16 Casey, David, 'The Emerging Role of Set Advisers in Action Learning Programmes', *Journal of European Training*, Vol 5, No 3, 1976

17   Garrett, Bob, *Management Groups: A guide for set advisers*, Action Learning Associates, Rugby 1982

18   Lawlor, Alan, 'Group problem solving can help the individual as well as his company', *Works Management*, Vol 33, No 11, November 1980

19   Casey, D. and Pearce, D., *More than Management Development,* Gower, 1977

20   Revans, R. W. *The Origins and Growth of Action Learning*, Chartwell Bratt, 1982

21   Revans, R. W., *Developing Effective Managers*, Praeger, 1971

9 Three case studies

Methods for studying and measuring productivity have now been examined and in the previous chapter the action learning approach was presented as a means of actually improving productivity and dealing with the associated open-ended problems. There have now been many uses of action learning to bring about organisational change which Revans (1) has described in his analysis of its development over nearly forty years. This shows that the creative use of such a simple process can lead to endless applications. As an example of its potential the philosophy of action learning has been directed to the specific problems of productivity improvement described in the three case studies in this chapter.

The first programmes were launched in 1978 and are still being developed. In this chapter three practical applications are examined. The first is briefly outlined, with the last two being treated in more depth. The first, shorter example is called a performance improvement programme (PIP) and involves a combination of productivity audits, external action learning group meetings composed of different companies, and in-plant action learning.

The second case study is an in-plant action learning programme conducted in a telecommunications factory which is part of a large

UK electronics group, during 1982/1983. The last case study involved a productivity improvement programme within a single industry. Each application presents a contrasting picture of ways of changing organisational performance for the better. They are also complementary, with each one dealing with particular aspects of the common aim of increasing productivity. The first and last are examples of methods for assisting a number of companies, whereas the second was concerned with bringing about change within one large company. For all of the cases presented the basic model is described so that they can be applied by others.

1   PERFORMANCE IMPROVEMENT PROGRAMME

In 1980 the Manpower Services Commission gave support to an experimental programme to bring together three aspects of the task of organisational change. Each one includes strengths and weaknesses and had previously been used separately. These three aspects are described below:

1   Productivity audits: as stated elsewhere a productivity auditing system consists of a regular monitoring of individual company performance plus comparisons of the results with other companies. While the interfirm comparison aspect is already a stimulant for change, some additional human interaction is considered necessary to ensure lasting improvements. The action learning process provides this human catalytic effect.

2   External action learning: a group of people from different backgrounds and companies who meet regularly to tackle real, topical problems shed fresh light on seemingly intractable difficulties. This climate of mutual support and constructive but critical debate is a powerful device for developing individual problem solving skills. However, unless there is a similar supportive climate in each organisation one person will have great difficulty in bringing about change.

3   In-plant action learning; to overcome the one-man-against-the-organisation problem of external action learning, the in-plant approach is applied. This type of programme, now used in a number of companies, is the equivalent of setting up a number of external action learning groups within the same organisation. In this way a critical mass of people share the difficulties and the blame for the problems that need resolving. Project 'Management Efficiency' (1) is an earlier

example of action learning within a large Belgian metal processing plant employing 7,000 people. The senior manager who initiated the programme considered that lasting change was a very human process and one should therefore recognise the following conditions:

- Change is a social or collective process: blame to one person should be avoided and seen rather as the responsibility of a wide group (the critical mass) of people or even a whole service.
- Change should be related to some observable activity; it demands reciprocal change on the part of others and so may set in motion a process that makes for more effective teamwork. Revans describes this as 'the principle of insufficient mandate'; you cannot change any human system unless you also are prepared to change yourself.
- Change is effected by a process of learning (or 'autonomous formation' in the original French expression): one perceives the deficiency, one tries to find a way around it and one eventually changes – provided that other members of the group are also willing to change.

The 'PIP' project combined the three aspects productivity audits, external and in-plant action learning, in one programme. It began at the end of 1980 and involved a total of twelve mixed companies. Eight were based in the West Midlands region and four in the North East region of the UK. The aim was to gain experience in small and large companies engaged in different kinds of activity. It was also intended that the West Midlands, which was influenced by the motor car industry, and the North East, with a heavy engineering base, might also reveal the effects of differing cultures.

'PIP' OBJECTIVES

The 'PIP' experiment was seen as a new initiative to improve productivity. It sought to bring together the three elements previously mentioned to achieve two objectives: to assist a number of companies at the same time, the multiplier effect described more fully in the third case study; and to interpret productivity audit information at external action learning meetings. These meetings were also to provide the support and guidance for each company representative to set up and conduct their own internal action learning groups.

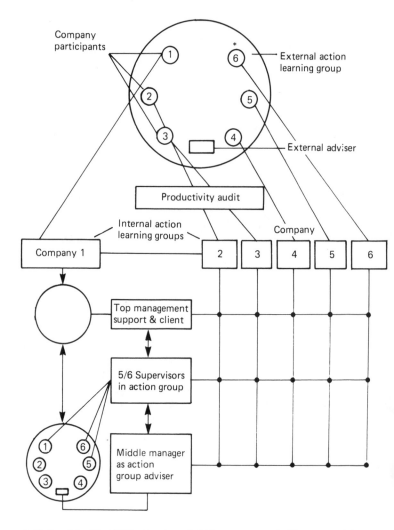

* Three of the West Midlands group of eight were represented by one participant

Figure 9.1   How PIP works

PROGRAMME STAGES

The 'PIP' scheme commenced with launch seminars in the Midlands and the North East during the spring and summer of 1980. Nearly 100 managers from a wide range of organisations attended these seminars and from these meetings the twelve companies who were to take part were selected. Only twelve companies took part for two reasons: (i) the Manpower Services Commission support was given for this number of companies and (ii) due to its experimental nature twelve companies were considered the maximum we could deal with. After these initial presentations the programme proceeded through the following four stages:

1. One-day workshops were held to explain the basis of the programme and how it works; this is shown in Figures 9.1 and 9.2. Such details as the measurement system, the audit procedure and action learning meetings were also explained.
2. Productivity audits were administered on a monthly basis for six months similarly to the procedure described in Chapter 5. The audits used were identical to Figures 5.5 and 5.7 (pages 105 and 107).
3. Monthly external action learning meetings were conducted.
4. The entire programme was reviewed at the end of six months.

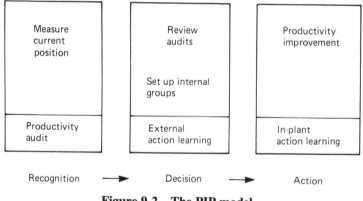

Figure 9.2   The PIP model

PROFILE OF COMPANIES

The companies and the managers who took part covered a wide range of manufacturing industry. They included the very small to the large with two managing directors, a general manager, two owners and the rest middle-level functional managers. It was this spread of company and job that led to the difficulties described later. Figure 9.3 lists the number of employees in each company, their principal type of production and the job of those who participated in the external action learning group meetings.

Co. No.	No. of Employees	Type of production	Job of participant
1	80	Electroplating	Managing Director
2	145	Needles	Organisation and Methods Officer
3	180	Heat exchanges	General Manager
4	450	Wire products	Operations Manager
5	740	Defence equipment	Production Engineering Manager
6	1100	Defence equipment	Productivity Services Manager
7	1170	Defence equipment	Factory Accountant
8	2000	Defence equipment	Factory Accountant
9	6	Welding and fabricating	Owner
10	18	Radiographic shields	Owner
11	20	Equipment for the disabled	Production Manager
12	60	Castings and heavy machining	Managing Director

Note: Companies 1 to 8 are the West Midlands Group and 9 to 12 are from the North East.

Figure 9.3   PIP: profile of 12 participating companies

RESULTS

All of the twelve companies took part in the monthly audit, though after four months the active involvement reduced to nine, with four continuing for twelve months. Six monthly meetings also took place in the two locations with an average attendance of 70 per cent.

The total earnings productivity performance of the eight West Midlands companies is shown in Figure 9.4. This shows an average of 1.39 over the nine-month period April to December 1981, with a variation between the highest and lowest individual company results of the order of over 2 to 1. Even bigger variations were found in plant productivity and the percentage of wages to sales.

Total
earnings
productivity

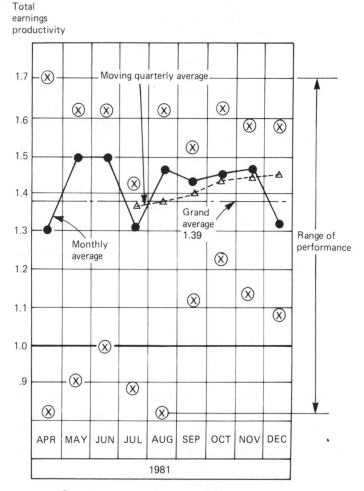

Note: (X) Highest and lowest individual figures

Figure 9.4 PIP: Total earnings productivity for 8 manufacturers

The programme inspired most of the companies to improve their productivity information systems, with a number actually increasing their productivity, as the quarterly moving average in Figure 9.4 indicates. But the scheme was less successful in getting the intended in-plant action learning activities started, due to a combination of the following reasons:

1   Due to the variation in types of company there were doubts

about the comparability of audit data. While this was partly true, the total earnings productivity index is considered to be a common measurement. Moreover, it was considered that the different backgrounds of the participants should have stimulated the fresh thinking desired.

2 Some participants, due to their managerial level, were not in a position to influence decisions within their companies.

3 The companies should have been persuaded to start in-plant programmes in the early stages of the action learning meetings rather than half-way through.

4 Over half of the companies felt the effects of the developing recession soon after the programme commenced. One was near to liquidation and several had considerably reduced their workforce. The economic climate in the North East was particularly depressed, but due to a past history of adverse conditions management seemed to be more acclimatised to their difficulties. But the West Midlands, which had weathered previous downturns with little upset, were finding it difficult to adjust to a situation of high unemployment and company closures.

This raises the need for the early warning system previously mentioned; attacks on productivity have to start before a company is beyond help and certainly must continue even if the going is difficult.

In spite of these difficulties the programme does have potential, especially in the aim of assisting a number of companies at the same time. The lessons learned in this first experiment led to the more successful programme described in the third case study.

2 IN-PLANT ACTION LEARNING

There is a good deal of accumulated evidence to show that improving the performance of organisations should involve as many people as possible. The Hospital Internal Communications Project mentioned in Chapter 7 at one time included around 500 people ranging from porters to consultants. This project, which spanned the period 1965 to 1969, involved 10 leading UK hospitals and, amongst a number of points relating to organisational performance, showed that the productivity of bed occupancy was statistically related to how well nursing staff participated in decision making.

The Belgian project 'Management Efficiency' mentioned earlier is another example where different levels of management support each other in tackling problems of efficiency improvement. This second case study describes a further development of using the action learning approach to involve a significant group of people within the same company. The programme now described was first used in a Motorola semiconductors plant in Scotland. It was further developed in a Bowaters factory on the North East coast of England, with yet another variation being applied in the tyre division of Dunlop. All of these developments are contained in references 2,5 and 13 of Chapter 8.

Apart from the aim of involving the total management team, this form of in-plant action learning is particularly directed to the solution of open-ended productivity improvement problems which cross functional boundaries. The case study was run at a tele-communications plant also in the North East during 1982/1983.

THE COMPANY

The company is a large UK electronics and telecommunications manufacturer which at the end of 1981 employed around 47,000 people, with sales per employee of nearly £18,000. While this did not compare favourably with the almost £30,000 of Racal Electronics, one of its competitors, it had improved profit per employee during 1981 by 54 per cent. The telecommunications division concerned had a total employee strength of about 370 divided between two plants. One employed 250 on traditional switchgear manufacture and the other, where the programme took place, had 120 people working in three shifts using high technology to produce printed circuit boards (PCB). Figure 9.5 is an outline organisation chart for the PCB factory. It will be seen that the programme included the not unusual problems of dual functional responsibilities. The quality, engineering, sales and finance managers who took part served the interests of the older switch-gear plant as well as the higher technological PCB plant.

PROBLEM BACKGROUND

During the early discussions about the programme the problem was seen as one of attitudes and relationships within the PCB unit. Some people considered the situation was caused by recruiting people for the new plant from within the company. Although the entire workforce, including supervision and management, would be involved in information age technology and quite different methods of working, many of the people concerned found it difficult to forget the working practices of the older technology. The three shift systems, for example, required different methods of organisation. There was a tendency to give lower priority to quality towards the end of the shift and give more importance to output, especially as there was poor feedback between shifts. The inspection system was also rooted in the existing technology with the consequence that quality problems were discovered too late in the production cycle.

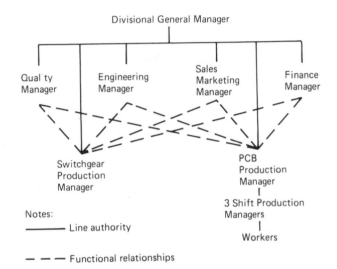

Figure 9.5   Telecommunications division: organisation chart

During the two and a half years before the programme commenced, the complete plant had been installed, the management team was set up and the workforce of 150 had been trained. The target set by the parent company was for the plant to be producing at agreed levels of output and returning budgeted profitability within three years. Within six months of this date the expected results did not seem to be in sight. The situation was either high output and low quality or low output and high quality. All of the technical aspects of manufacture seemed all right, so was it a human and organisational problem? It was proving difficult to pinpoint causes or to locate the areas where the problem was occurring, because it seemed to move from section to section for no apparent reason. In these conditions management were in a mood to consider fresh initiatives.

PROGRAMME OVERVIEW

As the result of the initial discussions with senior management it was agreed that a real-time problem solving programme would be an effective way of dealing with the situation. The programme was designed to involve all managers, supervisors and functional specialists in finding solutions to their own productivity problems over a 6/9-month period.

Similarly to the earlier Motorola and Bowater schemes, the programme began with a team building/management skill development workshop for the supervisors and functional specialists. The principal thrust of this workshop was a simulation of the actual conditions existing in the plant. It involved the making and selling of actual products to a certain quality specification with an outside workforce which the workshop participants had to train and manage. It was thus a highly realistic way of enabling those taking part to set up a manufacturing organisation similar to their own, manage it and then evaluate in a 'safe' situation the technical/economic/social lessons. During this period those taking part were also given the opportunity, in an open-ended way, to reveal the productivity problems in the plant as they saw them. This was an alternative way of gaining problem recognition instead of using productivity audits.

This introductory stage was followed by a six-month in-plant action programme with senior managers as clients, middle managers as advisers and the supervisors/functional specialists as fellows. This is the model described in Chapter 8. Details of the complete programme are shown in Figure 9.6.

CONDUCT OF PROGRAMME

This model has now been successfully used on a number of occasions. It does involve risk but any programme of change will not be without some difficulties. While the approach will need some modifications to suit particular circumstances, what follows is a practical account of starting and running a programme of this kind.

Team building workshops

It was agreed that these introductory workshops would take place on two consecutive weekends to suit shift patterns and to ensure that all managers, supervisors and functional specialists could take

OBJECTIVES

To solve the productivity problems of the plant.
To build more effective working teams.
To develop management/interpersonal skills.
To introduce the delegates to the philosophy of integrated group problem solving.

Method
The main emphasis will be on learning by doing as shown in Figure 9.7.

Programme

Part 1   3-day team building workshop organised around a learning simulation and exposure of problems for investigation and action.
Part 2   Action learning part involving five stages:
  Stage 1   Programme introduction, form action learning groups, choose projects and advisers. Half a day.
  Stage 2   Investigate – get information, suggest solutions, choose and test. 2 months.
  Stage 3   All groups present recommended solutions to clients. 1 day.
  Stage 4   Clients respond to group recommendations on an individual basis and agree action plan which groups implement. 3 months.
  Stage 5   Final review of the whole programme to be organised by fellows. 1 day.

Figure 9.6   In-plant action learning programme

part. In this way all those who were to participate could be catered for within two weeks. They were run on a residential basis due to the intensive nature of the work to be done; this was especially necessary for the simulation, which was designed around the PCB plant. Each workshop commenced shortly after the end of the 6 (0600 hours) till 2 (1400 hours) shift on the Friday and finished in time for the commencement of the 2 (1400) till 10 (2200) shift on the Monday. Those taking part were a mixture of line supervisors, chemists, engineers, quality staff and so on.

The workshop commenced with a general introduction to the whole programme, of which the weekend was just the first part.

During the early stages each individual was asked to write down what they saw as the main problem which was stopping them

---

Technical (25)[*]

Lack of training in new technology
Technical expertise can only be got on the job and with time; will the company support this? Should we buy this expertise?
No planned maintenance, resulting in breakdown of essential production equipment
Poor drawings for new items of production
Excessive manual backup required for computer systems
Lack of complete customer information until after job has started.

Resources (4)[*]

Lack of in-house training
Underfunded projects
Lack of reference books.

Management/Motivation (47)[*]

Attitudes to change
Lack of communication of the when and why of process changes
Management decisions without involving those concerned
Only partial communication between shifts
Union demarcation
Restrictions on the use of personal initiative
Others doing my job for me
Doing what is not really required causes frustration
Operations don't care
Lack of clear management decisions and failure to stick to them
Relevant information difficult to come by
Lack of information on how faults really occurred for fear of reprimand
Delays in information from engineering
General apathy towards quality

Note: ( )[*] total responses in each category.

Figure 9.7   What stops you doing a good job?
Summarised replies from supervisors and support on introductory action learning workshops.

personally doing a good job. This is a significant aspect of the whole model. The intention is that, without any strings, those who can affect output and quality problems should participate in the identification and solution of their own problems. The answers to this question were typed and passed back to the delegates so as to provide a composite view of problems. An edited version of the replies to this question, categorised under the main problem headings of Technical, Resources, Management/Motivation are listed in Figure 9.7. It is significant that the last category considerably outnumbers the first two. They were also used as a basis for the open forum with senior management which took place on the Monday morning.

In preparation for the simulation the Saturday morning was devoted to management skills and styles of leadership. The simulation ran from 1400 hours on Saturday until 1600 hours on Sunday, which necessitated working late into Saturday night. After dinner on Sunday the General Manager talked about the plant, its problems and the reasons for the programme, which was then followed by a general discussion.

Up to 1030 on Monday morning the delegates planned the conduct of an open forum with senior management from 1100 until lunchtime. They decided upon a question and answer approach, the important point being that the conduct of this session was left completely with the group.

The experience gained from this introductory weekend revealed the importance of participation and genuine involvement. It showed the inherent commitment and enthusiasm that exists at the grass roots. By the Saturday afternoon a high team spirit had developed, with the women participants being very supportive of the programme. The simulation required the group to organise all aspects of a business including design, marketing, production, quality, costing and budgeting. In preparation for the Sunday morning, when outside workers had to be hired and trained, many did not get to bed until the early hours. The consensus was that the experience had been rewarding and informative, highlighting many of the actual problems back in the plant. There was a general feeling of personal self-discovery and achievement. Those participating felt they had a better understanding of their own problems together with those of other departments. By the Monday morning open discussion with senior management, a group of people present had become more forthcoming and committed to tackle the problems of the plant. The management team reacted with mixed feelings. Some felt insecure, were uncertain about the programme, and some found the experience threatening, while others were more positive.

Selection of projects

The choice of projects was made at a one-day meeting of the senior management team. They used the responses to the question posed during the workshops as a basis for identifying relevant projects. These have been summarised on Figure 9.7. It was a long meeting which raised a number of issues, notably, feelings of personal criticism for managers and that involving people in management problems might weaken the position of some managers. These reactions are to be expected as the realities of actually bringing about organisational change. It also gives support to the earlier findings in Project 'Management Efficiency' (1) that somehow the blame for company problems should not fall on the shoulders of one person but should be shared.

Comments like, 'They don't understand' and 'If we promise to talk to our people more can we go away and forget about this?', highlight the defensive feelings present. However, the General Manager was convinced of the wisdom of the programme and agreement was eventually reached to proceed with the following five projects:

1 Training
2 Shift communication
3 Provision of manufacturing information
4 Quality/inspection
5 Pre-production procedures.

Five managers agreed to act as clients for each of the above projects. They also agreed to produce an expanded statement of their project in preparation for a meeting with the entire group in two weeks' time.

Five other managers volunteered to act as advisers, one to each one of the five groups. The aim was therefore to have five groups of about five participants per group with a common project for each group, a senior manager as a client and another in an advisory capacity to one of the five groups. In this way the whole management would be involved in the project and get a hands-on feeling for how the groups felt. They would also get first-hand experience of the difficulties in solving problems, and at the same time it should increase their commitment to the solutions produced.

Matching projects

The next phase in getting high participation in group working was to match the five projects with group participants and advisers; having created a climate where those concerned with the perceived problems of quality and output have identified them they should continue to freely decide how to tackle them.

Shortly after the clients' meeting, the whole group (ie the fellows, advisers and clients) met at a local hotel to achieve six objectives.

1   To introduce the action learning phase;
2   The clients to present the five projects;
3   To present the potential advisers;
4   To give the opportunity for the fellows to decide which project group they preferred and to choose the advisers they wished to work with;
5   The fellows to meet their clients and seek, if necessary, further information about their projects;
6   To agree arrangements for the first action learning group meeting.

It had been stated previously that group members could select their own advisers from within their group if they so wished. Furthermore, they would have complete freedom to choose the project they wanted to tackle.

After the five clients had made a brief presentation of their projects individuals were asked to decide the project they would like to work on by writing their name on one of five flip charts. This was followed by the choice of advisers, which in every case was one of the proposed advisers. Finally, preliminary meetings were held with clients and advisers and details of the next meeting agreed.

Thus by 1630, when the meeting concluded, the six objectives had been achieved and the action learning phase had begun.

Action learning part

During the three-month investigation, stage 2, each group carried out the fact-finding research for its project. The realities of trying to resolve problems in real time were ever present: a company/union dispute caused some supervisors to withdraw from the project; shift working posed difficulties for regular meetings; power struggles within groups and general frustration were the main examples. However, in spite of the difficulties, quite fresh insights and information about the five problems were obtained and as planned a presentation, including recommendations, was end of the three-month period. A synopsis of the five projects and the recommendations is outlined in Figure 9.8.

---

1 *Training*: Client, Company Training Manager.
Project brief: Consider how training could provide employees with knowledge/understanding of products, processes, technical aspects costs, job requirements and how to become more flexible.
Recommendations: safety training, provision of standard terminology on manufacturing processes, types of circuit and faults and one-week induction courses for new employees with updates every six months.

---

2 *Shift Communications*: Client, Production Manager.
Project brief: Study ways of improving shift communication including the function of production control, production engineering, quality and maintenance. Give attention to feedback and main problem areas.
Recommendations: launch videos as a communications vehicle, continue the initial questionnaire study, include all operators and seek information on individual job needs and what people need to know.

---

3 *Provision of manufacturing information:* Client, Information Systems Manager.
Project brief: Study the effectiveness of information provision on products, process utilisation, performance objectives and performance achievements.
Recommendations: introduce real-time information systems including visual display units (VDUs) for all foremen, distribute up-to-date reports to all departmental heads, incorporate work routing and scrap reporting in the real-time system.

---

4 *Quality/Inspection*: Client, Quality Manager.
Project brief: Review and make suggestions for improvements in inspection points, quality statistics and materials handling.
Recommendations: make operators responsible for their own quality and scrap levels, install quality assurance at critical points,

Figure 9.8 Synopsis of projects

install a daily fault recording system and an as-they-occur fault diagnosis procedure. Set up a good housekeeping procedure for all processes.

---

5 *Pre-production procedures*: Client, Engineering Manager.
Project brief: study pre-production activities and suggest ways to reduce lead times, anticipate manufacturing problems and improve material yields.
Recommendations: In the short term define scope of pre-production and appoint a co-ordinator. In the medium term, establish a central information area on specifications, drawings, customers, process tolerances and do's and don'ts of manufacturing. In the longer term, use computer to facilitate first-off production and inspection.

Figure 9.8   (concluded)

In some cases the studies had produced some improvements, in others clients wanted time to consider the recommendations – some thought they were putting off making a decision. An action phase did follow on from the presentations with many of the proposals being implemented. A final review meeting was held some five weeks later.

RESULTS AND LESSONS

During the nearly 12 months of the programme some 100 people were directly and indirectly involved. Company performance was increased from 60 per cent of potential to 90 per cent, cost savings were achieved and plant productivity was back on target. More specifically, the changes included the installation of VDUs for foremen and more effective quality reporting procedures. But there are a number of lessons for anyone interested in the management of change.

It is one thing to ask people for their views on problems and even to involve them in the problem solving process. But it is something quite different to trust them to implement the solutions themselves. This poses great risks for management, as mistakes might be made and they could lose status. However, management must recognise that, once the involvement process has started, even greater feelings of frustration and apathy will occur if the involvement is halted. This programme continued to reveal attitudes of fear, defensiveness and uncertainty, mainly on the part of management. The General Manager, who had initially been positive, became less so, giving more support to the client group than the project group. This raised a number of issues for the company. What was the management's real belief in the philosophy of group problem solving? How will a group feel if they are not involved in the implementation phases when other groups are? How do those at the grass roots help managers to overcome their feelings of defensiveness? In spite of all these natural human reactions a good deal was achieved in economic, technical and social terms.

The programme demonstrates that people at work do have an interest in improving the performance of their organisations. Furthermore, it is possible to work together towards meaningful solutions and most people are willing to contribute if the conditions inspire it. The overriding problem is not in encouraging workers, supervisors and functional specialists to become part of their own problem solving but in persuading management to create and maintain the conditions for it to take place. In a fast-changing world an open group problem solving climate of this kind will become more necessary. The principal aims of in-plant action learning are shown in Figure 9.9.

The in-plant action learning approach has been applied with equal success in another international electronics company and a medium-sized manufacturer of doors and related joinery.

Focuses within one company.

Involves the majority of people in the organisation.

Uses common problems worked on by groups.

Changes reference points of participants

      Client   – Senior management
      Adviser – Middle management
      Fellows – First line managers and workers

Produces effective solutions owned by all.

Overcomes re-entry and expectation problems.

Very cost-effective.

Figure 9.9   In-plant action learning: the principal aims

3   DYNAMIC INTERFIRM COMPARISONS

This case study describes a productivity improvement programme involving 24 companies within a single industry (horticulture). It combines productivity audits, an interchange of performance data and action learning – what we have called dynamic interfirm comparisons.

Apart from the objective of productivity increases within one industry the aim was also to develop a multiplier effect, that is to assist a number of companies at the same time. The multiplier concept should be of particular interest to most countries who want to help as many as possible of their numerous small to medium-sized enterprises to survive and grow.

Some reference has previously been made to the development of the 'PIP' concept, but it is briefly repeated here to put the case study into context. In 1978 eight small to medium manufacturing companies were the first to be involved in this more dynamic approach to interfirm comparisons, dynamic in the sense that the comparative figures would be used to bring about improvements in performance, rather than being of passing interest. This was followed by 12 retailers and then a further 12 manufacturers in two different regions of the UK.

By the end of 1981 32 manufacturers and retailers had been involved and considerable experience gained. Throughout this period many of the managers taking part had expressed the view that if more similar companies could participate then the scheme would be of even greater value. As the result of the great interest shown by two garden centre owners present at a small business workshop it was decided to approach the trade association for their industry. Discussions with the Horticultural Trades Association (HTA) were productive but the director of HTA thought that, although there was a need for a service of this kind, initially the scheme would have to be free to member companies. This was considered necessary because of the innovative nature of the project and because many member companies were very small businesses.

In 1982 the Training Division of the Manpower Services Commission (MSC) in the UK gave financial support to conduct a pilot project. The project objectives are listed below:

1   To gain experience on how to measure and improve productivity in one industry.
2   To involve 10 retailing companies (it was decided to conduct the first project for retailers and leave the growers for a possible later project) in a combined programme of a

productivity audit on a monthly basis for six months with
monthly action learning meetings.
3   To eventually enable HTA to include the scheme as a part of
their normal service to member companies. The design and
conduct of the first project was undertaken by Action Learning Associates (ALA).

The response to the invitations sent out by HTA was
greater than expected, with 31 expressing a strong interest.
Some companies also suggested that a 12-month audit should
be considered so as to obtain a more representative picture
of company performance. This was a valid proposal bearing
in mind the pronounced seasonal nature of the horticultural
trade.

It seemed a pity to lose the chance of productivity data for
31 instead of 10 companies and covering double the period
anticipated. The MSC in the light of this development gave
further support to the following modified programme:

1   Conduct the original audit plus monthly meetings for
10 companies.
2   Involve the additional 21 companies in a postal audit. The
experience with this aspect provided unexpected benefits as
described later on.
3   Continue the productivity audits for 12 months for all 31
companies.

The additional funding also made it possible to purchase an
Osborne portable Micro Computer and a printer. This was to
improve data processing; the portability would enable demonstra-
tions of the computer processing aspect at meetings.

PROJECT STAGES

The programme commenced in October 1983 and proceeded
through the following stages:

1   Guidance manual: guidance notes were prepared to explain
the complete programme for all 31 companies. These instructions were particularly important for those taking part
on a postal audit basis. The contents of this kind of manual
have been presented in an earlier chapter. The contents were
principally directed to:

    – definitions of information on Basic Information Sheet
      (BIS)
    – the procedure for completing the BIS
    – explanations of the monthly return
    – how to understand the figures.

2 Project initiation: the launch of the project took two forms.
The 10 companies who were selected to take part in the audit
and meetings attended a one-day introductory workshop.
The initiation of the postal companies was carried out with
explanatory letters and the guidance notes.

3 Conduct audit: this stage has been described in some detail
in Chapter 5 but it involved the following steps:

---

1 Return on capital employed $= \dfrac{\text{Net profit}}{\text{Capital employed}}$

2 Total earnings productivity $= \dfrac{\text{Total earnings}}{\text{Total cost}}$

3 Sales per employee $= \dfrac{\text{Total sales} - \text{VAT}}{\text{Total employees}}$

4 Sales per hour $= \dfrac{\text{Total sales} - \text{VAT}}{\text{Total hours worked}}$

5 Profit per employee $= \dfrac{\text{Net profit}}{\text{Total employees}}$

6 Profit per hour $= \dfrac{\text{Net profit}}{\text{Total hours worked}}$

7 Sales per square foot $= \dfrac{\text{Total sales less VAT}}{\text{Selling Area}}$

8 Wages to sales as a % $= \dfrac{\text{Total wages and salaries}}{\text{Total sales less VAT}} \times 100$

9 Rate of stock turn $= \dfrac{\text{Total sales less VAT}}{\text{Average stock at sales value}}$

**Figure 9.10 The measurements used in the garden centre
productivity improvement project**

a) Each company completes a Basic Information Sheet (BIS) and forwards it to the central processing base (ALA).

b) Process BISs and produce productivity ratios for each company and comparisons between them. The nine ratios used are summarised in Figure 9.10.

c) Each company receives three returns
    – their own individual comparison
    – sorted data for all companies
    – actual monthly sales, selling area, costs and total earnings productivity.

Actual examples of these returns are shown in Figures 9.11 and 9.12 and an example of the last one was included in Chapter 6. So as to give confidentiality of figures each company was given a code number.

4 Review meetings: these took place about every month during the twelve months of the programme. The principal aims of the meetings were:
    – clarifying queries on information required
    – discussions on the implications of the measurements, ie getting underneath the figures
    – identifying productivity priorities
    – discussions on methods for involving staff in improving productivity.
    – development of problem solving skills
    – creating an opportunity to exchange ideas on various ways for improving the performance of garden centres, ie to inject fresh thinking into the participants.
    – above all else to use the figures to actually improve productivity

```
************************************************************************

           INDIVIDUAL COMPARISON FOR COMPANY CODE NO.   17

                FOR PERIOD     9.1983  TO   10.1983

************************************************************************


     INDEX              THIS MONTH      LAST MONTH    % CHANGE
                          10.1983         9.1983

RETURN ON CAPITAL           1.21           1.84        -33.95
TOTAL EARNINGS              1.18           1.27         -6.98
SALES PER EMPLOYEE       1813.18        1861.25         -2.58
SALES PER HOUR             11.10          10.14          9.47
PROFIT PER EMPLOYEE       100.00         160.88        -37.84
PROFIT PER HOUR             0.61           0.88        -30.15
SALES PER SQ. FT.          0.66           0.64          3.51
TOTAL WAGES TO SALES       17.51          18.74         -6.61
RATE OF STOCK TURN          0.39           0.34         15.23
```

Figure 9.11   HTA productivity project: example computer printout of an individual company

```
* * * * * * * * * * * * * * * * * * * * * * * * * * * * * * * * * * * * * * * * * * * * * * * * * * * * * * * * * *
```

SORTED DATA FOR ALL COMPANIES FOR MONTH/YEAR   10/1983

```
* * * * * * * * * * * * * * * * * * * * * * * * * * * * * * * * * * * * * * * * * * * * * * * * * * * * * * * * * *
```

POSITION	RETURN ON CAPITAL		TOTAL EARNINGS		SALES PER EMPLOYEE		SALES PER PER HOUR		PROFIT PER EMPLOYEE		PROFIT PER PER HOUR		SALES PER PER SQ.FT.		WAGES TO SALES		RATE OF STOCK TURN	
1	-2.861	13	0.542	13	1055.81	13	5.279	13	-450.567	13	-2.455	6	0.124	20	6.152	7	0.110	5
2	-2.837	6	0.729	6	1319.17	21	8.245	21	-425.5	6	-2.253	13	0.134	13	12.696	6	0.112	13
3	-2.145	15	0.870	5	1344.25	5	8.402	5	-201.75	2	-0.870	8	0.530	2	12.778	22	0.206	2
4	-1.729	2	0.895	8	1378.85	20	8.874	20	-150.714	8	-0.863	2	0.538	5	13.320	8	0.208	21
5	-1.577	5	0.906	2	1813.18	17	9.022	2	-137.125	5	-0.857	5	0.628	4	13.778	11	0.227	12
6	-0.879	8	0.973	15	2106.59	10	11.096	17	-88.186	15	-0.557	15	0.663	17	15.122	4	0.232	4
7	-0.435	12	0.976	12	2108.92	2	12.949	10	-62.791	12	-0.356	12	0.670	12	15.696	9	0.284	20
8	0.628	7	1.153	10	2376.74	3	14.270	4	58.136	10	0.357	10	0.804	3	17.339	2	0.293	10
9	0.997	4	1.175	7	2395	4	15.845	3	86.500	4	0.515	4	1.044	11	17.506	17	0.376	3
10	1.214	17	1.183	17	2644.12	15	16.488	8	100.000	17	0.612	17	1.309	15	18.127	12	0.393	17
11	1.482	10	1.231	4	2857.14	8	16.698	15	162.211	3	1.081	3	1.389	21	18.512	3	0.447	11
12	1.641	3	1.307	3	2987.5	6	17.239	6	196.863	7	1.136	7	1.818	8	19.581	10	0.479	9
13	3.987	9	1.442	9	2998.62	9	18.635	9	289.615	20	1.810	9	1.992	6	20.022	15	0.498	6
14	5.557	11	1.531	11	3310	12	18.777	12	291.177	9	1.864	20	2.317	10	20.642	20	0.500	8
15	8.367	20	1.580	20	3477.69	22	20.365	22	353.833	21	2.211	21	3.014	22	24.244	13	0.790	7
16	10.615	21	1.610	21	4294.53	11	29.889	11	416.316	11	2.897	11	4.078	9	24.344	5	0.876	22
17	13.836	22	2.152	22	7745.1	7	44.683	7	741.846	22	4.344	22	8.977	7	24.877	21	1.200	15
AVERAGE	2.1095		1.19137		2718.42		16.2791		69.4038		.506913		1.76638		17.3374		.425374	

Note: * = company code numbers

Figure 9.12   HTA productivity project: sample computer printout of interfirm comparisons

5   A meeting to review the whole programme at the end of the 12 months.

PROFILE OF COMPANIES

For the purposes of the project a garden centre was defined as a horticultural selling outlet, with perhaps a growing facility, which included a car park for customer use. It is the parking facility which distinguishes garden centres from 'High Street' shops. Other characteristics were as follows:

1 Number of employees: 1.5 to 43, average number 11.6. The fractions arise from adjusting part-timers to a full-time basis.
2 Sales: average monthly sales ranged from a low of £1,583 to £113,697, with a grand average of £31,137.
3 Selling area (precisely defined and agreed as those parts of garden centres where customers were free to go): varied from a low of 2,200 square feet to 86,871, with an average of 24,635 (or 204, 8,070 and 2,288 square metres respectively).
4 Geographic location: the companies were predominantly in the South East region of the UK (there is a heavy concentration of horticultural businesses in this area), with about one-third from the Midlands to Northern regions.
5 Type of business: two indicators were employed.
   a) Product mix between green goods (ie plants) and hard goods (eg garden furniture, tools etc). The averages for all companies were 39 per cent green goods and 61 per cent hard goods.
   b) Business mix between pure retailing and a mixture of retailing and growing. The average breakdown was 43 per cent pure retailing and 57 per cent retailing and growing.

Apart from the geographical bias to the South, the companies taking part were considered a representative cross-section of the industry.

PRODUCTIVITY RESULTS

As expected, there were productivity variations between the companies taking part, due to two interrelated factors.

1 Some of the garden centres had better positions than others, eg easier access from the main road, better car parks and sites in the more prosperous catchment area of the South East, which supports higher prices.
2 The resources of some businesses were better managed.

The main thrust of the project was to convince all companies, even those enjoying the better positions, of the second point. While poor site position was considered to be partially out of their control and was a longer-term problem, it was accepted that it should be given attention. So as to obtain further insights into this, a survey was conducted during the project to seek views on the following factors:

1   Ease of access from road;
2   Proximity to main roads;
3   Car parking facilities;
4   Number and proximity of competitors;
5   Quantity, proximity and type of customers in catchment
    areas.

In overall terms 33 per cent thought their sites were good and 53
per cent gave a moderate assessment, with 13 per cent considering
their sites were poor. Though a subjective assessment, it suggests
that the general quality of sites needed improvement. Factors 4
and 5 were interesting because a number of the companies had
very scant information about both competitors and customers.

A detailed productivity analysis of the 10 companies (those
taking part in the audit and meetings) was made for the 12-month
period October 1982 to September 1983 for the review of the
project in December 1983.

The following six measurements from the nine used were
chosen:

Total earnings productivity   (2)
Sales per employee   (3)
Profit per employee   (5)
Sales per square foot   (7)
Wages to sales   (8)
Rate of stock turn   (9)

The figures in brackets show the position in which they appeared
in the monthly returns. These six indicators were chosen for two
reasons: firstly, they were agreed to be the key measurements in
assessing garden centre retailing performance, and secondly, to
simplify the presentation at the review meeting; the information
overload problem requires constant attention.

Each of the six measurements was analysed for each company as
follows:

1   The average for each measurement for the 12-month period;
2   The lowest and highest figure recorded. This reveals the
    dramatic seasonal effects;
3   The grand averages for items 1 and 2 above.
4   Each company has been ranked against their performance
    for all of the six indicators, their average rank and the
    number of times for each measurement they are below the
    grand average for the measurement.

The results of this analysis are shown in Figure 9.13. Some significant aspects of the analysis are highlighted below:

1 The range between the grand average highest and lowest is about 4 to 1. To put it another way, business results are four times better in the spring/summer than the winter months. It was also revealed that approximately 75 per cent of garden centre sales take place in four months of the year (ie April, May, June and September).

2 There was considerable variation in the performance of individual companies. The averages for each measurement and the range for each average (ie ratio of the highest to lowest average) revealed the following results.

Measurement	Range
Total earnings	2.2 to 1
Sales per employee	2.7 to 1
Profit per employee	8.5 to 1
Sales per square foot	6.2 to 1
Wages to sales	2.2 to 1
Rate of stock turn	3.5 to 1

These variations are due to a mixture of the two previous points, ie quality of sites and effectiveness of management, though the differences in sales per square foot were also influenced by the subjective nature of the original decision to acquire the site. There was little evidence that a given site was sought to suit predetermined market requirements.

3 All companies are below the averages in varying degrees. The best code numbers, 1 and 9, are only below average on one measurement, with six companies out of the ten being under average on three or more of the six measurements.

This all suggested plenty of scope for improvement using actual current industry standards, ie assessments made against the best and lowest performers as they were operating then, in other words, internal standards. But how much better could they be? For example, Marks and Spencer, an acknowledged top achiever in retailing, were obtaining an annual rate of stock turn of 18 and sales per employee of £100,000 compared to the highest for the garden centres of 7.2 and £57,120. Marks and Spencer are in a different kind of retailing to horticulturists but still provide some idea of the standards that could be reached.

Notes: Av = average, L = low, H = high, 1 = rank order, * = below average
G/Av = grand averages

Code No.	Total earns.			SPE £'000			PPE £'000			SD' £			W÷S %			ROST			Assesst.	
	Av	L	H	Av	L	H	Av	L	H	Av	L	H	Av	L	H	Av	L	H	Av Rank	No below * Av:
1	2.36 [1]	1.4	4.4	3.4 [3]	0.64	6.5	0.85 [1]	0.23	1.9	1.5 [3]	0.8	2.42	12.4 [1]	6.7	17.8	0.27 *[8]	0.12	0.4	2.8 [1]	1 *
2	1.46 [4]	0.5	2.9	2.66 *[6]	0.91	4.95	0.25 *[3]	(0.35)	1.1	0.92 *[6]	0.12	1.87	18.5 [4]	6.9	32.6	0.29 *[7]	0.12	0.62	5 [5]	4 *
3	1.05 *[9]	0.5	2.6	2.63 *[7]	1.08	4.42	0.04 *[8]	(0.44)	0.83	1.11 *[4]	0.46	2.1	23.2 *[9]	7.07	34.1	0.6 [1]	0.22	0.83	6.3 [7]	5 *
4	1.51 [2]	0.5	3.3	3.14 [4]	1.23	5.79	0.22 *[5]	(0.43)	0.17	0.74 *[8]	0.21	1.79	16.3 [5]	5.8	33.3	0.34 [5]	0.12	0.6	4.3 [4]	2 *
5	1.09 *[8]	0.2	2.2	1.69 *[10]	0.81	3.12	0 *[9]	(0.65)	0.48	0.82 *[7]	0.36	1.56	21.5 *[8]	9.1	26.3	0.17 *[10]	0.06	0.31	8.6 [10]	6 *
9	1.4 [5]	0.7	2.4	2.91 [5]	1.81	4.76	0.24 *[4]	(0.30)	0.97	4.06 [1]	1.7	7.99	17.1 [4]	9.7	29.8	0.46 [2]	0.19	0.63	3.5 [2 =]	1 *
10	1.22 *[7]	0.7	2.0	2.38 *[8]	1.48	4.26	0.10 *[7]	(0.23)	0.68	2.54 [2]	1.29	4.7	19.06 [6]	10.3	27.4	0.36 [3]	0.18	0.61	5.5 [6]	3 *
11	1.33 *[6]	0.6	2.3	4.76 [2]	2.62	8.99	0.39 [2]	(0.49)	1.68	1.09 *[5]	0.47	2.3	16.36 [3]	6.9	23.6	0.35 [4]	0.19	0.67	3.5 [2 =]	2 *
12	1.04 *[10]	0.4	2.1	3.54 [2]	1.66	6.6	(0.08) *[10]	(0.76)	0.74	0.69 *[9]	0.31	1.37	20.0 *[7]	7.2	33.4	0.26 *[9]	0.10	0.51	7.8 [9]	5 *
17	1.5 [3]	0.4	2.9	1.75 *[9]	0.46	3.3	0.19 *[6]	(0.34)	0.79	0.65 *[10]	0.16	1.56	27.7 *[10]	9.7	59.8	0.3 [6]	0.08	0.62	7.3 [8]	4 *
G/Av	1.4	0.6	2.7	2.9	1.3	5.3	0.3	(0.37)	0.93	1.4	0.6	2.8	19.2	7.9	31.8	0.3	0.13	0.6		

Figure 9.13   HTA productivity figures 12 months
(October 1982 to September 1983) analysis.

In the light of the above the companies who participated were made aware of three aspects of their performance:

1 How could those who were below average increase their productivity to reach the 'average' standards internal to their industry?
2 Within the constraints of each company (eg siting, catchment area etc) what increases in performance were possible? (Standards set by each company consistent with their own particular circumstances.)
3 They should help in the development of agreed standards for the industry. These should be influenced by points 1 and 2 above and external standards, eg Marks and Spencer.

GENERAL RESULTS

The three project objectives were satisfied.

1 Practical experience has been obtained in the problems of measuring and improving productivity in a single industry.
2 Twenty-four of the 31 companies maintained an active involvement in the project for the 12 months planned. The audit forms were returned regularly and attendance by the 10 companies in meetings was about 95 per cent. The multiplier effect of assisting a number of companies did work. An unexpected benefit was the postal audit aspect. Through a combination of personal comments on audit returns, letters and telephone calls it was possible to assist companies at a distance. The MSC have given further support to a 'self help' manual to assist smaller enterprises to improve their own productivity. The aim is to extend the postal audit concept through trade and productivity associations.
3 The trade association (HTA) have adopted the programme as a part of their service to members.

The specific results achieved which formed part of this experiment in dynamic interfirm comparisons are listed below:

1 The majority of the companies taking part continued with the audit, with another 30 also joining.

2   A similar programme is being introduced to the growing side of the industry. The ultimate aim is to link the audits for retailers and growers. Their productivities are clearly interdependent; an efficient growing operation means more competitive retailing and vice versa.

3   The mixture of simple audit procedures, the careful preparatory groundwork of guidance manuals and an introductory meeting, plus the personal aspects of meetings, telephone contacts etc, all helped to create an action-oriented climate.

4   Many companies improved their productivity in a number of different ways. Interviews reported in the *Observer* (2) (a UK Sunday newspaper) show one owner improved his rate of stock turn and another redesigned his house plant department. For one company the results were even more dramatic. It was a partnership of two and the audit revealed the business could not support two, so one sold his interest to his partner.

An independent survey of the project by Clutterbuck (3) provided valuable feedback from participants such as: 'I am now setting targets for departmental managers by way of monthly budgets.' 'The meetings have caused me to question my location and marketing techniques.' 'I am getting staff to complete hourly activity sheets to establish patterns of customer flow and staff availability.' See Figure 9.14 for the activity sampling form used for this purpose. Figure 9.15 shows the results of analysing these data for one day. It illustrates that staff availability was lowest when there were most customers. The owner of this business has now introduced a development plan for his entire staff of six to improve this situation.

Other reactions were: 'We have decided to move to weekly buying rather than big bulk orders at the beginning of the season.' 'The monthly figures gave us a new insight into our business never previously provided by accountants or bank managers.' 'I have increased gross profit on unbranded goods by 5 to 10 per cent.' 'It confirmed we were in the wrong location. Unless we move we have no hope of improvement.'

Those who took part in the postal audit were unanimous that the information and telephone contact had been useful. As one owner said, 'It removes the sense of loneliness.' The other benefits included tighter stock control, and an exchange of new ideas, with some managers visiting each other's garden centres. Some of the companies made a detailed study of the rate of stock turn (ROST) of their house plant product group. The aim was to discover for

SALES ACTIVITY STUDY

Observer **M DAVIS**   Time **9·05**

Date **16·5·198—** Day **MONDAY**   Weather: wet   dry ✓ sunny ✓

Area	Activity	Customer	Staff with customer	Staff ancillary work				
				P/s	Cl'g	Wg	Till	Cp
Car park	Arriving	₴₴₴						I
	Looking/selectg.							
	Carrying/loadg.		I					
	Sales talk							
Shop	Entering/walking	I						
	Looking/selectg.	I						
	Carrying goods							
	Sales talk	I	(					
	Paying	I					I	
	Queueing	I II						
Outdoor	Walking thru'	(						
	Looking/selectg.	II						
	Carrying goods	I						
	Sales talk	I	I				I	
	Paying	I						
	Queueing	II						
	Totals	20	3				2	I

Remarks

P/s   = pricing/stockg.
Cl'g   = cleaning
Wg   = watering
Till   = Till duty
Cp   = Car Park duty

Figure 9.14   Activity sample

themselves that ROST varies about overall averages for the company. Figure 9.16 is an example for the month of February 1983 for company code number 1. It can be seen that house plants turned over 22.5 times more than the overall company ROST. Within the divisions of house plants ROST also varies from 6.9 to 1.04 or 6.6 to 1. This is a good illustration that overall ROST is only the beginning. The individual items will vary as shown here.

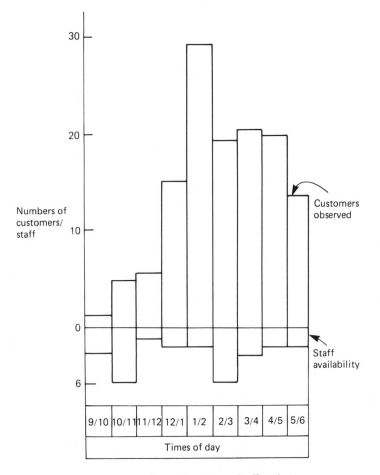

HTA productivity audit: customer/staff study

Figure 9.15   Customer/staff study Monday 25 May 1983 – observations every hour

The task, as this company discovered, is to increase the turnover of the slow movers.

LESSONS

A project of this scope was bound to present a number of lessons for those involved. These are especially the project managers

(Action Learning Associates), the trade association (Horticultural Trades Association), the supporting agency (Manpower Services Commission) and in a more abstract sense the task of productivity improvement. The lessons for each one of these are now examined.

Company code no. 1   Date   February 1983

Product group (by price band) £	Stock		Sales		Rate* of stock turn ROST
	No of items	Value £	No of items	Value £	
0–99p	88	42.80	150	122.25	2.9
1.0–1.99	140	215.70	441	648.60	3.01
2.0–2.99	54	125.05	226	498.40	3.9
3.0–3.99	58	198.98	89	271.02	1.37
4.0–4.99	34	152.21	37	158.10	1.04
5.0–7.50	7	45.40	19	107.85	2.4
7.51–9.99	2	15.90	13	104.10	6.9
10.0–24.99	14	204.20	20	291.20	1.4
> 25.0	1	27.50	2	55.10	2.04
Totals	398	1027.74	997	2256.62	
Average ROST					2.7
Range highest to lowest	6.9 ÷ 1.04				6.6 to 1
Overall company ROST					0.12
Ratio houseplants to company ROST	2.7 ÷ 0.12				22.5 to 1

Figure 9.16   House plant ROST study

Project managers (ALA)

An important lesson for us in the project management role was how to achieve a balance between the self-learning climate of action learning and the directive consultancy advice expected by company owners. On the one hand it was considered that changes for the better had to be self imposed if real commitment was to be gained; people have to decide for themselves what they believe their problems to be and what they are capable of doing about them. On the other hand, the project had by implication directed which measurement would be used, but only as a device for those concerned to recognise they could be better.

Meaningful productivity improvement is really a process of technical and human change. Therefore those who initiate programmes of change must recognise at the outset the problem of getting the right balance between giving advice and enabling people to learn for themselves. The dilemma revolves around the 'reinventing the wheel' debate. For example, during the project some managers decided they wished to know more about the flow of customers during the day and the availability of staff to deal with them. They might have been able to develop their own method for getting the information but we decided to give guidance on activity sampling. As a general rule advice will be accepted and used if it meets a perceived need. But the overriding aim must be to get people to claim ownership of their problems and methods for solving them.

Throughout the review meetings there was a feeling of 'tell us what to do'. There were times when we misjudged their need for direct guidance. Some appreciated that the project adviser allowed discussion to flow and he taught us how to look for weak areas in our businesses. Equally, some managers felt the need for more advice. With a group of ten, each with differing problems, personal guidance was not easy. The usual problems of group size were evident, especially the domination of discussion by 3/4 extroverts with the reserved ones making little contribution. It was for this reason that the original intention was to conduct meetings in groups of five, but as most had travelled some distance they preferred a full day's meeting for all 10 companies. For future programmes the lessons are fivefold:

1   Keep group size to around six to allow more personal attention and to facilitate group interaction.
2   Spend more time at the introductory meetings explaining the action learning method and the periodic need for expert advice. Ideally, a group adviser skilled in both aspects is preferred. If this is not possible the ongoing adviser would be concerned with the group processes of problem solving, listening, questioning and challenging established beliefs. Experts would then be brought in as the need arises. These

roles have been described in some depth in Chapter 8.

3   The project confirmed the prior view that many companies, especially the smaller ones, do not have basic productivity information. As many participants said at the monthly meetings, 'Getting detailed monthly stock figures is a project in itself.' While estimating methods were established for overall company stock figures, information, for specific products, of the kind obtained for the house plant survey (Figure 9.16) was receiving attention towards the end of the project.

4   More work is necessary to integrate existing financial information with productivity measurement. A number of the managers taking part stated that the audit told them more about the operating aspects of their businesses than their accountants and banks. Both are clearly important, but they should complement each other.

5   HTA and in turn their member companies will require advice for 1 or 2 years to

a)   establish the scheme as a normal part of their service.
b)   help with the figure processing problems caused by more companies joining the scheme.
c)   as 12 months' figures become available, to assist in the annual monitoring of performance with allowance being made for price changes.
d)   assist in the determination of published industry standards.

The trade association (HTA)

The total project concept is of significance to any trade association and equally productivity associations. Both types of body have access to many companies and therefore the multiplier effect should be of interest to them. In this way they could act as a powerful lever for improving the productivity of large numbers of enterprises. The main challenges to them for introducing this dynamic approach to comparing productivity are listed below:

1   Initially it will require an investment in time and money, though with the HTA scheme companies were eventually prepared to pay for the service. We have had discussions with some overseas productivity centres and they agreed that they did have to be prepared to invest in proactive ventures of this kind. The problem is that either external agencies (eg government or industry) have to give support or they have to do it out of their own income.

2 Companies have to be convinced of the reliability and comparability of the measurements used.
3 Computer facilities, including software, are necessary for processing the data.
4 Group advising skills are necessary.

HTA met the first two challenges and are hoping the group advising role might be provided from within member companies, but it seems some kind of training/development task will be necessary.

Supporting agencies (MSC)

Creating a climate for continuing productivity improvement seems to require one of two policies: either industry should be self supporting and let the lame ducks die, or government should intervene to promote industrial regeneration, at its extreme a social programme to provide employment.

While there has been an emphasis of the first policy in countries like the USA and the UK, in practice it is not quite as clear-cut as this. Clearly indiscriminate handouts are wasteful of resources. However, innovations of the kind described here do require funding to get them proven. It would have taken much longer, if it had occurred at all, without the encouragement and support provided by the MSC.

But even when funding is given, whether by government agencies or productivity associations, there is still the dilemma of deciding when the development has concluded and the programme has become so natural a part of the organisation that self sufficiency is possible. How to sustain the change process once it has started is a highly significant problem for helping agencies like the MSC or trade associations or the individual organisations. For the HTA project we believe the second stage was reached.

Productivity improvement

Helping companies to get better information is an important part of improving productivity. Helping a number of companies at the same time – the multiplier – is a worthwhile aim but it also raises the question 'who does it?' But a number of other pertinent questions are raised:

1 Should productivity standards for industries be based on the current performance of companies in the industry? Or should they be developed from scratch on what they are capable of? The former is a current efficiency approach with

the latter what is possible or effectiveness policy. The HTA project used current efficiency but in two years could be moving to the second.

2 The action learning meetings bring figures to life, but they depend on experienced advisers with preferably process skills and expert knowledge which is relevant to the organisations concerned. But if they do not exist how will they be trained?

CONNECTIVE SUMMARY

The three case studies examined provide contrasting approaches to productivity improvement and yet they are also complementary. The second case study, involving large numbers of people in the same company, was shown to have a powerful influence on gaining commitment to change. Although the first and third examples were directed to involving numbers of different companies, the 'in-plant' concept is still recognised as the tool for improving garden centres. Involving staff in activity sampling of customer flow is one example of this.

For the medium to large organisation, all our experience suggests that a critical mass of people at all levels need to be involved if ownership of the productivity improvement problem is to be obtained. This is the principal aim of the in-plant programme. The philosophy is a 'bottom up' approach, because the main thrust of problem identification and solutions comes from grass roots operating management, whereas the HTA project was a 'top down' policy, due to the active involvement of the owners of the garden centres. In our opinion the aim should be a blend of both. Each programme is stronger on some factors than others. In general, for bringing about change in medium to large organisations, some form of in-plant action learning should be considered. But for the improvement in performance of numbers of small to medium-sized enterprises, the dynamic interfirm comparison scheme does have possibilities. Both methods need to take account of the process skills of problem solving and the expert technical inputs of knowledge. No matter how well people work together, they are unlikely to improve their situation if they do not know how to analyse their underlying organisational and technological weaknesses. These technical inputs could vary from simply giving guidance on doing an activity sampling, to an extensive analysis of the organisation. Action learning creates a climate where people firstly recognise the need to change and secondly admit their ignorance. The action learning method also helps to avoid relying on outdated knowledge and experience 'P' and to assist those concerned to learn to ask the totally new question 'Q'. In varying ways these case studies recognised these requirements. A comparison of the principal factors for both approaches is shown in Figure 9.17.

No	Factor	In-plant programmes	Interfirm comparisons
1	Involves a critical mass of people	Initial aim of programme	May do eventually
2	A 'Bottom Up' approach ie involves the grass roots	Initial aim of programme	May do eventually
3	A 'Top Down' approach ie starts with top managers	Will involve top management	HTA programme did start with owners
4	Includes a multiplier effect	Not part of programme	A principal aim of the approach
5	Crossfertilisation of new ideas and posing new questions 'Q'	Will occur but generally within the company	Highly probable
6	External agency to initiate and conduct the programme	Will be so but company concerned will pay for programme	Requires funding to get programme started
7	Problem identification	Determined by participants in programme	Influenced by productivity audits

Figure 9.17   In-plant programmes and interfirm comparisons compared

This chapter concludes Part III on methods for improving productivity. In the final chapter, the question posed at the beginning 'Where should you be?' is examined. For purposes of short-term survival, organisations will have to make the best use they can of existing resources and the situation in which they find themselves. But their longer-term continuance will mean making radical alterations to all aspects of the organisation. The next chapter aims to create awareness of the nature of these changes with some suggestions for adapting to them.

Before you proceed further we suggest you consider the question stated earlier, 'How to sustain the change process once it has started?' In a fast changing world where productivity in its totality will need constant attention it seems to us an important question.

REFERENCES

1 Revans, R. W., *Project 'Management Efficiency', The origins and growth of action learning*, Chartwell Bratt, 1982
2 Clutterbuck, David, 'Show me yours . . .' *Observer*, 23 October 1983
3 Clutterbuck, David, 'How does your garden centre grow?', *Management Today*, July 1984

Part IV
New Perspectives

10 What should you be doing?

In the previous chapter the emphasis was on making the best use of existing resources alongside operating within the constraints of the present environment. This was illustrated in Figure 1.5 (page 23) with the two questions 'Where are you now?' and 'How much better could you be?' The measurement systems described have been concerned with providing quantitative and qualitative answers to these questions. While these issues are important they are to do with the short term. For longer-term survival every organisation will need to adjust to the consequences of rapid change. Revans, (1) as stated in Chapter 1, has expressed this adaptation process in two simple equations:

1 $L \uparrow C$ = Failure
2 $L \leqslant C$ = Success

where L = learning or adaptation and C = rate of change.

To aspire to equation 2 and therefore to deal effectively with the third question in Figure 1.5, 'What should you be doing?', will mean becoming more aware of the nature of the changes taking place, and knowing how to adapt, both technologically and in human terms. An inability to recognise the changes taking place or inappropriate skills in introducing change can have the kind of dramatic effects so prevalent in many parts of the world. The near disappearance of UK motor cycle manufacturing and shipbuilding and the decline of US 'smokestack' industries are good examples. The future is here today if only we can see it, but equally, we create our own futures if we continue to behave in the same way.

This chapter will explore what is known about the future and those aspects of it which are here now as well as its particular significance to productivity. But firstly, what are the sources for increasing our awareness of the future?

SOURCES OF AWARENESS

It can be argued that organisations which are aware of their internal and external functions are more likely to survive, ie their learning is at least equal to the rate of change. This means not only that they have good intelligence systems but also that learning takes place; the information sensed leads to personal and organisational change. Awareness of changes is likely to spring from two overlapping sources:

1   *Current activities:* During the day-to-day management of the organisation, verbal and written information will give clues to significant changes. These might include the introduction of substitute materials, and shifts in the product mix with the consequent efforts on processes. The signs are there, but they may go unnoticed.
2   *Not readily available:* There is a rich store of information and the new reference points on the changes affecting organisations which may necessitate going outside our usual sphere of operations. For example:

   –   Newspapers, especially if studied over a period of time, provide valuable pointers to likely economic, political, social and technological change. John Naisbitt (2) has developed a method for analysing, on a daily basis, the content of American newspapers. The 10 'megatrends' resulting from this analysis are shown in Figure 10.1. But apart from the messages in these trends it is the technique of analysis which is just as important for any organisation interested in the change process. The method called content analysis involves the monitoring of significant news items and how long they continue to claim newsspace, but also watching for holes in the news, that is, items that disappear.

- Radio/television, particularly live broadcasts, also give clues of likely swings in attitudes and behaviour.
- Books/articles provide valuable pointers to the future as it is now happening. The problem is knowing which material to read. For many busy managers the first difficulty seems to be finding the time to read. But if keeping abreast of change means reading then somehow the time must be found. Once the process has started one book generally leads on to others.

However, whether our awareness is aroused within or from without the most important requirements for being sensitive to a changing world are an open mind and a willingness to act on what we see.

What follows is an analysis of the significant changes which will affect productivity and the 'What should you be doing?' question. It is based on three sources of information:

1 The experience of conducting productivity improvement programmes;
2 Discussions with various overseas productivity centres;
3 Newspapers, articles and books.

The analysis considers energy/materials, wealth, viability and economic performance, challenges for industry, new style measurements, white collar productivity, computer conferencing, reward systems and attitudes to productivity.

ENERGY/MATERIALS

The high-volume growth economies of the Western World during this century were based upon abundant supplies of cheap energy and raw materials. With the continuing low-cost supplies of these two basic commodities a continuous cycle of economic growth was possible. Wages could be increased to support higher standards of living and hence the production of even more goods. In these conditions energy-rich capital was introduced to achieve the economies of scale considered necessary to provide an even greater supply of goods. This state of affairs continued until 1973 – the year OPEC quadrupled the price of oil and by 1981 it had increased by a total of six times.

TREND No. 1 Restructuring of Europe and the US from an industrial society to a society based on information and knowledge. Inherent are changes as profound as those encountered when we moved from an agricultural to an industrial society.

TREND No. 2 Demand for personal contacts and expanding human interrelationships is going to skyrocket as people are exposed to high technology – 'High-tech/high-touch', a constant search for balance between technology and human contact.

TREND No. 3 Global economic interdependence of nations – a major trend in which developing countries supply the world's industrial products; developed nations emphasize high-tech and information products.

TREND No. 4 The computer is a liberator rather than a tyrant and slavedriver as many had supposed. Home computers give individuals quick access to information formerly available only to companies. Also, with computers to keep track, companies can – and will – have different contracts with each of their employees.

TREND No. 5 Decentralisation of all our institutions: business, governmental, social and political. For example, the computer is allowing big companies to disperse profit centres; local governments and administrations are given increasing power.

TREND No. 6 Return of old-fashioned self-reliance. We have accelerated the moving away from dependence on institutions – including government, the medical establishment, corporations and the school system.

TREND No. 7 The traditional line-up of political power is undergoing such a profound change you won't recognise it in a few years. Voter interest will centre almost exclusively on local and regional issues. National politics will be secondary.

TREND No. 8 The long-dominant business management pattern is undergoing a revolutionary upheaval. The old 'top-down' corporate system is giving way to the innovative 'bottom-up' system where employees have a saw in how their companies are run.

TREND No. 9 The shift from North to South in the US will continue and profoundly change the character of regional business and investment opportunities. But not the entire South will benefit – the trends predict **specific** areas and cities of greatest growth and opportunity.

TREND No. 10 The 1980s is a decade of unprecedented diversity among people, groups, institutions and geography, and an incredible market-segmented, decentralised society. Finding your market niche will be the business trick of the 1980s.

Figure 10.1   The 10 megatrends which will change our lives and businesses.

With acknowledgement to John Naisbitt, *Megatrends,* Macdonald and Warner Books, 1983.

During this period other fundamental changes had been taking place. Oil had overtaken coal as an energy source and consequently there was a dramatic, nearly threefold, increase in its consumption between 1960 and 1980. Because of these dramatic price increases the older industrialised parts of the world like the European countries, the USA and Japan are now using less energy. This reduction in demand could continue when it is remembered that energy inefficiencies still exist in the Western World. However, the developing world will want to use more as they continue to industrialise. This dramatic increase since World War II and perhaps a more modest rise to the turn of the century has meant the tapping of fresh supplies of oil. This has been achieved with such oil finds as the North Sea, Alaska and Point Arguello off the California coast. But while more oil is being discovered and extracted the cost is increasing, eg seagoing oil platforms cost $1 billion dollars to construct. As Odum (3) points out, the idea of net energy costs is becoming significant. It costs energy to get energy. Two American researchers (4) predict that in twenty years drilling for oil may consume more energy than it gleans!

The last twenty years have also been marked by similar rises in the price of raw materials used in industry. This has been so because, as with oil, their extraction costs have increased, partly because they are more difficult to get at and partly due to higher energy costs to extract them. Another factor is that the Third World sources of many raw materials have increased their prices to pay for the dramatic rise in the cost of their oil imports.

There are some who argue that the cost of energy will come down. The available evidence suggests that this is improbable, but even if it does it is very unlikely it will ever again reach the low levels existing prior to 1973, the year of the first OPEC price rise. This means that the balance between energy, capital and labour which formed the basis of pre-1973 mass economies is disappearing. Paul Hawken in his penetrating analysis (5) suggests that we are now moving into what he calls the 'Next economy'. As he states, in these conditions national economies and their enterprises can adopt one of three approaches. Firstly, some nations must cut back so as to share the finite resources of energy with the less well-off. Secondly, through a technological fix involving a combination of nuclear energy, oil shale and solar power we can return to our former period of economic growth. Thirdly, the current energy position provides opportunities to use energy more wisely. It will be interesting to see which policy is adopted.

Whichever view of the energy position is adopted it does have some significant implications for the productivity issue and especially for industry.

1 Productivity measurement will need to be directed to energy
   content in processing and products. Energy-rich capital
   equipment and their resulting goods produced will become
   less and less competitive. The same attention will be
   necessary to material content. Toshiba refrigerators consume only 70 per cent of the electricity of an average
   American make. At the same time the American automobile
   industry, through its policy to reduce material consumption,
   has saved some 250 million tons of iron, steel, aluminium,
   glass, rubber, plastic, copper, zinc and lead in 10 years.
2 Organisations of the next economy, the processes they
   employ, the goods made and services produced will be
   characterised by:

   – a low energy to capital/labour ratio.
   – partially replacing energy by labour and a more in-
     telligent use of energy and materials.
   – a purposeful policy of designing intelligence and in-
     formation into what is produced, how it is produced,
     services provided and the way organisations function.
     This is already taking many forms, for example, less
     maintenance (an American truck that will go one million
     miles before overhaul), products that last longer and
     more predictable and reliable processes controlled by
     microprocessors. But information is also important in the
     service organisation. The Briar Patch (6) network of
     small businesses in California is a good example of honest
     information being an accepted part of the 250 or so
     enterprises in the Network. Their philosophy is right
     livelihood, that is, identifying with the real needs of their
     customers, suppliers and staff in a very open style of
     management, balance sheets and profit statements being
     freely available. Stanford University's Values and Life-
     style project provides support to this philosophy and
     suggests that Briar Patch businesses will predominate by
     1900. As Hawken (5) says, 'Companies that try and fool
     their customers or manipulate their employees will find
     themselves threatened by a (Briar Patch) company that
     does no such thing.

Larger organisations will also have to recognise the role of
information as crucial resource. Perhaps the success of the
Japanese economy comes from their acceptance of this need and a
consequent climate of probing, questioning and a willingness to
unlearn.

This transition from what Hawken (5) describes as a mass economy (mass production and high energy/material content) to an information-based economy is already taking place. It is affecting some industries sooner than others, but the impact on smokestack industry is here for us all to see. Toffler (7) comes to a similar conclusion when he describes the change from 'second wave' economies to 'third wave'. However these changes are affecting individual organisations, two facts are difficult to disclaim: energy and capital are both more expensive than they were at the height of the mass economy, and at the same time labour has become cheaper. This shift in the balance between energy, capital and labour is of profound importance to productivity and how it is measured. The sheer economic and commercial implications of this situation can be approached in two ways. We can react when the problem claims our attention. As with most reactive policies, when we do take action it may be too late. Alternatively, a proactive stance can be adopted by making adjustments before the situation has become imperative. There seems to be little doubt that productivity in the next economy will be concerned with being proactive and using our wisdom to produce more using less of the world's resources.

All organisations, especially those which consume energy and materials, will need to use different ways of measuring their productivity. Notable amongst these measurements are comparisons between the following factors:

Capital	*Now*	*Future*
Energy consumed		
Products		
Raw material content		
Energy consumed		

A summary of the likely effects of these energy/material changes is shown in Figure 10.2. This whole question of the potential influence of energy and raw materials on organisational performance requires serious study. After all, the whole basis of world economics depends upon them and as far as we know they are finite and irreplaceable. Moreover, the move towards a more intelligent use of energy presents opportunities and many challenges, not the least the awesome problems of unemployment. The flow of energy and the productivity of its usage are shown in Figure 10.3. The concept of the energy sink may become increasingly important in measuring the productivity not only of energy but of all resources, physical and human.

Factor	Mass economy Pre-1973 oil rise	Information economy Post-1973
Energy/materials	Cheap and abundant, rising consumption	Expensive, more costly to obtain, consumption rates slowing down
Capital	Replacing labour, rich in energy consumption. Aimed at high volume production	Increased costs due to higher interest costs. Lower energy consumption, more predictable processes, smaller quantity production. Intelligent processing
Products	High volume, short life, mediocre quality, high maintenance, rising consumption	Low volume, longer life, high quality, low maintenance, reduced consumption. Less energy content, more intelligence
Labour	Rising wages and standard of living, short supply	Lowering of wages, reduced material standard of living, increased quality of work life, long on supply
Environment	High volume production led to waste, pollution and low quality of work life	Lower volumes, less consumption and more intelligent use of resources will mean a higher quality of work life
Skills	Highly specialised narrow skills	Broad-based skills, high use of intelligence and creativity

Figure 10.2   Productivity in an information economy

WHAT IS WEALTH?

Productivity improvement is often associated with the related aim of creating wealth. But what is wealth? There is probably just as much confusion over this question as over the earlier, similar one

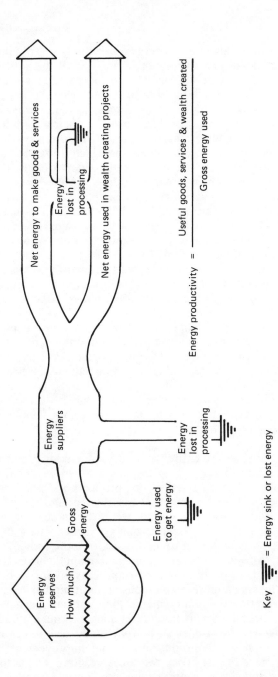

Key  = Energy sink or lost energy

$$\text{Energy productivity} = \frac{\text{Useful goods, services \& wealth created}}{\text{Gross energy used}}$$

Figure 10.3   The productivity of energy usage

Adapted, with acknowledgement, from the *Co-Evolution Quarterly*.
Office of the Governor, Oregon, USA

on productivity. In the analysis of energy productivity was put into the broader context of producing more using less of the world's resources. This may provide some indications of the real nature of wealth. It should not be confused with income, as it often is. Because the wages of individuals, the earnings of organisations or the GNP of a country go up, this does not mean their wealth has also increased. After we have consumed part of this income in day-to-day living expenses any surplus remaining which is invested for safeguarding tomorrow's income can be regarded as wealth. But judging by their large deficits, many countries are in a negative wealth position. The United States, for example, is reckoned to owe \$5.2 trillion against assets (wealth) of \$7 to \$8 trillion – what is now being called the debt bomb. Debts of this magnitude arise partly because of the tremendous increase in the price of oil and the great difficulties of moving away from a mass economy. Countries and individual organisations have been living off past wealth and have consequently built up huge debts, a situation which has led to the prevailing high interest rates with a similar effect on the cost of capital.

Wealth may therefore be defined as the intelligent investment of surpluses from income in future wealth creation, intelligent in the sense that the investment makes a wise use of resources. In other words, through the combined application of human creativity and information age technology, energy and materials are more effectively utilised. The ways in which money has been used to create wealth vary considerably. Revans (1) describes four ways which have all been regarded as wealth creation.

1 Real radical: these are entirely new ways of making products with quite new processes accompanied by more creative ways of organising work. Designing products and processes that use less energy and materials, last longer and fulfil the genuine needs of the community would be radical wealth creation; for instance aeroplanes that go further on a gallon of fuel, last longer and, through the use of more intelligent machines, consume less energy in their manufacture. The Briar Patch previously described represents an innovative way of achieving a more harmonious relationship between a business and the community of customers and suppliers.

2 Real incremental: this involves developing existing methods and products. The use of such work study techniques as activity sampling can produce surprising improvement in obtaining more from existing resources, cf, for example the warehouse and garden centre studies previously described.

3 Spurious incremental: trying to give the appearance of im-

provements that have not really been made. For those
organisations that continue to make products by second
wave methods with all the consequent increased costs, the
reaction is to make a smaller product but package it to
appear the same size as before. Because the charge is close
to the original price, we think we are getting good value.

4 Spurious radical: giving the appearance of growth and
change when no real wealth creation has taken place. The
spate of company mergers and property investment during
the 1960s was a good example of what was then called wealth
creation.

Item 1 will provide the true answer to the title of this chapter
'What should you be doing?' Though some idea of the areas where
answers might be found has been suggested, we shall have to
develop the skills of asking entirely new questions. It is unlikely
that the answers will be in our existing experience and second
wave value systems. There is, however, little doubt that organisational survival will depend upon real radical wealth creation.

Item 2, real incremental wealth creation, provides short-term
answers to organisational development. The previous attention to
the two questions, 'Where are you now?' and 'How much better
could you be?', has been directed to this aspect, but with the
caution that a continued reliance on this policy leads to the conditions described by Hayes and Abernathy, reference (8) in
Chapter 8, 'Managing our way to economic decline'. As they note,
the crisis facing American industry in the '... preference of
(managers) for serving existing markets rather than creating new
ones and by their devotion to short term returns and management
by numbers'.

Items 3 and 4, though they still have credence, are what Revans
calls spurious. But it is also accepted that genuine wealth creation
projects will tax all our creative abilities and the courage to
implement them.

Even if organisations through the efficient management of
resources can produce surpluses (wealth), these can still be
squandered on items 3 and 4-type investments. Some of the surplus should be directed to incremental projects (item 2), with most
of the mental energy and resources going to real radical changes.
Investment in wealth creating projects should be judged against
the following criteria:

1 Will it lead to products, processes and services that consume
less energy/materials and have higher intrinsic value?

2   Will the equipment and people spend more time on pro-
    ductive (and more satisfying) work?
3   Will a useful output be generated, ie is the product or service
    really needed by the community?

Georgescu-Roegen (8) suggests that the true 'output' of the
economic process is the enjoyment of life and to minimise the
physical production of waste.

VIABILITY AND ECONOMIC PERFORMANCE

The economic assessment of organisational performance has received a good deal of attention. We need to know, with as much
notice as possible, if the enterprise continues to be viable. If this
question is put to the managers of most commercial organisations
their answer will probably be expressed in economic terms. It will
most likely be some combination of return on capital profit, or
levels of liquidity. Although these measurements are clearly important, the assessment of the viability of any enterprise based
solely on this single economic variable could be dangerously
misleading.
    Just as organisations do not fail when they cease to make profit,
so too economic soundness on its own is not a good guide to total
viability. If the innovative risk taking climate has been discouraged
and there is a powerful desire to maintain the status quo, the
organisation has become unviable even if it is making profit.
Furthermore, if the people working in the organisation have
become wholly concerned with preserving their job status and an
outdated structure the seeds of decline are there. The organisation
may be being preserved through government funding or slow
changes in market conditions but in terms of fulfilling real needs it
is not satisfying its fundamental role of meeting the changing
requirements of the environment. Stafford Beer in his impressive
study (9) defines a viable system as one that is capable of responding to environmental changes even if they were not foreseen at the
time the enterprise was set up. Beer continues with the simple
truth that we should not delude ourselves that systems behave as
they were set up or how we would like them to. What is important
is what they actually do. If they are not responding to real needs
change the system! But Beer also reminds us that if the system
becomes so complex that we cannot model it then we cannot
manage it!
    Beer's Viable System Model (VSM) developed in detail in *The*

Heart of Enterprise also provides fresh thinking on the effective performance of organisations. The interdependency of all systems is emphasised. While all systems, to be viable, should be capable of an independent existence they nevertheless depend on other systems of which they are a part. Therefore, to be viable the management of the internal system must be balanced with the external environment and other systems to which it relates. In the VSM there are five functions which are fundamental to the management of any system. These are:

1 Policy: can be related to the top management function, whose main task is to enable a continuous adaptation to external changes with internal capabilities. To do this the efficient operation of the four functions below is essential.
2 Intelligence: is the sensing device that scans the environment for significant changes, especially threats and opportunities. The results of this scanning need to be presented to the policy function in a form they can relate to information about the internal state of the system.
3 Control: the effective implementation of policies is the task of the control function. It also includes reliable information on the true state of the organisation.
4 Co-ordination: is a damping function, that is, the job of trying to relate what can easily be unco-ordinated decisions between the various subsystems.
5 Implementation: is the doing part of the system, ie the productive work aspects.

The Viable System Model also includes two other principles which have a significant bearing on productivity measurement and the information systems that support it. The first is self-regulation on the internally set reference standards which organisations and their subsystems use to assess their performance. Secondly, self organisation is the ability of the organisation to change these reference points to better suit the changed external circumstances and hence continued viability.

A simplified diagrammatic version of Beer's model is shown in Figure 10.4. While it may be interpreted in the conventional hierarchical sense it should rather be viewed as an analysis of any viable system. It is noted that every viable system contains and is part of other viable systems. The idea of interdependency is an essential aspect of all viable systems. It can also be seen that the policy functions purpose is to balance intelligence from outside with internal capabilities. Beer aptly describes this interface with

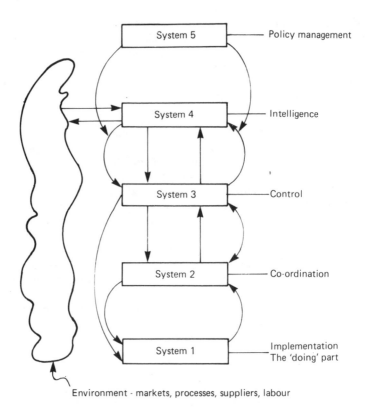

Note: each viable system contains its own viable system down to each
        person in the organisation who is also a viable system

Figure 10.4   Beer's viable system model

the environment as 'the outside and then' and the internal functioning of the organisation as 'the inside and now'.

From the foregoing, viability is more than just one variable of
economic performance. It must include the equally important
factors of innovation, risk taking and how well the five fundamental functions perform in maintaining viability. Figure 10.5 is a
method for evaluating these main variables.

Variable	Evaluation method
Economic	Financial (eg return on capital and profitability). Productivity measurement such as efficiency, effectiveness, comparisons and trends.
Innovation	Number of entirely new ideas (ie real radical) and mistakes made in last 2/3 years.
Learning	Evidence of willingness to unlearn. How many established methods have been abandoned?
Policy	Is the task of balancing the demands of the environment and internal capability and use of intelligence and control information understood? Does the policy function spend too much time at the lower levels of co-ordination and implementation at the expense of the above?
Intelligence	Who does it? How is it used if at all?
Control	Is there adequate information on how the organisation functions, rather than how it is assumed it works?
Co-ordination	Is there evidence of fluctuations in activity and conflicting decisions?
Implementation	Does the system enable the doers to do their jobs or does it impede them?

Figure 10.5 Variables in viability evaluation

CHALLENGES FOR INDUSTRY

STATUS QUO OR CHANGE

The opportunities for wise investment in viable wealth creating projects will occur in all organisations in both the public and private sectors. However, a significant proportion of the potential for getting more for less will come from industry. While manufacturers, especially in the older established countries, are now face to face with the realities of the information economy, they can still adapt. What is required is to be proactive about the entirely new situation they face rather than wait for events to overtake them; the 'plan or be planned for' plea challenge. The penalties for adopting a status quo policy are vividly described in the Hayes and Abernathy article (see Chapter 8), 'the Reindustrialisation of America' (10) and the British *Production Engineer* article 'For America Read Britain'. (11) They all illustrate the results of relying on incremental and spurious wealth creation.

FORCES OF CHANGE

The principal changes that manufacturers will need to adapt to are: a move away from products and processes rich in energy and materials to intelligent systems that consume less; and a redistribution of traditional manufacturing industry to the developing world. This is particularly true of the low added value products which depend upon well-tried production skills.

The analyses made by Hawken (5), Naisbitt (2) and Toffler (7) provide a good insight into these fundamental shifts in the structure of manufacturing industry. Goldhar and Jelinek (12) have also made a detailed study of the factors requiring urgent attention and, of more importance, the need to adjust to them.

NEW-STYLE MANUFACTURING

From all the above studies, the manufacturers who survive will have to exhibit the following characteristics:

1 High added value: products and processes that include designed in intelligence and creativity will mean higher added value than traditional low skill mass produced goods.
2 Flexibility: due to a combination of more selective customers, rapid change and the microprocessor making possible customised production, greatly increased flexibility will be necessary in design, product mix and manufacturing personnel of all kinds. John Atkinson in the UK *Guardian* newspaper (13) suggests that a new flexible firm will be necessary to meet these conditions of extreme flexibility.

Such an enterprise will consist of three groups of people, a small core group of permanent staff and two peripheral groups consisting of sub-contractors and those on short-term contract. All this will mean a move away from mass production to jobbing/batch systems.

3 Adaptation: companies will need to make rapid adjustments to changes in their markets; this will apply just as much to suppliers as it does to customers. As Toffler has said, the successful enterprise will need to adjust like trees in the breeze, going in whatever direction the winds of change take them.

4 Process control: the microprocessor now makes possible much greater control of quality, accuracy and repeatability of processes.

5 Throughput times: the times for introducing new designs and the times to change over from making one batch to another will be considerably reduced. Japanese manufacturers are aiming for zero set up times.

6 Reduced waste: for sound commercial reasons as well as the wider environmental issues waste reduction in all its forms will be a high priority. This will include poor quality showing itself in scrap and rework, wasteful use of energy and materials and the maintenance costs of downtime.

FACILITATING CHANGE

The application of Beer's five systems necessary for viability will aid this adjustment and particularly the intelligence and control functions. The adaptation task for manufacturers is certainly a total one which must involve design, manufacturing, marketing and accounts. Adjusting to the kinds of challenge now described provides some of the clues to what manufacturing industry should be doing to remain productive. A piecemeal approach is not the answer and the following two-stage programme is suggested to facilitate the change to new-style manufacturing:

1 Create awareness of the characteristics of new-style manufacturers. This would involve two- to three-day residential workshops for the main functions involved, ie design, manufacturing, marketing and accounts.

2 Implementation stage consisting of an in-plant action learning approach divided into diagnostic and action phases. The diagnosis would involve a study of the changes considered

necessary in products, processes and organisation structure. In the action phase project groups would implement the results of the diagnostic phase.

We suggest that manufacturers might evaluate their enterprises against the six factors previously described, ie added value, flexibility, adaptation, process control, throughput time and waste. The evaluative method should consist of a quantitative assessment of each of the six items as they are now compared with what they should be. The new standards for what should be could be determined in a combination of two ways, (i) internally determined, (ii) external intelligence.

Industry will have to face the productivity connection between how much is produced and with what resources, when it is available and the quality of what is produced together with the service offered. Getting this balance right will determine whether the organisation survives.

NEW-STYLE MEASUREMENTS

THE END OF GNP

Just as there are fundamental changes in economics, so there are in the approaches to measuring economic performance. The overall achievements of most countries are still assessed on the basis of gross national product (GNP) per capita, GNP per employee or output per worker in industry, a more refined version. A principal aim of countries is growth in their GNP. As we have noted earlier this kind of indicator is only a partial measurement of productivity with no indications of the use of other inputs like capital charges and employee costs, although the Bureau of Labor Statistics in Washington is now adopting the total factor method developed by the American Productivity Center in Houston.

These moves towards total measuring devices will provide a more reliable economic picture. But in an age of such profound changes we should also be questioning the suitability of GNP and its growth for judging the total economic and social wellbeing of any country.

GNP, being the total of all wages, salaries, rents, profits and royalties received, may give some indication of our standard of living, but does it really? We now know only too well that continued economic growth has been accompanied by such social costs as pollution and as Hazel Henderson (14) says of Ralph

Nader 'Every time there is an automobile accident the GNP goes up.' There are many other costs, including the 36 million unemployed in the OECD, which all add to the GNP. The Japanese have already recognised this problem and are to replace GNP with net national welfare (NNW). The new indicator will deduct from GNP such social costs as auto accidents, pollution, congestion and so on. But as Hazel Henderson reminds us, we should also find a way of adding to GNP the vast amount of unrecorded work like housework and voluntary activities. Therefore, in future growth in NNW will be a lot more meaningful in economic and social terms than increases in GNP.

PRODUCTIVITY AND COMPLEXITY

The dilemma of low productivity/efficiency is still meeting mixed reactions across the world. In some cases it is rising even if measured on partial indicators, while for others it remains stubbornly low. Much of the confusion arises from a failure to understand the nature of the productivity problem we now face. The factors which must be included are the net energy concept previously mentioned and the social costs of trying to manage the increasing complexity caused by rapid change. Our attempts to control this situation include increased legislation, larger policing (public and private security forces) and rising bureaucracy to the ridiculous situation where the costs of control exceed production costs. Hazel Henderson describes this situation as the 'Entropy State', where society has reached a stage where the transaction costs of complexity and interdependence exceed society's productive capabilities. Entropy may be defined as the natural evolutionary process, considerably advanced by manmade economic processes where low entropy usable energy is irrevocably converted into high entropy unusable energy. Within the context of energy, fossil fuels like coal, gas and oil exist in an ordered usable low entropy form and become high entropy and disordered ie unusable when we burn them. So we are attempting to measure and improve productivity in a rising state of complexity and disorder.

While little known at present, entropy will become a common part of economic debate within the next few years. The profound analysis by Georgescu-Roegen(8) reminds us that the economic system is advancing the natural entropic process. Furthermore, if we are to survive we must learn to manage the earth's resources more wisely. In the long run the entropic degradation of the sun will be a crucial factor, as Georgescu-Roegen has said, 'for surprising as it may seem, the entire stock of the earth's natural resources is not worth more than a few days of sunlight'. Indeed we owe it to future generations to use nature's endowments wisely and productively. By the turn of the century productivity and entropy will be synonymous.

EFFICIENCY FOR WHOM?

It was stated earlier that productivity measurement is influenced by what is measured and the frames of reference of who does the measuring: eg chief executives will use different criteria for measuring company performance from trade unionists. But apart from the influence of those affected by the measurements we should also pay some attention to time horizons; we could easily achieve short-term improvements in productivity while storing up high long-term costs, eg by the use of asbestos. These are all issues which in the here-and-now of survival may seem out of place but will still eventually become significant issues. Figure 10.6 is a modified diagram used by Hazel Henderson (14) as a basis for discussion on these wider aspects of productivity, and especially, what efficiency is.

The longer-term aim is to become a more balanced economic system, or a state of syntropy.

'WHITE COLLAR' PRODUCTIVITY

STRUCTURE OF EMPLOYMENT

The last twenty years have seen significant changes in the kinds of job we do. During the period 1973 to 1982 the movement away from agriculture and industry to professional service type occupations continued. Table 10.1, prepared by the Israel Institute of Productivity, (15) illustrates the large increases in those parts of the economy not covered by agriculture and industry. Studies made within industrial enterprises would also reveal shifts away from the blue collar manual type of work towards the knowledge/information-based job. This whole area of work, where it is difficult to measure output as easily as with the blue collar operative, can be generally called white collar or information jobs. It is a significant part of the economy of all countries and therefore requires attention for three reasons:

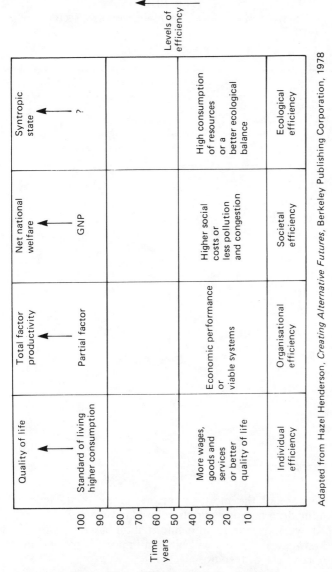

Figure 10.6 Efficiency and time horizons

1 White collar workers now constitute a half to two thirds of the workforce in many countries, eg in the USA and Canada it is nearly 70 per cent. They, therefore, consume high proportions of human and physical resources.

Table 10.1
Increase of employees by main economic sector

Period 1972 to 1982

Country	Percentage change in employees, 1973/1982			
	Total change for all sectors	Service and related sectors	Industry	Agriculture
Israel	+ 23%	+ 36%	+ 9%	− 12%
USA	+ 21%	+ 31%	+ 5%	− 1%
Canada	+ 29%	+ 41%	+ 11%	+ 1%
UK	− 3%	+ 12%	− 22%	− 11%
Japan	+ 10%	+ 25%	+ 6%	− 27%
Italy	+ 13%	+ 53%	− 5%	− 23%
Germany	− 4%	+ 11%	− 14%	− 33%
Sweden	+ 9%	+ 25%	− 9%	− 17%

2 Because of the more intangible nature of the work it is difficult to measure and therefore improve.
3 As we move more into information-based economies the knowledge workers will play an important role in the productive use of resources.

DEFINING WHITE COLLAR WORKERS

There are various interpretations of what a white collar worker is, but the following list of jobs by Mali (16) is a useful analysis.

> White Collar Workers: in general terms professional and
> technical workers, that is, managers, teachers, accountants,
> engineers, medical doctors, dentists, nurses, lawyers, super-
> visors, public administrators, publishers, government
> workers, social workers, real estate workers, quality control
> staff, draughtsmen, bank tellers, computer programmers and
> analysts, sales representatives, production controllers and
> planners, clerks and the self employed.

This type of occupation thus spans all the economic sectors of
agriculture, industry, commerce and the public organisation.

In this general area of white collar work is also included the
rapidly increasing service sector for reasons 1 and 2 above. Typical
service type workers are: retail sales staff, cashiers, waiters, bar-
tenders, hotel staff, fire-fighters, police, security personnel, hair-
dressers, domestic workers, cleaners and medical support staff.

IMPROVING WHITE COLLAR PRODUCTIVITY

A high proportion of the attention to productivity has been
directed to labour productivity in blue collar jobs. The field of
white collar efficiency is, therefore, comparatively new territory. If
we add to this a belief that the work of the professional/knowledge
worker cannot be measured, then it is clear we are entering a new
and difficult area. But bearing in mind the size of the resources
consumed it becomes evident it is a subject that must be tackled.

The nature of this kind of work makes it clear that measurement
will be more of the qualitative than quantitative kind. Even so we
should keep in mind the dictum that you cannot improve anything
unless you first measure it.

There are seven factors to be considered before trying to improve white collar productivity:

1 Objectives: what aspects are to be covered, eg professional
   workers, accountants, or maybe design productivity;
2 Awareness: gain the understanding of those concerned,
   arouse their interest in the nature of the problem and seek
   suggestions.
3 Measurements: the inputs (ie the resources used) should be
   comparatively easy to obtain; it is what constitutes an output
   that will be difficult to define and agree upon. However,
   every organisation and its parts must have some kind of
   output for it to exist. Getting agreement on what is productive work, that is, the most significant activity should be an
   important first step. Involving people in self-reporting

diaries as a means of individual and group study will provide valuable information. The engineering assessment questionnaire, Figure 10.7, is a method for both seeking information and promoting discussion on improving engineering design performance. Through this approach self study and improvement (ie diagnosis and remedies) become one process. A similar method was used to enable professional mental health workers to improve the services for the mentally handicapped (17). In this project parents, family doctors, health visitors, mental welfare officers and training staff all played a part in designing methods for measuring and improving the services provided. Six quantifiable indices were produced, thus:

D – the disability of the handicapped person
A – the activity of the parents
C – the co-ordination of the services
M – the activity of the mental welfare officers
S – the services received by the handicapped
F – the satisfaction or fulfilment of parents

The model of interaction of the parents and the professional people involved is illustrated in Figure 10.8. This study has been included to demonstrate that if the productivity of a professional service for the mentally handicapped can be measured and improved by letting those concerned do their own studies, then other white collar jobs can also be measured and improved.

4 Interdependency: the output is most likely to be a service to some other part of the organisation. Therefore any approach to improving efficiency must include the other functions concerned; improving one part could be to the detriment of the other parts. The mentally handicapped project and adjusting to new-style manufacturing are examples of the need for interdependency and the dangers of suboptimisation.

5 Team aspects: unlike some blue collar jobs most white collar work depends upon effective group activity.

6 Participation: discretion is a characteristic of white collar jobs, therefore participation in the design and conduct of the improvement programme is important. The participative research approach was described in Chapter 7.

7 Environment: designing a climate which meets personal and group needs is an important requirement for the improvement of white collar productivity. This should include opportunities for personal development, recognition, an effective reward system, adequate discretion and appropriate resources.

Instructions : There are 17 questions divided into the four areas of Achievement/productivity, Organisational, Information and Personal factors. There are five possible responses to each question. Reply 'uncertain' if you do not know or are unsure. All five responses range from 1 *Very low* (VL) to 5 *Very high* (VH). In some cases values are placed on responses. Please be frank and express *your* personal view as *you* see the company at present.

● Average response from 20 engineering managers

No.	Question	VL 1	Replies 2	3	4	VH 5
1	Achievement/productivity What is the degree of technical success? How well do you achieve your design objectives and performance specifications?			●		
2	How long does it take to get new ideas into the market place?	24> ●	— Months— 12-24	6-12	3-6	0-3
3	How well do you get first production units available by planned dates?	6> 	— Months late — 3-6	1-3 ●	0-1	On time
4	Is there any increase in the added value to your latest products?	VL		●		VH
5	What is your current achievement in minimising design modifications after release of drawings?	VL	●			VH
6	Organisational How effective is *your* planning of engineering work?	VL		●		VH
7	How well do functions (e.g. design, manufacturing, marketing and accounts) communicate with each other?	VL	●			VH
8	How much do other functions participate in design?	VL		●		VH
9	How well do *you* understand design/engineering objectives and problems?	VL		●		VH

Figure 10.7   Engineering assessment questionnaire

No.	Question	Replies VL 1	2	3	4	VH 5
10	How well is project management integrated as a single function?		•			
11	Is the climate in the company conducive to an effective engineering function?	VL	•			VH
12	Information Is relevant engineering cost information available to *you*?	VL		•		VH
13	Are time standards set for engineering work?	VL			•	VH
14	Do you consider the information you do get is complete?	VL	•			VH
15	Is there a satisfactory feedback and review of results achieved? - that is, the learning aspects	VL		•		VH
16	Personal How do *you* consider *your* abilities match *your* job needs (i.e. technical competence and human skills)	VL		•		VH
17	What is *your* current level of motivation?	VL			•	VH

Figure 10.7   (concluded)

COMPUTER CONFERENCING

The combination of interfirm comparisons and action learning involves an interchange of productivity data and a sharing of problem identifying/solving methods. Some 100 companies have taken part in this kind of activity and with some success in improving productivity. Fresh insights into the productivity problem have also been revealed. However, any new initiatives that can make this process even more effective should be considered. How desirable would it be to have the following additional advantages?

● instant feedback of individual company productivity figures combined with access to past data;

- instant comparisons past and present, with other companies' productivity information;
- minimising the problem of the time to attend meetings and the difficulty of large distances between interested companies;
- completely flexible communication (ie any time of the day or night or any venue) between all the companies taking part in productivity audits/action learning meetings;
- decreasing the problem in face-to-face meetings of dominance by one or two people, insufficient time to deal with all matters and a low contribution by the more passive members of the meeting.

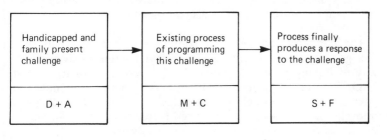

Key to indices: expressed in degree of factor stated

D = disability	M = mental welfare activity	S = services received by handicapped
A = parental activity	C = co-ordination of services	F = parental fulfilment

With acknowledgement to Ali Baguer and Prof. R.W. Revans, *But Surely that is their Job*, ALP International Publications, 1973.

Figure 10.8   Model of interaction: project to improve services for the mentally handicapped

The American Productivity Center (APC) are pioneering the use of computer conferencing as a means of satisfying the above needs.

Computer conferencing (18) makes use of the facilities of high-capacity low-cost microcomputers to improve communication between widely dispersed people. It is not video conferencing, electronic mail or local area networking, and it does not replace them. The unique and distinct advantages of computer conferencing are listed below:

1   A computer conference has a specific subject/objective,

eg increasing productivity awareness or exchanging technological information. It is thus action-oriented, with specific
time limits of the order or 3 to 12 months.

2   A moderator (a kind of action learning group adviser) guides
the conference to achieve its objectives.

3   Conferences are interactive, that is, a form of electronic
action learning.

4   Many people can interact: the first American Productivity
Conferences (19) involved 175 top leaders spread across the
continent.

5   Those who participate can see the results of past and present
dialogue on a visual display unit (VDU) and get printouts as
required. Editing, searching, analysis, summarising and
graphic presentation are also all possible.

The APC-inspired computer conferences on productivity provide good examples of what can be achieved in this highly effective
way of linking people together. In the period April to August
1983, 175 senior leaders from business, labour, academia and
government were brought together electronically. They exchanged
information and ideas and produced recommendations for action
in each of the following seven conference issues:

1   Co-operation in the workplace
2   Health care
3   Information workers/measurement
4   Quality
5   Rewards
6   Technology
7   Training

One participant at the APC productivity computer conference
expressed his concern one Sunday evening, thus,

'There is some feeling that this productivity problem we face
is temporary. That it will go away with the recovery, or that
we merely have to find the right combination of magic incan-
tations or techniques.

I am convinced it is far more serious. . . . There is no question
in my mind that the forces loose in the world today will
inexorably force us to face the problem of producing competitively or sinking from the scene as did Greece and Rome.'

As we are already part of the information revolution it does
seem appropriate that this kind of technology should be used in
the task of increasing understanding about productivity and for

improving it. The APC describes computer conferencing as productivity bartering, which is acting as a catalyst for change in both private and public organisations. However, like most innovations it does require investment in time and money for its implementation.

REWARD SYSTEMS

Productivity in the kind of changes now described raises a number of motivational problems. These include job security; many people identify productivity with unemployment – the growth situation of the 1960s also led to pay outpacing productivity, which resulted in overpaid employees. Consequently there is now a need to overhaul reward systems to suit the new conditions being experienced. A total approach will be necessary which takes account of objectives, security, information disclosure, participation and measurement.

REWARD OBJECTIVES

The introduction of any system of reward or sharing the gains in productivity should be based upon clear objectives. Because organisations are interdependent units, narrowly based systems are generally not effective. Systems should relate rewards to achievement, be linked to an agreed output measurement, eg added value or total earnings, and be credible to everyone concerned.

SECURITY

This is probably the most difficult area with the high level of unemployment throughout the world. However, it is an issue that must be faced. People will need some assurance that co-operation in productivity will not result in job losses. Lifetime employment in one organisation is probably not possible in today's fast-changing situation, but nevertheless national and local strategies to deal with the problem must be included.

INFORMATION DISCLOSURE

People will feel more confident if they are given regular feedback on how they and the organisation as a whole are doing. An informed workforce is not only more secure but, of equal importance, it can contribute ideas for improving productivity. But information disclosure cannot be solved with quick fix approaches like distributing copies of the balance sheet. It is a long educational process to produce information that is believed and causes positive responses.

PARTICIPATION

Throughout the book the participative theme has been stressed. One of the findings of the APC Computer Conference on Reward Systems was that greater employee involvement in decisions will be one of the main sources of productivity improvement in the years ahead. Autocratic-style organisations and short-term improvements from cost cutting (cutting the workforce) are unlikely to secure the co-operation needed to cope with the necessary changes. The Scanlon suggestion-based reward system, now growing again, is a good example of a participative approach to incentives. We should also remember that rewards do not just depend upon financial incentives; simply recognising people's efforts is highly important.

MEASUREMENT

Effective incentive systems have always depended upon reliable measurement. They are still too often devices to enable people to earn higher wages with little connection to actual productivity gains. A good system should reflect: physical output and quality achieved; the impact on the organisation as a whole; productivity as well as cost improvements.

Incentive systems should also be reviewed on a regular basis to see if they are meeting these criteria. If not productivity will drift down and wages up.

ATTITUDES TO PRODUCTIVITY

MIXED REACTIONS

The attitudes to productivity both within enterprises and from across the world present a mixed picture. A study of newspapers and comments from individuals produces a kaleidoscope of opinions and beliefs. The word itself is part of the problem, for in the minds of many people it is still regarded in the narrow sense of production and blue collar productivity. It is therefore seen as only applying to industry. The current economic crisis, which, as we have suggested, is more than a 1930s-style recession, is creating a pattern of reactions. Feelings of bewilderment and uncertainty are resulting from the failure of conventional economic wisdoms to produce the expected results. Increased productivity and growth do not seem to be producing a reduction in unemployment as they did at the peak of the mass economy. In these conditions managers are preoccupied with keeping costs down, trying to get more out with a reduced workforce and dealing with all the problems of satisfying world markets. Giving up precious time to reflect on the underlying productivity problem is difficult to justify. Moreover, people working in all types of organisation view productivity with very mixed feelings, notably thinking that productivity = unemployment.

ATTITUDE STUDIES

Four studies provide information on attitudes to productivity, one conducted by the ALA, a second an international study by an American consulting firm, thirdly another American study of the views of 236 top executives and, lastly, a survey of the views of UK executives on the social implications of change. The results are summarised below.

Action Learning Associates study

This was a questionnaire study conducted by the ALA in the UK during 1982. It involved 100 industrial organisations and 25 helping agencies (eg banks, educational bodies, employers' associations and productivity centres). It provides some useful pointers to how industrial managers and those who provide guidance think about productivity. The significant points are:

● The low response of 20 per cent may suggest a mixture of indifference and productivity being low on the list of priorities;
● There was a contrast between industry and the helping agencies on the factors having the greatest influence on productivity. This is shown in Figure 10.9. It can be seen that the two groups show large differences of opinion in costs, the order book and quality. On the other hand their

views coincide on the influence of management and, surprisingly, both put information the lowest on their list of priorities.

● Industry's views on the factors most likely to increase productivity were increased sales, better production methods and more up-to-date technology. Restrictive labour practices and more efficient suppliers were listed as the main influences that restricted productivity.

A survey of 100 industrial organisations and helping agencies conducted in 1982 by Action Learning Associates. Questionnaires received = 24

Factor	Average rank order* of importance	
	Industry	Helping agencies
1 Costs	1	8
2 Plant	5	4
3 Order book	2	5
4 Management	2	1
5 Information	8	8
6 Products	7	6
7 Attitudes	4	2
8 Quality	6	3

*   a rank order of 1 signifies the highest importance

Figure 10.9   Attitudes to productivity

AMERICAN INTERNATIONAL SURVEY

This survey by Peter Small and Associates (20) was carried out in 1981 to gain international views on employee attitudes to productivity in Australia, Japan, the USA, the UK and Western Germany. Some of the significant points, shown below, reveal areas of agreement and disagreement.

1   Significant proportions of employees in Australia, the UK and the USA believed that declining productivity will be a problem for many years.

2 British employees feel there is less investment in new equipment than 10 years previously, whereas employees in Australia and America hold the opposite view.

3 Australians do not believe that standards of living and quality of life have to be sacrificed to achieve acceptable levels of growth, the Japanese are divided but the British and West Germans believe it will be necessary.

4 The Australians, Americans and British would accept lower spending on health and welfare, and higher prices if it led to investment in higher growth. In America there would also be an acceptance of less spending on the poor and higher levels of air and water pollution. For the same aims the Australians would not be willing to accept higher unemployment whereas the Americans and British would.

Top executives study

This is a survey (21) of 236 top-level executives from a cross-section of 195 US industrial companies. The main findings listed below confirm the various observations made throughout the book:

1 The focus is too narrow, generally concentrating on cost savings in one part of the company, usually manufacturing. It was rare for the interactions of functions to be included.

2 The efforts were disjointed and addressed the symptoms rather than the underlying causes. More often they were reactions to what was hurting the most at the time, eg reducing scrap, tightening standards etc.

3 Time horizons were short, generally less than a year. Only a small proportion of those questioned claimed plans that were integrated with overall business plans.

4 Top management's involvement was lukewarm.

The principal reasons revealed in the study for disappointments in improving productivity are listed in Figure 10.10. As the survey concludes, the managers admitted the real enemy in the problem of productivity improvement was themselves.

Social implications of change

This survey was conducted in the spring of 1983 by Francis Kinsman (22) among 30 leading people involved in various aspects of British business. These 30 people were interviewed using the single question 'What do you imagine will be the most important social issues facing British management by 1990?'

No.	Factor	Size of response %
1	Piecemeal unplanned approach	66
2	Inadequate departmental co-ordination	42
3	Insufficient investment in management/ supervisory development	41
4	Lukewarm commitment by top management	40
5	Insufficient awareness by design of their effect on manufacturing	39
6	Weak industrial and manufacturing engineering	39
7	Weak first-line supervision	35
8	Poor communication	32
9	Insufficient workforce training	32
10	Poor financial control/information systems	24
11	Weak middle managers	21
12	Decline of the work ethic	20
13	Lack of appropriate reward systems	20
14	Insufficient capital for improved plant and equipment	17
15	Poor employee relations	9
16	Poor relationships with trade unions	9

Figure 10.10   Causes of disappointment in improving productivity listed in size of response

With acknowledgement to *Harvard Business Review*, September/October 1982

There was a general acceptance that while life for many in the UK was good it might not remain so if the competitive challenges were not faced. The significant points emerging from the interviews were:

- a gradual emergence from the world recession to a tentative economic improvement.
- an intolerable pressure on many traditional and some new industries from Japan and the Far East.
- survival and triumph is possible for those industries that are flexible, innovative, dogged and aware, maintain the very best of employee relations and build bridges with the USA and the Far East by means of a two-way flow of trade, technology and people.
- a convergence of all communications to continue with a resultant integration of the global village – hence the UK like everybody else staying boxed in by world problems as well as suffering its own.
- a worsening of the international currency crisis but with ultimate salvation with some kind of Bretton Woods 11 agreement.
- probably no serious oil crisis before 1990 though continued instability in the Middle East.
- no World War III unless caused by unimaginable stupidity. Instead Soviet pragmatism realising the need of its internal economic priorities leading to a high release of economic energy.

These four studies reveal the importance of understanding attitudes to productivity. They provide information on the factors that are limiting it and the areas which need attention, these being top management and relationships between workers and management as well as those between management/government and trade unions. In a personal letter to the 15,000 chief executives in the UK Confederation of British Industry, the Director General, Sir Terence Beckett, stressed the high importance of productivity in remaining competitive. During 1984 in spite of the increases in efficiency made in manufacturing industry UK unit labour costs rose by 2.6 per cent compared to falls in the USA and West Germany of 2.5 and 2.3 per cent.

CONCLUSIONS

Nine areas have been explored and chosen as a guide to the chapter title, 'What should you be doing?' The future is with us now and we have therefore suggested that by various means we should become more aware of its implications both for the individual enterprise and at national levels.

The nine aspects of the future described are briefly summarised below in an attempt to place them, as an interrelated whole, within the productivity context.

1 Energy: our social and economic wellbeing depend upon energy. The dramatic increase in the price of energy and its finite availability have had equally powerful influences on resource management and the structure of economies. But as the result of these changes we shall have to give more serious attention to the influence of energy on productivity and the as yet esoteric concept of entropy.

2 Wealth: productivity and wealth are positively linked. The more efficient use of resources (especially energy) should produce the surplus (wealth) which can then be invested in an even better utilisation of resources. But we need to be aware of spurious wealth and the increasing situations of negative wealth.

3 Viability: economic indicators are not good guides to long-term viability. Innovation and risk taking are also important. However, with organisations becoming more complex the fundamental nature of organisations described in the viable systems model will claim greater attention.

4 Challenges to industry: due to the changes caused by the transition to an information age economy industry must also make fundamental adjustments. The characteristics of the changes were listed together with the new-style productivity measurements (eg added value increases, time to make changeovers and total throughput times).

5 New-style measurements: in the climate of profound change now being experienced it is to be expected that our established measuring devices will also change. GNP as an indicator of the total wellbeing of a country is questionable. Apart from its narrow partial factor basis it takes no account of the social costs of economic activity. Furthermore, the methods for judging efficiency will need to be set against the criterion of time horizons and the interdependencies of all the factors concerned. Figure 10.6, already used by Hazel Henderson, is intended as a device to promote discussion on how productivity affects various parts of society and the world environment or what is called the ecosytem. For individual organisations and for countries the question 'Where are you now?' could be used to see how you appear on the following scale:

Partial productivity measures	←——————→	Total factor measures
Second wave organisation	←——————→	Information age organisation
Fragmented reactive programmes	←——————→	Co-ordinated/ proactive short- and long-term programme

6 White collar: this significant and growing part of national economies needs specific attention. Methods have been described for measuring and increasing the productivity of those who work in white collar areas. Even in difficult tasks like services for the mentally handicapped productivity can be defined and measured. The common requirement is to involve those who do the work in the defining and measuring.

7 Computer conferencing: the idea of dynamic interfirm comparisons and action learning is aimed at setting up networks of people for exchanging productivity data and methods for improving it. Computer conferencing is the application of information age technology to improve this process. Apart from linking large numbers of individual enterprises it could also bring together productivity centres.

8 Reward systems: how we reward people in financial and psychological terms is a significant part of the productivity problem. But it has to be placed in the total context of job security, what the aims are and the measurement system on which the rewards are based.

9 Attitudes to productivity: whatever our views may be on the need to respond to change and improve productivity, our attitudes will influence what we do.

We have shown that concentrating on short-term survival diverts our attention from the kind of longer-term problems described here. Attitudes to productivity also seem to present a contrasting picture both between organisations and across countries. This is probably partly due to different value systems and to misunderstanding about the nature of the productivity problem. It is also understandable that people should hold differing views when the widely varying situations within organisations are considered. At one end of the scale there are companies with inadequate productivity information trying to survive still using second wave technology. But as we have shown we are already in the midst of the information economy. Between these extremes we also find the growth of new companies using 1950s-type management techniques. The barbershops described by Drucker (see Chapter 7) which used simple work study methods show what can be done.

Our aim has been to present productivity as a total problem of managing resources in a fast-changing world, with our social well-being depending on it. The first chapter set the scene with the following nine chapters dealing with the five main areas, namely:

1 Elements of measurement and information systems;
2 Finding out where you are now and how better use could be made of existing circumstances;
3 The participative use of techniques to combine investigation and improvement into one process;
4 How to improve using action learning;
5 New perspectives as a guide to what you should be doing.

Figure 10.11 is a framework of the book showing the relevant chapters for these five areas and appropriate references. We suggest you use the diagram as a device for exploring the productivity issue. Both the material we have presented and the reference material should be seen as a development tool. Add to the references and decide which are the areas to which you need to give attention.

Productivity has been presented as a subject requiring continuing attention and which should be regarded as the management of total limited resources for all kinds of organisation. In this respect it clearly also requires attention at the national level. Whether it be at micro or macro levels the main stages in introducing programmes of productivity improvement should involve the following six main steps:

1 Awareness: create an awareness of the nature of the productivity problem;
2 Commitment: there has to be commitment initially of top leaders and then everyone concerned;
3 Plan: agree upon a total plan of action divided into a short-term plan of one year and a longer-term one covering four to five years. Where you are now and how much better you could be are short-term aspects, with where you should be involving longer-term horizons. The long term may involve

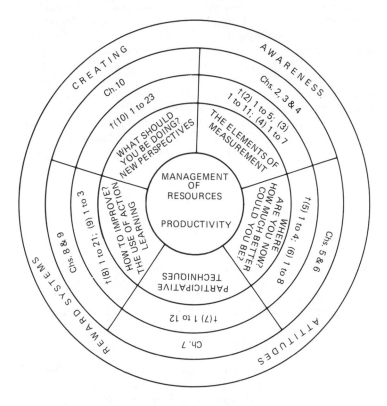

Figure 10.11 Framework of book

ideas as yet unattainable but still worth aiming for.
4 Measurement: develop an appropriate measurement system.
5 Programme: set up an improvement programme which must involve the critical mass of people in both the design and implementation of the programme.
6 Control: regularly review the programme and modify where necessary to suit changing circumstances.

When countries are trying to keep inflation at bay and organisations are striving to keep their heads above water it will be difficult to persist with a total approach of this kind. But the alligators will keep snapping if the swamp is not drained. Furthermore, there are the alternative strategies of trying to convert existing companies to the information age or creating new ones.

We have covered a lot of varied material, which may have appeared a bewildering picture. This has been done by design to portray the complex nature of the productivity problem. Moreover, because it is a total problem the interaction of economic, social and technological factors has to be considered. Whether it be a small manufacturing enterprise, a government department or a hospital ward, productivity is a priority issue. The resources of labour, capital, materials, and energy concern them all. How they apply technical and managerial know-how to these resources to produce the right level and quality of goods and services alongside enjoyment of life is the essence of productivity.

REFERENCES

1 Revans, Professor R. W., *Management, Productivity, and Risk, The Origins and Growth of Action Learning*, Chartwell Bratt, 1982
2 Naisbitt, John, *Megatrends*, Macdonand and Warner Books, 1983
3 Odum, Howard T., *Environment, Power and Society*, John Wiley, 1971
4 'Increased drilling for Oil May Consume More Energy than It Gleans', Study Finds, *Wall Street Journal* 3 February 1982
5 Hawken, Paul, *The Next Economy*, Holt, Reinhart and Winston, 1983
6 *The Briar Patch Book, experiences in right livelihood and living,* A New Glide/Reed Book, San Francisco, 1978
7 Toffler, Alvin, *Previews and Premises,* William Morrow & Co., 1983
8 Georgescu-Roegen, Nicholas, *The Entropy Law and the Economic Process*, Harvard University Press, 1971
9 Beer, Stafford, *The Heart of Enterprise*, John Wiley, 1979
10 'The Reindustrialisation of America', *Business Week,* special issue 30 June 1980
11 'For America Read Britain', *The Production Engineer*, November 1980
12 Goldhar, Joel D., and Jelinek, Marianne, 'Plan for Economies of Scope', *Harvard Business Review*, November/December 1983
13 Atkinson, John, 'The New Flexible Firm', *The Guardian*, 18 April 1984
14 Henderson, Hazel, *Creating Alternative Futures, The End of Economics*, Berkeley Publishing Corporation, 1978
15 *Productivity in Israel, An International Perspective* Israel Institute of Productivity, Tel Aviv, No 9, October, 1983

16 Mali, Paul, *Improving Total Productivity*, Wiley Inter-
    science, 1978
17 Baquer, Ali and Revans, Professor R. W., *But Surely That Is
    Their Job? A study of health and social services, designed and
    conducted by those who work in them*, ALP International
    Publications, 1973
18 Hiltz, Starr Rozanne and Turoff, Murray, *The Network
    Nation*, Addison Wesley, 1978
19 *Computer Conferences on Productivity, A final report for the
    White House Conference on Productivity*, American Produc-
    tivity Center, Houston, September, 1983
20 *Perspectives on Productivity: A Global View*, Peter Small &
    Associates, 400 Madison Avenue, New York 10017, USA,
    1981
21 Judson, Arnold S., 'The Awkward Truth about Produc-
    tivity', *Harvard Business Review*, September/October, 1982
22 Kinsman, Francis, *The New Agenda, An exploration of the
    new human issues facing British management*, Spencer Stuart
    Management Consultants, Brook-House 113 Park Lane,
    London W1Y 4HJ, 1984

Appendix 1
Glossary of terms

Relevant references are also made in the index.

Accountants' productivity   Financial measures of efficiency, eg return on capital employed.

Activity sampling   A low-cost method for collecting information on the utilisation of materials, plant and people.

Actuality   Productivity levels being achieved using existing resources and with current constraints.

Added value   Defined by economists as gross value added, is sales value less all outside purchases.

Ancillary work   Work to support productive work, eg materials handling, cleaning up after the last job and preparing for the next.

Audit   A regular and systematic measuring of productivity, can take place at the primary and secondary levels. Generally quantitative but can also be qualitative.

Blue collar   People directly engaged in transforming materials, also generally physical work.

Capability   Productivity levels that could be reached using existing resources with current restraints.

Comparisons Number four of the five aims of productivity measurement, compares productivity performance with other organisations, industries and countries. Called levels in the USA.

Controls Part of a productivity monitoring system which aims to modify resource management to achieve desired levels of performance – it is an action-inducing mechanism.

Deflating Adjustment of output and input figures for the effects of inflation and price increases.

Depreciation Allowances for the wear and tear costs of using fixed assets. In productivity measurement should be included as a real cost of conversion and not a nominal cost as in accounting.

Direct labour People directly engaged in productive work, generally physically working on materials or selling them.

Economists' productivity Gross value added generated per person, eg GNP per employed person.

Effectiveness Number three of the five aims of productivity measurement, reveals the productivity potential within the organisation. Theoretically cannot exceed unity.

Efficiency Number two of the five aims of productivity measurement. Indicates the level of utilisation of input resources.

Engineering productivity States that efficiency can never exceed unity.

Entropy The level of disorder in systems, particularly energy sources. Fossil fuels naturally exist in an ordered state and become disordered (unusable) when burnt. The entropy in organisations can be reduced by effective information (negantropy).

Feedback Part of the productivity control system. Provides information on actual performance for use in making appropriate adjustments.

Feasible capacity The hours available for productive and ancillary work.

Gross Domestic Product (GDP) An indicator of national output, when divided by total population or employed persons is a measurement of a country's productivity. Is the equivalent of added value at the company level. It is the total of all wages, salaries, rents and dividends paid or the total of all income less purchases between organisations to avoid double accounting.

Frequency The regularity with which productivity information is made available.

Gross National Product (GNP) Is GDP plus payments made to overseas claimants.

Gross factor cost Total of all costs incurred in making and selling products or providing services. Includes materials (where appropriate), purchased services, wages and salaries and depreciation.

Haphazard information Production information made available on an *ad hoc* basis.

Idle time Time when labour, materials and plant are not involved in ancillary or productive work.

Indexing Comparison of output, input and productivity measures with a base year which is given an index of 100.

Inflation adjustment see Deflating.

Information Productivity data which are published on a regular basis and which are used for taking action.

Input The resources used in the conversion process generally comprise wages and salaries, purchased services and depreciation, but could also include materials, numbers of people employed and total hours worked. The denominator in productivity ratios.

Interfirm comparison Productivity comparison between companies mostly within the same industry.

Labour productivity Generally output per unit of labour input, often added value divided by total employees; at national level it is GNP divided by employed population. Still tends to dominate the assessment of productivity.

Levels see **Comparisons**. This is the term used in the USA.

Macro Measurements of productivity at national, regional or industrial levels, eg output per worker.

Maximum theoretical capacity The time available if organisation worked 365 24-hour-days per year.

Measurement The use of output/input information to judge productivity; will mostly take the form of some ratio of output to input.

Method study A systematic technique for observing, recording and analysing the use of materials, equipment, people and space.

Micro Measurements of productivity within individual organisations, eg plant productivity.

Mix Generally the different products and processes in a manufacturing company and their effects on productivity.

Monitoring Systematic checking of productivity movements over a period of time. See also Controls and Trends.

Negantropy The flow of information in a system, the opposite of entropy.

Net National Welfare (NNW) A more refined version of GNP. Reduces GNP by social costs but also increases it by unpaid work.

Net Value Added (NVA) Gross value added less depreciation.

Objectives   Number one in the five aims of productivity measurement. Shows the degree to which organisational objectives are being met.

Output   The results of the conversion process, the numerator in productivity ratio. Examples, GNP, sales, total earnings and added value.

Partial productivity   Productivity measurements which only include one input in the denominator, eg labour productivity.

Participative techniques   Methods for studying productivity which involve people in the design and conduct of the investigation.

Piecemeal approaches   Only tackling one part of the productivity problem, eg introducing incentive systems or quality circles.

Planning   Agreeing in advance how objectives are to be achieved and regularly reviewing progress.

Plant economics   The degree to which the 'size' capacity of plant is utilised.

Potential   The potential in every organisation to achieve higher levels of resource utilisation than at present. See also Effectiveness.

Price adjustment   see **Deflating.**

Price recovery   The extent to which profits can be maintained or increased through price increases.

Primary measurements   Productivity measurement at the overall organisational level.

Productivity   The ratio of output to input, how efficiently and effectively resources are used. A more physical measurement of organisational performance.

Productive work   The work activity that has the most significant impact on productivity. In manufacturing it is what actually changes materials in some way.

Profitability   A financial indication of performance, eg ratio of profit to assets or sales. Profitability can increase with low productivity and vice versa.

Purchased services   All services purchased from outside and used in the conversion process.

Qualitative   The subjective aspects of productivity; difficult to quantify. Includes attitudes, beliefs and value systems.

Quantitative   Those aspects of productivity which can be numerically assessed, for example the percentage of time spent on productive work.

Real time control   Making available productivity data on a continuous basis rather than after the event.

Rewards   Methods for rewarding the results of productivity achievements. Generally take the form of financial rewards but should also include psychological recognition.

Rate of Stock Turn (ROST)   A measure of the utilisation of stock, that is, sales divided by average stock.

Secondary measurements   Productivity measurement at the lower (grass roots) levels of organisations.

Social costs   The costs incurred in any economic system, also called externalities. Typical examples are congestion and pollution. Also a measure of friction or entropy in the system.

Social surplus   Interests, rents, royalties, and profits retained in a country, or NVA less labour costs.

Stocks   Materials, work in progress and finished stocks existing in a production system.

Syntropy   A balanced economic/social system particularly with regard to energy consumption and low social (friction) costs.

Throughput materials   In manufacturing and retailing the materials which are contained in the sales. Regarded as a temporary investment.

Time horizons   The timespan over which productivity is to be measured.

Timeliness   The degree to which productivity data are available when required.

Time study   A technique for obtaining times for completing work activities.

Total employees   The total people employed in an organisation on the conversion process.

Trends   The last of the five productivity aims. Shows the static, growth or declining aspects.

Utilisation   The extent to which available resources are used to generate output.

Validity   Productivity measurements which accurately reflect changes in productivity.

Viability   The ability of an organisation to adapt to changes, even the unforeseen ones. It is more than just economic factors.

Wages and salaries   Total costs of remuneration for everyone working in the organisation.

Wealth   Surplus money and resources which are wisely invested in the future. It is what is left from income after meeting daily consumption needs.

Weighting   Methods for comparing differing output and input mixes.

White collar   The growing number of professional/service workers.

Working capital   The day-to-day resources necessary for sustaining the conversion process. Includes work in progress, stocks and liquid funds.

Work measurement   Includes the range of techniques for

determining work times, eg time study, synthetics, analytical estimating and so on.

Appendix 2
Productivity Network

The management of productivity should be continually enriched by fresh thinking. This is considered to be particularly necessary in such a fast changing world. Below is an international list of organisations who have a particular interest in productivity in all its forms. Perhaps it is not too optimistic to hope that this kind of network might soon be linked by the computer conferencing method mentioned in the last chapter. By this means an interchange of productivity information could enable real-time enrichment to take place.

Country	Contact	Organisation
Europe & Middle East		
Belgium	A. C. Hubert Secretary General	European Association of National Productivity Centres Rue de la Concorde, 60 1050 Brussels Tel. 571 71 00

Country	Contact	Organisation
	M. Pierre Administrateur général	Institut pour l'Amélioration des Conditions de Travail (IACT) Rue de la Concorde, 60 1050 Bruxelles Tel. 511 81 55
Cyprus	H. Constantinou Director	Cyprus Productivity Centre (CPC) Ministry of Labour and Social Insurance PO Box 536 Nicosia Tel. 47991
Denmark	M. Kring Director	National Agency of Technology 135 Tagensvej 2200 Copenhagen N Tel. 85'10 66
Egypt	Prof Saad El-Din Ashmawy	Consultancy & Action Learning Centre 6 Aisha Taimoria St Garden City Cairo Tel. 28227-634368
France	P-L Remy Directeur	Agence Nationale pour l'Amélioration des Conditions de Travail (ANACT) 7 Boulevard Romain Rolland 92120 Montrouge Tel. 657 13 30
	Ms Sylvia Ostry Director of Economics and Statistics	OECD Division of Statistiques Economiques Et Des Nationaux 2 Rue Andre-Pascal, 75775 Paris Cedex 26
Germany	H. Hüller Geschäftsführer	Rationalisierungs-Kuratorium der Deutschen Wirtschaft (RKW) Postfach 5867 6236 Eschborn Dusseldorfstrasse, 40 Tel. (6196) 495-1 Telex 04 18362 rkwd
Greece	D. Paleothodoros Director General	Greek Productivity Centre Kapodistriou Street, 28 Athens 147 Tel. 3600 411
Hungary	Z. Roman Director	Institute of Industrial Economics Research of the Hungarian Academy of Sciences Postfach 132 1502 Budapest 1112 Budapest Budaörsi ut 43-45 Tel. 853 779

Country	Contact	Organisation
Iceland	I. Hannibalsson Managing Director	Technological Institute of Iceland Keldnaholt 110 Reykjavik Tel. 91-854 00
Iran		Industrial Management Institute Mosadegh Road Jame Jam Avenue Tehran Tel. 294130/9
Ireland	J. Lynch Director	Irish Productivity Centre (IPC) IPC House 35-39 Shelbourne Road Dublin 4 Tel. 686 244
	Senator Noel Mulcahy	The Irish Management Institution Sandyford Road Dublin 14
Israel	Israel Meiden Director	Israel Productivity Institute 4 Henrietta Sold Street Tel Aviv 61336 Tel. 422411
Luxembourg	J. Faltz Secrétaire général	Office Luxembourgeois pour l'Accroissement de la Productivité (OLAP) Rue A. Lumière, 18 1950 Luxembourg Tel. 48 92 60
Netherlands	C. A. M. Mul Secretary (Corresponding member)	Commissie voor Ontwikkelingsproblematiek van Bedrijven (COB) Bezuidenhoutseweg, 60 Postbus 90405 2509 LK Den Haag Tel. 81 43 41 Telex 32377 ser nl
	R. V. Creutzberg Deputy Director (Corresponding member)	Rijksnijverheidsdienst (RND) Postbus 20104 Lutherse Burgwal, 10 2500 EC's-Gravenhage Tel. 60 19 32
	Dr Angus Maddison	Faculteit Der Economische Wetenschaapen Van der Rijksuniversiteit Postbus 800 9700 Av Groningen Tel. 011-31-501-11.6722

Country	Contact	Organisation
Norway	W. Meyn Acting Director	Norsk Produktivitets Institutt (NPI) PO Box 8401-Hammersborg Oslo 1 Akersgaten 64 Tel. 20 94 75
	Knut Wollebaek Head of Department	Norwegian Employers Confederation Hansteensgt 2 Oslo 2 Tel. (02) 20 25 50
Spain	L. Escuriaza Director (Corresponding member)	Instituto de le Pequena y Mediana Empresa Industrial (IMPI) Agustin de Foxa, 29-6a Madrid-16 Tel. 733 00 26
Sweden	Lennart Strandler	Swedish Employers Confederation 10330 Stockholm
Switzerland	G. Kanawatty	Management Development Branch Training Department International Labour Office 4 route des Morillons CH1211 Geneva Tel. 022 996111
Turkey	H. Gurtan Secretary General	Milli Prodüktivite Merkezi (MPM) Mithatpasa Caddesi 46 Yenisehir-Ankara Tel. 17 91 96
UK	D. Savage Editor	National Institute of Economic and Social Research 2 Dean Trench Street Smith Square London SW1P 3HE Tel. 01 222 7665
	J. Robertson	Turning Point Spring Cottage 9 New Road Ironbridge Shropshire TF8 7AU Tel. 095 245 2224
	R. Edwards Director	British Productivity Council The Management College Henley on Thames Oxfordshire RG9 3AU Tel. 049 166 676
Yugoslavia	M. Kecman	Jugoslovenski Zavod Za Produktivnost Rada (Yugoslav Productivity Institute) Uzun Mirkova, 1 Belgrade Tel. 626 899

Country	Contact	Organisation

North America

Canada	G. Rivest Director	Productivity Improvement Service (xjmd) Market Development Branch— Industry Trade & Commerce 235 Queen Street Ottawa, Ontario KIA OH5 Tel. (613) 992-1722
Quebec	F. Major Directeur général (Corresponding member)	Institut National de Productivité (INP) C.P. 157-Succursale Desjardins Complexe Desjardins-Tour Sud-Bureau 1509 Montréal H5B 1B3 Tel. 514-873 7601
USA	E. Milbergs Director (Corresponding member)	Office of Productivity, Technology and Innovation Department of Commerce 14th & Constitution Ave. N.W. Washington DC, 20230 Tel. 202-377 2059
	Jerome T. Mark Associate Commissioner for Productivity & Technology	U.S. Bureau of Labour Statistics U.S. Department of Labour 200 Constitution Avenue, NW Room S4325, Washington, DC, 20212 Tel. 202/523-9294
	C. Jackson Grayson Jr Chairman	American Productivity Center 123 North Post Oak Lane Houston, Texas 77024 Tel. 713/681-4020
		OECD Publications and Information Center 1750 Pennsylvania Avenue, NW Suite 1207 Washington DC, 20006 Tel. 202/724-1857
	Jajo Arai Director	U.S. Office Japan Productivity Center 1901 North Ft. Myer Drive Arlington, YA 22209 Tel. 703/243-5522
		World Bank International Bank for Reconstruction and Development 1818 H Street Washington DC
	Hazel Henderson	PO Box 448 Gainsville Florida 32601

Country	Contact	Organisation

Australasia, South Africa and South East Asia

Country	Contact	Organisation
Australia (Corresponding member)	I. D. Jowett Executive Director	Productivity Promotion Council of Australia (PPCA) 228 Victoria Parade East Melbourne Victoria 3002 Tel. 663 3861
South Africa	Dr Jan Visser Executive Director	National Productivity Institute PO Box 3971 Pretoria 0001 Tel. (012) 323 2306
Bangladesh	M. Asghar Ali Secretary Bangladesh Industrial Technical Assistance Centre S. M. Al-Husainy Secretary Ministry of Industry Government of Bangladesh	Bangladesh Industrial Technical Assistance Centre (BITAC) Tejgaon Industrial Area Dhaka-8 Tel. 300121-4
Republic of China	Wang Sze-Cheh General Manager China Productivity Center Joseph K. T. Li Manager, International Cooperation Office China Productivity Center	China Productivity Center (CPC) 201-26, 11th Floor Tung Hua North Road Taipei, Taiwan 105 Tel. (02) 773-2200
Hong Kong	Graham Cheng Deputy Chairman Hong Kong Productivity Council Ms Cissy Wu Administrative Assistant Hong Kong Productivity Centre	Hong Kong Productivity Centre (HKPC) 21st Floor, Sincere Bldg 173 Des Voeux Road, Central Tel. 5-443181
India	Waris R. Kidwai Secretary General S. K. Chatnagon Chairman National Productivity Council	Standing Conference of Public Enterprises First Floor, Chandralok 36 Janpath New Delhi 110001 Tel. 322283 National Productivity Council (NPC) Institutional Area, Lodi Road New Delhi-110003 Tel. 615002, 618480, 618807
Indonesia	Danang Joedonagoro Director General for Manpower Development and Utilization Ministry of Manpower and Transmigration	National Productivity Centre Dept. of Manpower Jalon Gatot Subnoto Kay 51/52 PO Box 358 Kby Jakarta Selartan

Country	Contact	Organisation
	Rusli Syarif Director National Productivity Centre	
Fiji	Wang Kangway Principal Labour Officer	Ministry of Employment & IR PO Box 2216 Suya
Japan	Masahiro Goshi Director, International Cooperation Department Japan Productivity Center	Japan Productivity Center (JPC) No. 1-1, Shibuya 3-chome Shibuya-ku, Tokyo 150 Tel. (03) 409-1111, 409-1126/7 (Direct)
	Mr Hiroshi Yokota Secretary General	Asian Productivity Organisation 4-14 Akasaka 8-chome Minato-Ku Tokyo 107 Tel. (03) 408-7221
Republic of Korea	Pork Pil Soo Chairman & Chief Executive Koo Il-Hae Managing Director	Korea Productivity Center (KPC) Korea Herald Building 1-12, 3-6A Hoehyon-Dong Chung-Gu 100
Malaysia	Ir. Hj. Arshad Bin Hj Marsidi Kmn Director	National Productivity Centre Jalan Sultan, PO Box 64 Petaling Jaya Malaysia Tel. 03-563267, 563688
Nepal	Ajit N. S. Thapa Joint Secretary Ministry of Industry His Majesty's Government of Nepal Ishwari Lal Shrestha Secretary Ministry of Industry His Majesty's Government of Nepal Tej Kumar Sharma Industrial Extension Service Division Industrial Services Centre	Industrial Services Centre (ISC) Balaju Industrial District Balaju, Kathmandu Tel. 11522, 15830, 13522
Pakistan	Brig. M. A. Faruqui General Manager Pakistan Industrial Technical Assistance Centre Imtiaz Ahmad Chaudhry Joint Secretary Ministry of Industries Government of Pakistan	Pakistan Industrial Technical Assistance Centre (PITAC) Maulana Jalal-Ud-Din Roomi Road Post Office, Lahore 16 Tel. 854171/2

Country	Contact	Organisation
The Philippines	Arturo L. Tolentino Managing Director Productivity & Development Center Development Academy of the Philippines	Productivity & Development Center Development Academy of the Philippines (PDC/DAP) PO Box 74, Araneta Center Cubao, Quezon City Tel. 673-5242-50 Loc 253
Republic of Singapore	Low Choo Tuck Asst. Director Field & External Relations Unit Lim Jit Poh Executive Director National Productivity Board	National Productivity Board (NPB) 8th Storey, Cuppage Centre 55 Cuppage Road, Singapore 0922 Tel. 7345534
Sri Lanka	N. S. Arumugadasan Director, Research National Institute of Business Management	National Institute of Business Management (NIBM) 1205 Wijerama Mawatha Colombo 7 Tel. 93404
Thailand	Thamnu Vasinonta Director Thailand Management Development and Productivity Centre Samnao Chulkarat Deputy Director-General Department of Industrial Promotion Ministry of Industry	Thailand Management Development and Productivity Centre (TMDPC) Dept. of Industrial Promotion Ministry of Industry Rama 6 Road, Bangkok 10400 Tel. 2815780, 2817148, 2817359

Index